Cracking the

AP®

ENGLISH
LANGUAGE &
COMPOSITION

Exam

2013 Edition

Richard Hartzell, Ph.D.

PrincetonReview.com

Random House, Inc. New York

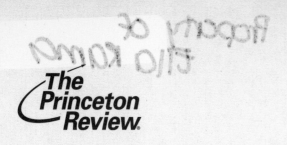
The Princeton Review, Inc.
111 Speen Street, Suite 550
Framingham, MA 01701
E-mail: editorialsupport@review.com

ISBN: 978-0-307-94511-2
ISSN: 1558-9676

Editor: Meave Shelton
Production Editor: Kathy G. Carter
Production Coordinator: Deborah A. Silvestrini

Printed in the United States of America on partially recycled paper.

10 9 8 7 6 5 4 3 2 1

2013 Edition

Editorial

Rob Franek, Senior VP, Publisher
Laura Braswell, Senior Editor
Selena Coppock, Senior Editor
Calvin Cato, Editor
Meave Shelton, Editor

Production

Michael Pavese, Publishing Director
Kathy Carter, Project Editor
Michelle Krapf, Editor
Michael Mazzei, Editor
Michael Breslosky, Associate Editor
Stephanie Tantum, Associate Editor
Kristen Harding, Associate Editor
Vince Bonavoglia, Artist
Danielle Joyce, Graphic Designer

Random House Publishing Team

Tom Russell, Publisher
Nicole Benhabib, Publishing Director
Ellen L. Reed, Production Manager
Alison Stoltzfus, Managing Editor

ACKNOWLEDGMENTS

Even though there is only one author, a team of people contributed to the creation of this book.

First of all, I want to thank Paul Tipton for his sage counsel and Kamilla Khaydarov and Rachel Newman, who wrote the student essays. Also, thanks go to my assistant, Kathryn Lee. Her cheerful manner and professional support proved invaluable; I could not have completed the text without her help.

Thanks to Dawn Shepherd Wolfe and Jeff Soules, who updated and reviewed this book.

I cannot fail to mention both my wife, Susana, and Laura, who for months on end allowed me to replace them with my computer screen and tolerated the very, very occasional bouts of bad humor that resulted from my sequestration.

And finally I'd like to thank my colleague and friend Robb Cutler for suggesting that I take on this project; I have forgiven him.

CONTENTS

PART VI: THE PRINCETON REVIEW AP ENGLISH LANGUAGE AND COMPOSITION
PRACTICE TESTS AND EXPLANATIONS 171

Introduction

WHAT IS THE PRINCETON REVIEW?

The Princeton Review is an international test-preparation company with branches in all major U.S. cities and several cities abroad. In 1981, John Katzman started teaching an SAT prep course in his parents' living room. Within five years, The Princeton Review had become the largest SAT prep program in the country.

Our phenomenal success in improving students' scores on standardized tests is due to a simple, innovative, and radically effective philosophy: Study the test, not just what the test claims to test. This approach has led to the development of techniques for taking standardized tests, techniques based on the principles the test writers themselves use to write the tests.

The Princeton Review has found that its methods work not just for cracking the SAT, but for any standardized test. We've already successfully applied our system to the GMAT, LSAT, MCAT, and GRE, to name just a few. Obviously you need to be well versed in language and grammar to do well on the AP English Language and Composition Exam, but you should remember that any standardized test is partly a measure of your ability to think like the people who write standardized tests. This book will help you to brush up on your AP English Language and Composition skills and to prepare for the exam using our time-tested principle: Crack the system based on how the test is created.

We also offer books and online services that cover an enormous variety of education and career-related topics. If you're interested, check out our website at **PrincetonReview.com**.

PART ◆ I

Welcome to the Exam

1

A Brief Introduction to the AP English Language and Composition Exam

WHY DO YOU NEED THIS BOOK?

This book was written for a student whose goal is to achieve the best possible score on the AP English Language and Composition Exam. We at The Princeton Review believe that the best way to achieve this goal is to understand the test—and especially how the test is written. If you understand the limitations that test writers face, you will approach the test in a way that enables you to earn your maximum score—and that's probably what matters most to you right now. Even if your English Language teacher spends most of the class time discussing her favorite books instead of teaching you about rhetoric, you can still ace the exam with the help of this book. However, if you had excellent English instruction in a course specifically centering on the nuts and bolts of AP English Language, then this book will help you review what you learned and give you valuable test-taking strategies that will ensure your success.

Despite the diversity that might result from differing teachers and curricula, the courses share a common task: to teach you to read and write English at a college level. Likewise, the AP English Language and Composition Exam shares the same goal—it attempts to test you on whether you read and write English at a college level.

How Is This Book Organized?

In this book, we start by giving you a brief overview of the test—we tell you about the history of the test, what it looks like, how to sign up for it, and what your score means. Then, in Parts II and III, we go through some strategies and techniques for approaching the two parts of the exam: the multiple-choice section and the essay section. The content review portion of the book, Parts IV and V, prompts you to use the techniques you learned in Parts II and III to answer the sample questions and drills you see there. You need to get as much practice using these techniques as you can, and that means using them whenever you have an opportunity.

Got it? Now let's find out more about the exam itself.

Know the Exam, and Practice, Practice, Practice

There's more to doing well on a standardized test like the AP English Language and Composition Exam than simply knowing all about English. After all, how often have you answered questions incorrectly on a test even though you really knew the material? To do well on the AP English Language and Composition Exam, you need to know not only *what* will be tested, but also *how* it will be tested. How many multiple-choice questions are there, and what are they like? This is helpful knowledge to have, if only so you know how to budget your time on test day. What kinds of essays are on the exam, and what do the essay readers expect? If you know what they expect, you can practice giving it to them on practice tests—well before test day.

This knowledge brings us to our next point: It is absolutely essential that you *practice* before going into "the big game." Doing some trial runs—answering AP-type multiple-choice questions and writing AP-style essays—is one of the best ways for you to get ready for the AP English Language and Composition Exam. Think about it. If you are a tennis player, you probably practice every day. You practice serving, you practice your backhand, and you play matches against your teammates. This helps you become as prepared as you possibly can for real matches. In the same way, going through drills and taking some full-length practice tests will help you be as prepared as you can be for the AP English Language and Composition Exam.

So what can you do besides faithfully complete the drills and practice tests in this book? Well, there are practice questions and essay questions from past tests on the College Board website, and you can go through those if you feel like you want more practice after you've finished this book. Their website is: **www.collegeboard.com**. You can also get more information by contacting the College Board directly at:

Phone: 609-771-7300 or 888-225-5427 toll-free in the United States and Canada

TTY: 609-882-4118

E-mail: apexams@info.collegeboard.org

A BIT OF HISTORY YOU MAY WANT TO KNOW

Once upon a time, in Ancient Greece, there were scholars who decided that rules for written and oral expression needed to be formalized; among these were Plato and Aristotle. This marked the birth of rhetoric. The Roman rhetoricians continued to develop this important art because they understood the importance of speech in ruling a vast empire.

In Europe, during the Middle Ages, the rules of rhetoric became even stricter. It was determined that to give "proper" form to thought, one had to follow certain rules of expression. By the time the Renaissance rolled around, the goal of expression was to match the models of antiquity. Everyone was striving to live up to the brilliance of the past.

The rest of the story, as it pertains to your AP exam and you, can be summed up in this way: For centuries, writers struggled to liberate themselves from the yoke of formal rhetoric, to invent new forms, and finally to use no forms at all. By the second half of the twentieth century, they had succeeded. Freedom at last! Unfortunately, there was an unanticipated side effect: Reasoned discourse all but disappeared. Horrified professors began to complain that university students were handing in disorganized, illogical drivel. The pendulum began to swing the other way; freshman composition became a mandatory course at most colleges; the formal study of grammar, usage, and rhetoric returned. And high school students, hoping to place out of the freshman composition course in college, began to flock to AP English Language and Composition courses.

AP ENGLISH—DON'T CONFUSE THIS EXAM WITH ITS SISTER

When you sit down to take the AP English Language and Composition test in May, about 369,000 other students will also be sitting down in testing centers around the world to take the same exam. The sister exam to this one (which is often confused with this test) is entitled the AP English Literature exam. It is also given in May, and is taken by about 347,000 students each year. The reason for the existence of these two similar tests is that different freshman college English courses emphasize different things. The Language test assesses knowledge and skills in expository writing or rhetoric, while the Literature test assesses knowledge and skills in dealing with literature, including poetry, which is not tested on the Language test.

The tests are similar in format and are scheduled on different days during the AP weeks, so it is possible to take both exams in the same year. If you are a strong student of both rhetoric and literature, it may be a good idea to take both exams—many students do.

Interestingly enough, almost all of the students who take the Literature and Composition exam take a course that's specifically designed to prepare them for the test. However, many schools do not have a course that specifically covers AP English Language and Composition. In fact, more students take the AP English Language and Composition Exam without a specific preparatory class than any other AP subject exam. Like the other AP exams, there is no prerequisite for either AP exam in English; anyone who wants to take the tests may do so.

AND DON'T BE SHY...

As you know, AP English courses, like other AP courses, are essentially first-year college courses. Actually, AP English courses are sometimes better than their corresponding courses at college. This is partly because nearly everyone in an AP course is a strong student who wants to be in class; as a general rule, the more excited the class, the more inspired (and interesting) the teacher will be. So, if AP English is available at your school, and if you're motivated and interested, take it if you have not done so already.

Even if you cannot take the course, if you're a strong student and you're just thinking about taking the test, you should do it. Sign up for the AP English Language and Composition Exam, study the material in this book, and go for it! AP English credit enables you to skip ahead of the pack, saves money, looks great on your transcript, and opens up your college schedule so you can get to the really interesting courses faster. Even if you only place out of freshman English (but don't get any credit for that course), it will have been worth it. If you are wondering what kind of credit is given for AP courses and what score you need to get on the AP to get credit, ask the colleges that you'd like to attend.

SO WHO WRITES THE AP ENGLISH EXAM—AND WHAT DOES IT LOOK LIKE?

The AP English Development Committee writes the test, but ETS (Educational Testing Service) is involved in crafting it too. The AP people (English instructors from high schools and universities) pick the passages and write first drafts of the test questions, but then the ETS people step in and fine-tune the test. ETS's primary concern is to ensure that the test, especially the multiple-choice section, is similar to previous versions and tests a broad spectrum of student ability.

Luckily for you, ETS has predictable ways of shaping questions and creating the wrong answers. On multiple-choice tests, knowing how the wrong answers are written and how to eliminate them is very important. We'll discuss this topic in detail in the next chapter, entitled Cracking the Multiple-Choice Questions. So let's answer the second question in the heading of this section: What will the test look like?

The Format of the AP English Language and Composition Exam

Below is a helpful outline that describes the basic format for the exam. The total time allotted for the completion of this exam is 3 hours and 15 minutes, or 195 minutes.

Section I: Multiple Choice (60 minutes)—counts for 45 percent of your grade
Total number of questions: 50–55

Section II: Free Response (135 minutes)—counts for 55 percent of your grade
Composed of three essays, which the College Board describes in the following way:

1. Fifteen-minute reading period

2. Analysis of a passage and exposition/presentation of the analysis (40-minute essay on a passage that ETS provides)

3. Argumentative essay (40-minute essay that supports, refutes, or qualifies a statement provided by ETS)

4. Synthesis essay (40-minute essay that integrates information from a variety of sources that ETS provides)

WHAT YOUR FINAL SCORE WILL MEAN

After taking the test in early May, you will receive your scores sometime around the first week of July, which is probably right about when you'll have just started to forget about the entire harrowing experience. Your score will be, simply enough, a single number that will either be a 1, 2, 3, 4, or 5. Here is what those numbers mean.

Score Meaning	Approximate percentage of all test takers receiving this score	Roughly equivalent first-year college course grade	Will a student with this score receive credit?
5—Extremely qualified	10%	A	Usually
4—Well qualified	20%	A−, B+, B	Usually
3—Qualified	30%	B−, C+, C	Maybe
2—Possibly qualified	30%	N/A	Very Rarely
1—Not qualified	10%	N/A	No

Your Multiple-Choice Score

In the multiple-choice section of the test, you are awarded one point for each question that you answer correctly, you receive no points for each question that you leave blank or answer incorrectly. That is, the famous "guessing penalty" on the SAT and SAT Subject Tests does not apply. So, even if you are completely unsure, guess. However, it is always best to use Process of Elimination (POE), as discussed in Part II, to narrow down your choices and make educated guesses.

YOUR FREE-RESPONSE SCORE

Each AP essay is scored on a scale from 0 to 9, with 9 being the best score. Essay readers (who are high school or university English instructors) will grade your three essays, and the scores for your three essays will be added together. The resulting total (which ranges from 0 to 27) constitutes your free-response score.

We will go into the details of essay scoring in Part III, but in general an essay that receives a "9" answers all facets of the question completely, making good use of specific examples to support its points, and is "well-written," which is a catch-all phrase that means its sentences are complete, properly punctuated, clear in meaning, and varied (they exhibit a variety of structure and use a large academic vocabulary). Lower-scoring essays are considered to be deficient in these qualities to a greater or lesser degree, and students who receive a "0" have basically written gibberish. If you write an essay that is not on the topic, you will receive a blank ("—"). This is equivalent to a zero.

The essay readers do not award points according to a standardized, predetermined checklist. The essays are scored individually by individual readers, each of whom scores essays for only one prompt. Thus, you will have three different readers, and each reader will be able to see only the single essay that he or she reads. The readers do not know how you did on the other essays or what score you received on the multiple-choice section.

YOUR FINAL SCORE

Your final score of 1 to 5 is a combination of your scores from the two sections. Remember that the multiple-choice section counts for 45 percent of the total and the essay section counts for 55 percent. This makes them almost equal, and you must concentrate on doing your best on both parts. If you can get a score of 36 (number correct) on a multiple-choice section with 54 questions, you have exactly a 99 percent chance of getting at least a score of 3 on the exam.

You will have the opportunity to calculate your final score for each Practice Test in this book. Both Answers and Explanations chapters include a worksheet to guide you through ETS's formula step by step.

GETTING CREDIT

So how do you get credit from colleges for taking this exam? First, you must attend a college that recognizes the AP program (most colleges do); second, you need to get a good score on one of the two AP English exams (Language and Composition or Literature and Composition).

Your guidance counselor or AP teacher should be able to provide you with information on whether the schools to which you're applying award AP credit. They can probably also tell you how much credit you can get and what scores you need to get the credit. You can also sometimes get the information you need from the college's website. By far the most reliable way to find out what you need to know is to write or e-mail (do not call) the admission office of the schools that interest you and ask about their AP policy. When someone from admission responds, take the e-mail or letter with you when you register for courses (that's why you didn't call!). College registration does not always go smoothly, and you don't want to have to argue with an admission clerk over things like credit (or placement).

In general, the AP exams are widely accepted, but minimum scores and credits awarded vary from school to school. A 4 or a 5 will get you credit at many schools (with the exception of most of the Ivies). A 3 can work, especially at larger universities, but unfortunately, a score of 1 or 2 will get you neither credit nor placement.

As you saw from the table, only about 30 percent of the students who take the AP English Language and Composition Exam earn a 4 or a 5, and about 40 percent receive a 1 or a 2. The rest—30 percent to be exact, receive a 3. This isn't an easy test, but it's well worth the effort that it takes to do well. And again there's good news: With so many poorly prepared students taking the test, you can use this book and walk into the testing center with an important advantage.

Just a couple more topics and we'll move on to strategies and techniques.

HOW TO REGISTER TO TAKE THE EXAM (AND OTHER USEFUL INFORMATION)

This test is administered once a year, in early May, and the fee is $87. Your high school guidance counselor should have all the information you need to sign up to take the AP English Language and Composition Exam. You will have to fill out some forms and make sure the timing of this exam doesn't conflict with any other AP exams you may be taking. Since you'll be preparing so much for this exam, it would be a shame to encounter a scheduling conflict on test day.

On test day, be sure to wear comfortable clothes and shoes; consider dressing in layers if you don't know what the temperature in the testing room will be like. Bring a snack to eat during the break if you think you'll get hungry. Also, remember to bring at least two number-2 pencils and a few good blue or black pens (those are the only two colors allowed on the AP exam).

Finally, and most important, don't forget to get a good night's sleep before test day.

HOW TO USE THIS BOOK

While you may be tempted to skip right to the content review portion of this book—Parts IV and V—we strongly recommend that you read the chapters on test-taking techniques before you work through the content review. These chapters will give you a better idea of what you're doing and show you important techniques for approaching the sample questions, drills, and two full-length tests.

After you have taken the practice tests, we advise that you read all the explanations, even the explanations to the questions that you've answered correctly. Often, you will find that your understanding of a question or the passage will be broadened when you read the explanation. Other times, you'll realize that you got the question right, but for all the wrong reasons. Also, sometimes you could learn the most from other students, so we strongly recommend that you read the sample essays, which several well-prepared students wrote just days before they took the real exam.

Moving On...

At this point, we've described the basics of the AP English Language and Composition Exam. You probably have a lot of unanswered questions, such as *What are the passages like? What kinds of questions are in the multiple-choice section? How should I approach the essays to ace them? Does good handwriting count? When should I guess?*

We'll answer all these questions and many more in the chapters that follow.

PART ◆ II

Cracking the System: The Multiple-Choice Section

2

Cracking the Multiple-Choice Questions

RELAX!

The multiple-choice section of the AP English Language Exam will test your ability to take multiple-choice tests more than it will test your knowledge of English. If you're already an accomplished test taker, then wonderful! Our techniques can still help you, even if you don't need much help. Just focus on your weak subject areas. If you get high grades in class but consistently underachieve on standardized tests, you can relax—using our techniques on these multiple-choice questions will make a huge difference on test day. Finally, if you fall somewhere in between (most students do), using our techniques for the multiple-choice section will probably earn you half a dozen more points than you would have gotten if you hadn't used them.

WILL THE PASSAGES ON THE EXAM LOOK FAMILIAR?

Probably not. The multiple-choice section is made up of 4 to 5 passages, which are followed by 8 to 17 multiple-choice questions about each passage. Although most of the passages will come from works of the nineteenth and twentieth centuries, you should count on seeing at least one that was written before 1800. Typically, students have the greatest difficulty with the older passages since the style is so different from what they're used to seeing in their everyday lives. Again, don't worry. Our practice tests include passages from earlier works just like the real exam does, so that type will be familiar by the time you get to the test.

Think about it—almost any prose written in English or translated into English is a candidate for inclusion on this test. Variety is the byword! Imagine all the different *types* of writing that could be included: works of fiction, essays, biography (or autobiography or diary entries), speeches, letters, pieces of journalism, literary (or any aspect of cultural) criticism, science and nature writing, and writings about politics or history. Contemporary and classic, controversial and commonplace, and male and female perspectives are just some of the contrasts you should anticipate among the passages.

The passages will also run the gamut as far as types of diction, syntax, imagery, tone, style, and points of view. The teachers and professors who write the exam want to include as many rarely seen passages as they can. The idea is to get you to focus on rhetorical devices, figures of speech, and intended purposes of writings that you have not already articulated. Drawing inferences about a passage you've studied in class is less of a challenge than seeing how you deal with new material; this is a much more valid test of your ability to see how writers' language works.

Okay, let's start talking in more detail about how to approach the questions.

THE BIG PICTURE

Some people may advise you to read the questions that pertain to the passage before you read the passage. Do NOT take that advice! If you do this, you run the risk of automatically filtering your reading through the lens of a particular question or questions. You might ignore certain important aspects of the paragraph in your search for the answer to the questions you read. Get a real sense of the passage before you dive into specific questions. Imagine that the first question will be, "What's the gist of the passage?" In other words, the forest will have a quality of its own, and you need to be comfortable within that forest before you can analyze its trees; *read for the big picture*. Some of the multiple-choice questions will ask you to summarize the author's tone, style, and point of view. To do this, you'll need to have a sense of the big picture. In fact, several of the questions will probably try to trick you into identifying the wrong answer because you're focusing too narrowly on the sentence (or section) to which the question refers.

In a minute, we'll introduce you to a typical passage on the AP English Language Exam. First we'll talk more about two other important techniques you should use when tackling these questions—the Two-Pass system and POE.

PACE YOURSELF! THE TWO-PASS SYSTEM

There are 50–55 questions on the multiple-choice section of this exam, and you have a total of 60 minutes to complete it. This means that you have about one minute to answer each question. To most efficiently use your time, you should employ what we call the Two-Pass system. Basically, this means that you make a first pass at the multiple-choice section, answering the questions you easily can and circling the harder ones so that you can go back later. This system works well since, in this section, all the questions are worth the same number of points—regardless of whether you think they're easy or hard! Be careful when bubbling your answer sheet, especially when you skip questions using this technique.

As you know, on the AP English Language Exam, the multiple-choice questions are based on passages. We've also told you that there will be a total of 4 to 5 passages on your test (although some passages are repeated). Since you have 60 minutes total, this means you should be spending about 12 to 15 minutes on each passage and its questions.

Here are the steps to take when using the Two-Pass system.

1. Answer all the easy questions first.

2. Circle the hard questions.

3. Look at your watch to see how much time you have left out of whatever number of minutes you allotted for this passage (between 12 to 15). If you have 5 minutes left, tackle questions you circled. If you have no time left, then come back to the circled questions after you've safely finished the rest of the passages in the section (if there's time).

POE AND GUESSING

You've probably heard about the techniques called "process of elimination" and "educated guessing." Whatever you know about these techniques, you should know that on this exam, your chances of gaining points on a question will go up if you can eliminate one or more answer choices before you guess. This means that if there are questions on this exam that you don't know the answer to—and there will be—apply POE and guess.

But, does guessing really help? Sure! Let's say you end up blindly guessing on 15 questions. Random selection suggests that you will get 3 of these 15 right, which means you just earned a point. Because no points are deducted for wrong answers, the 4 wrong answers simply receive zero points. If you are going to guess without any POE, don't waste time wondering what the best letter is. Just pick a letter and move on.

While blindly guessing should gain you a point here and there, using POE *in conjunction* with guessing increases your odds of getting questions right. Let's say on the 15 questions above, you are able to narrow them all down to three choices through POE. Well, now random selection suggests that you will get 5 questions right. So, you picked up 2 more points on hard questions through POE rather than random guessing.

While five points won't get you to your goal score, you won't be guessing (whether blindly or with POE) on the entire test. The point is that even blindly guessing should get you a point here and there, and thoughtful guessing based on POE is an important strategy when you are faced with a hard question.

Let's recap:

- Read the passage for the big picture.
- Pace yourself (use the Two-Pass system).
- Use POE on *every question*!

Now you're ready to try your first sample passage.

SAMPLE PASSAGE #1—HERE'S HOW IT'S DONE

(The following passage is excerpted from Henry David Thoreau's Walden.*)*

One day when I went out to my wood-pile, or rather
my pile of stumps, I observed two large ants, the one
red, the other much larger, nearly half an inch long, and
Line   black, fiercely contending with one another. Having once
5   got hold they never let go, but struggled and wrestled
and rolled on the chips incessantly. Looking farther, I
was surprised to find that the chips were covered with
such combatants, that it was not a *duellum*, but a *bellum*,
a war between two races of ants, the red always pitted
10   against the black, and frequently two red ones to one
black. The legions of the Myrmidons covered all the hills
and vales in my wood-yard, and the ground was already
strewn with the dead and dying, both red and black.
It was the only battle which I have ever witnessed, the
15   only battle-field I ever trod while the battle was raging;
internecine war; the red republicans on the one hand,
and the black imperialists on the other. On every side
they were engaged in deadly combat, yet without any
noise that I could hear, and human soldiers never fought
20   so resolutely. I watched a couple that were fast locked
in each other's embraces, in a little sunny valley amid
the chips, now at noonday prepared to fight till the sun
went down, or life went out. The smaller red cham-
pion had fastened himself like a vice to his adversary's
25   front, and through all the tumblings on that field never
for an instant ceased to gnaw at one of his feelers near
the root, having already caused the other to go by the
board; while the stronger black one dashed him from
side to side, and, as I saw on looking nearer, had already
30   divested him of several of his members. They fought
with more pertinacity than bulldogs. Neither manifested
the least disposition to retreat. It was evident that their
battle-cry was "Conquer or die." In the meanwhile there
came along a single red ant on the hillside of the valley,
35   evidently full of excitement, who either had dispatched
his foe, or had not yet taken part in the battle; probably the latter, for he had lost none of his limbs; whose
mother had charged him to return with his shield or
upon it. Or perchance he was some Achilles, who had
40   nourished his wrath apart, and had now come to avenge
or rescue his Patroclus. He saw this unequal combat from
afar—for the blacks were nearly twice the size of the
red—he drew near with rapid pace till be stood on his
guard within half an inch of the combatants; then, watch-
45   ing his opportunity, he sprang upon the black warrior,
and commenced his operations near the root of his right
fore leg, leaving the foe to select among his own members; and so there were three united for life, as if a new
kind of attraction had been invented which put all other
50   locks and cements to shame. I should not have wondered
by this time to find that they had their respective musical

bands stationed on some eminent chip, and playing their
national airs the while, to excite the slow and cheer the
dying combatants. I was myself excited somewhat even
55 as if they had been men. The more you think of it, the
less the difference.

THE ANALYSIS

Having read the passage, what would you say the big picture is? The dominant rhetorical strategy Thoreau employs in this passage is the analogy that compares the behavior of the ants with that of human beings. Is he writing to shed some scientific light on the behavior of ants? No. He's dwelling on details about the insects to lead us to a revelation about human beings. He's asking us to see that people are like ants and is commenting on the inappropriateness of associating warfare with grandiloquence and romance. Thoreau is basically asking, *What difference do the struggles of the ants make, when we examine them from far above? Likewise, what difference does human warfare make, when seen from far above or even from a divine perspective?*

This is the big picture. As you read the passage, you need to keep in mind his reason for taking this strong interest in ants and not get waylaid by the particular events taking place in the narrative. The last lines of the passage should help you make the important conceptual leap. Thoreau outright says, "I was myself excited somewhat even as if they had been men. The more you think of it, the less the difference."

As we mentioned earlier, some types of big-picture questions you'll see on this exam will ask you to characterize the speaker's tone, style, or attitude in the passage. Another type of big-picture question that you'll see will ask you to describe how a particular detail fits into the big picture—what a particular word means in context or how the reader is meant to interpret a word based on the tone, style, or attitude of the passage as a whole. Let's look at a typical big-picture question.

1. The author's tone in this passage can best be
   described as one of

   (A) suspicion and confusion
   (B) horror and shock
   (C) detachment and criticism
   (D) condescension and bemusement
   (E) admiration and empathy

The correct answer is (D). While it may be tempting to take the words at face value and interpret the ants as heroic, remember that this is a big-picture question, so you need to consider the overall meaning or intent of the passage. Remember that Thoreau's intention is to make the point that the observer is to the ants as some higher being would be to humans. This is why *condescension* is a valid answer. In order to determine tone, you will need to frequently consider many different connotations of the answers.

When you're looking for the correct answer, remember that both elements of the answer choice must be correct, so the easiest way to approach this type of question is to try to eliminate just one of the elements; if one of them is wrong, then the whole answer choice can be eliminated. For example, *detachment* (C) is a plausible answer, but *criticism* is not; so (C) can be eliminated. Half wrong is all wrong.

In case you didn't notice, Thoreau makes three references to Greek history, literature, and art in this one paragraph. Do you know who the Myrmidons were? Do you know the story about the Spartan mother who says to her son, "With it or on it"? Do you understand the relationship between Patroclus and Achilles? If not, don't worry. Though you may be tested on whether or not you can spot a classical allusion, this kind of specialized knowledge will never be tested explicitly. If you miss certain pieces of the big picture, don't be disheartened! Just like when you put together a jigsaw puzzle, if you have the general outline and can fill in major portions of the content, then you can imagine the entire picture even if a few pieces are missing.

Here is another typical big-picture question that gets at pretty much the same issues as the previous one.

2. In this passage, the author exaggerates the greatness of the ants' struggle to

   (A) exaggerate the greatness of nature
   (B) show the true greatness of nature
   (C) demonstrate the importance of war
   (D) illustrate the fierceness of ants
   (E) suggest the exaggerated greatness of humans

The answer is (E). The other answers—(C) and (D) in particular, may have also looked good to you—were deliberately put in there to trap readers who didn't pay attention to the big picture.

Now, let's take a look at what types of details will be tested—and how.

DETAILS AND THE BIG PICTURE

You now know that for each passage you come to in this section, you'll read the passage to get the big picture. Big-picture questions often come either at the beginning of the question set or at the end, and the detail questions are sandwiched in between.

Let's assume that the passage by Thoreau was the first one on the test and that the two questions that we already looked at were the first two questions about the passage. The next two are as follows.

3. In lines 1-2, Thoreau changes "wood-pile" to "pile of stumps" because he wants to

   (A) enhance the sense of realism in the passage
   (B) trivialize the setting of the action
   (C) be thoroughly truthful in his depiction
   (D) create a sense of drama
   (E) make the setting more natural

You can immediately eliminate choices (A), (C), and (E); you know from getting the big picture that Thoreau probably wouldn't be trying to "enhance the sense of realism," or "be thoroughly truthful." Nor is he trying to "make the setting more natural." The setting is just about as natural as it can get. Even if you thought that (D) reinforced your view that the battle of the ants was a serious epic drama and chose that answer, you may have been saved at the last minute if you noticed that (B) lined up nicely with the answer choices from the first two questions. If you got those two questions right, then (B) would have been a choice that reinforced your confidence. Your answers should match each other.

Take a look at the next question on this passage.

4. All of the following humorously aggrandize the battle EXCEPT

    (A) it was not a *duellum*, but a *bellum* (line 8)
    (B) the hills and vales of my wood-yard (lines 11-12)
    (C) human soldiers never fought so resolutely (lines 19-20)
    (D) whose mother had charged him to return with his shield or upon it (lines 37-38)
    (E) Or perchance he was some Achilles (line 39)

Again, in case you missed the big picture, the exam writer goes so far as to *say* that the battle is humorously aggrandized. If there was ever any doubt about the seriousness of the author's point of view toward the ant war, that doubt should immediately disappear.

Let's look through the answer choices, starting with (A). Even if your Latin is weak or nonexistent, you can probably see the word "duel" in *duellum*, and *bellum* (war) is defined in the context; if you catch the pun (knowing that *duellum* is the ancient Latin word for war and the etymological root of *bellum*), then the humor is even more obvious. The "hills and vales" (B) are, of course, only minuscule piles of wood chips or sawdust. Hopefully the humor in the personifications in (D) and (E) was also apparent. The correct answer is (C); in fact, it is almost the only line in the passage that could be considered not tinged with humor.

THE DETAILS

After you have read the passage to get the big picture, don't read it again to try to get all the details. Instead, as you come to detail questions that refer you back to specific lines in the passage, go back to those places and read more closely. You should *always* reread those lines; do not rely on your memory, and do not reread the entire text. When a question refers you to words or lines in the same part of the passage, make sure you "read around the lines." That is, you should read the sentence before the sentence in question, read the sentence itself, and finally read the sentence that follows the one in question. You want to read as little as possible, but as much as is necessary, and this is an art that you must develop over time. Our practice tests at the end of the book will afford you ample practice for honing your skills.

Let's move on. Most of the non-big picture questions on the passage will focus on detailed information from very specific parts of the passage. Remember, do NOT go back and read large portions of the text; if you cannot answer a question without extensive reading, then you should leave the answer blank and return to it, in your second pass through the questions in the section. Here are a couple of examples of this type of question.

5. In context, "pertinacity" (line 31) most nearly means

    (A) pertinence
    (B) loyalty
    (C) perspicacity
    (D) obstinacy
    (E) attentiveness

On this type of question, oftentimes just knowing the definition of the word will not be enough to enable you to answer the question correctly, and the indication that you are to find the meaning "in context" almost guarantees that the answer won't be the first meaning that pops into your head. "Pertinent" wouldn't be right, and "pertinence" (being pertinent) is also incorrect. If you go back and look at the context—especially the word "bulldogs"—you should be able to eliminate all the answers except (D). Another clue is the adverb "resolutely" that appears slightly earlier in the passage. The ants are fighting resolutely and obstinately—like bulldogs.

Let's go through a couple more.

6. The phrase "who had nourished his wrath apart"
    (lines 39-40) most nearly means

    (A) who was hungry for battle
    (B) who worked up great anger in private
    (C) who was only partly angry
    (D) who fought alone
    (E) who feasted alone

7. The phrase "who had nourished his wrath apart"
    (lines 39-40) serves mainly to

    (A) create the impression of an epic tone
    (B) sustain the seriousness of the author's point of view
    (C) highlight the extent of the hatred between the enemies
    (D) underscore the loneliness of the combatants
    (E) emphasize the cannibalistic nature of the combatants

Question 6 is a translation question. What does "who nourished his wrath apart" mean in simple English? The answer is (B).

Question 7 is more of a big-picture question—remember that these generally occur at the beginning and ending of the group of questions that pertain to one passage. On a real test, you would not see two questions on the same quotation, but we want you to see how the exam writers can approach material from different perspectives. We have already determined that there is a playful humor in the humanization (*anthropomorphism*) of the combat of the insects, and this allows us to eliminate answer (B), which is there just to trick students who missed the big picture. The correct answer is (A). There is "the impression" of an epic tone (rather than a true epic tone) because, once again, Thoreau's aim is to have us understand the futility and insignificance of events in the grand scheme of things.

One final note about detail questions: Do not forget the big picture when answering the detail questions. Often, the test writer will inadvertently give away important information about the big picture in the phrasing of the detail questions and answers, as they did in the sample questions on this page and on page 20. Sometimes the detail questions will cause you to reevaluate your big-picture view of a passage; if your view is correct, the detail questions will probably confirm that view.

FURTHER PRACTICE

Try out the next passage and questions on your own, then check the answers and explanations that follow.

Questions 1-4. Read the following passage carefully before you choose your answers.

(*The following passage is from* The Word Museum, *by Jeffrey Kacirk.*)

Of particular interest to me have been the myriad elusive details of earlier times that tend to go unnoticed. In my schooling, I found that teachers and historians, because of their socially prescribed curricular attention toward larger social concepts, often bypassed the smaller and more personal expressions of social custom and conduct, often leaving the novel as the best lens with which to view forgotten elements of everyday life. Take, for instance, the long-defunct activity called *upknocking*, the employment of the *knocker up,* who went house to house in the early morning hours of the nineteenth century to awaken his working-class clients before the advent of affordable alarm clocks. Until encountering this entry, I had never thought about how people of this time managed to awaken with any predictability.

Line 5, 10, 15 (margin line numbers)

1. The author of the passage is most likely

   (A) a scientific researcher
   (B) a lexicographer
   (C) a historian
   (D) a sociologist
   (E) a teacher

2. The author has a particular interest in

   (A) old words and alarm clocks
   (B) social and political history
   (C) unusual activities and personal conduct
   (D) historical detail and social conduct
   (E) literature and the nineteenth century

3. In this passage, "*upknocking*" is viewed as

   (A) an interesting anachronism
   (B) a superannuated and silly word
   (C) a working-class word
   (D) a word devoid of historical interest
   (E) the key to understanding the nineteenth century

4. Which word from the passage gives the clearest indication as to where the author encountered the process of *upknocking*?

   (A) entry (line 13)
   (B) novel (line 7)
   (C) schooling (line 3)
   (D) employment (line 10)
   (E) clients (line 12)

EXPLANATIONS

1. **B** If you know that lexicon is roughly synonymous with dictionary (and you do if you've studied the Hit Parade), the question is an easy one. If you don't, then it's still a simple matter of POE. Given that the author refers to teachers and historians in a way that appears to set them apart, it is reasonable to assume that the author is not a member of either group. At this point, you could guess and go, or you could note the phrase "until encountering this entry," which is the clue that points to the correct answer—the entry is a dictionary entry.

2. **D** It is wise to use POE again and attempt to eliminate all but one of the answers. Remember that if one of the elements isn't relevant, then the entire answer is invalid. The first answer begins in a promising fashion; the author is interested in old words; however, that interest is only tangentially related to alarm clocks—and the entire topic (upknocking) is only an example used to illustrate a more sweeping interest. Eliminate (A). Answer (B) begins with similar promise, but there is nothing in the passage that addresses political history. All of the remaining answers are at least somewhat plausible, but remember that the example of upknocking is used to illustrate "the smaller and more personal expressions of social custom and conduct" rather than "larger social concepts." That is, the author is interested in the revelatory details of social conduct (or concepts), rather than in the sweeping generalities. The author is, indeed, interested in nineteenth-century literature and unusual activities of that century, but only as they reveal how discrete social groups (in this case, the working class) lived and functioned.

3. **A** If you are not familiar with the word *anachronism,* go back and review the Hit Parade. There are two important meanings of this word. If you were to write a story about one of Ulysses's forgotten adventures, in which the hero uses a machine gun to defeat Schwartzathon, the King of Califia, then you would have employed an anachronism (the gun); that is, you would have placed a thing (or a person) out of its proper time. But an anachronism can also be something that was once relevant, but no longer is—a definition almost synonymous with "superannuated."

    Once again, POE can help you eliminate the incorrect answers. *Upknocking* may sound like a silly word to you, but you should be able to understand the author's sincere, serious interest in such a word. Besides, the test writers would never expect you to choose an answer that referred to any aspect of the English language as "silly," so you can always eliminate this type of answer choice when you see it. Answer (C) is off base because, although the word applied to working-class life, there is no reason to suspect that only that class knew of or used the word. If you chose (D), then you need to go back and read the passage very carefully. Choice (E), the final answer, is simply hyperbolic; *upknocking* is a word that gives us a better glimpse into what the nineteenth century was like, but it is not the key to understanding the entire century.

4. **A** We addressed this in the explanation to question 1; at the very least, you should be able to eliminate answers (C), (D), and (E).

TO SUM UP

- Begin each passage by reading for the big picture.

- Concentrate on the author's goal, tone, and point of view.

- Do not read stubbornly; you do not need to understand or follow everything; some (even many) details may escape you—focus on the big picture!

- Always return to the passage when multiple-choice questions refer you to specific lines.

- Always read around the lines; the context of the lines is almost always critical in determining the correct answer.

- Pace yourself! Remember our Two-Pass system. Dividing the section into chunks for each passage should help you out.

- Don't forget about POE and educated guessing! If you can eliminate two answer choices, your chances of guessing correctly increase a lot.

A FINAL NOTE

Do NOT expect to be entertained by the passages! Every now and again, you will encounter a passage as clever and entertaining as Thoreau's, but that will be the exception. The test writers often (purposely?) choose passages that are dry, humorless, and downright boring. This exam is about toughness—mental toughness. Your ability to concentrate and think methodically and critically even *when you're not interested* is as important as anything when it comes to scoring high. You are in luck because the vast majority of the passages in the sample tests in this book are every bit as dry, humorless, and boring as the ones that you'll encounter on the real exam! If you read the passages and answer the questions under actual testing conditions, you will be ready for the rigors that await.

PART ◆ III

Cracking the System:
The Essays

3

Basic Principles of the Essay Section

THE FORMAT AND CONTENT OF THE ESSAY SECTION

The format of the AP English Language essay section underwent a significant change in May 2007, requiring a new essay—the synthesis essay. We're including all of the information you'll need for the post-2007 test.

The essay section of the exam will be made up of the following:

- One synthesis essay
- One rhetorical analysis essay
- One argumentative essay

In Chapters 4 through 6, you will learn more about each kind of essay and how to go about writing the best possible essays in the time that's allotted—a total of 2 hours, or 120 minutes (that does not include the 15-minute reading period). At the test site, you will receive all the paper you need (including scratch paper), and you will be instructed to write in pen. Remember to bring two or three blue or black ink pens with you.

As we mentioned, you'll have two hours to complete the essay section. While the test administrator will give you some approximate guidelines for time management, you will not be told how much time to spend on each essay or when to move on to the next essay. Time management is important! Before you set foot in the test center, you must practice writing 40-minute essays. Of course, if your school has not provided you with practice, the tests at the end of this book will give you an opportunity to hone your skills. Do not fool yourself into believing, as so many other students (and teachers) have, that any type of writing will prepare you to write the AP English Language and Composition Exam. Writing a cogent, organized essay under rigid time constrictions is a learned skill; writing three consecutive essays under such conditions requires special training, stamina, and lots of practice. Fortunately for you, this book provides you with all of those.

THE IMPORTANCE OF THE ESSAY SECTION TO YOUR SCORE

The essay section of the AP English Language and Composition Exam counts for 55 percent of your total score, which means that it's only slightly more important to your overall score than the multiple-choice section of the test. However, the essay section will *feel* like it's more important because two-thirds of your time will go into producing the essays. Students tend to look at the essay section with a combination of awe, fear, and excitement. It's one thing to send off some pencil marks on an answer sheet for mechanized correction; but it's quite another to submit your writing to an anonymous person for judgment. The essay section is the only place in this exam where your personality—at least to a limited degree—will shine through to test graders. Don't let this scare you: use it as an opportunity to show off what a great, cool writer you are.

Keep this in mind: Although the multiple-choice and essay sections are roughly equal in the ETS scoring process, there is a big difference between the way that you'll approach each of these sections. Preparing for the essay section of the exam is more than just memorizing and applying techniques.

READY, SET, WRITE!

As we've discussed, you will write your AP essays under intense time pressure and without a pre-paratory lesson. That is not what you're used to. In the past, editing and rewriting may have been an important part of your in-school essay writing. Perhaps your teachers have insisted that you turn in drafts of essays and required you to revise the drafts. If so, then you know that good writing takes patience and care; the "ready, set, write" attitude that test writers expect you to adopt when writing the AP essays runs opposite to the right way to approach most writing and is, hopefully, diametrically opposed to the way your teachers have trained you to write. Unfortunately, just because you have the ability to write a superlative essay when time is not a factor does not guarantee that you'll be able to write a good one in 40 minutes. That's why you're reading this chapter.

The closest thing you may have experienced to writing the essays for the AP test is probably an in-class essay test, but even in that case there are significant differences. For example, in-class essays usually come after you've spent several classes on the subject at hand and know what your teacher expects you to have learned. Also, on in-class essay tests, the teacher wants to see what you know, not just how well you write. On the AP exam, you will be writing cold on a passage you read just two minutes prior for the first time. You'll have no time to revise—only proofread—your work, and you'll be graded at least as much on the form and writing as on the content. The AP essays call for a kind of speed writing; you have to come up with good ideas and get them down efficiently—on the very first try.

This isn't the best way to write, but remember that everyone else is working under the same conditions. If you know how to make the most of these conditions, you will have a leg up on most other writers. It's a little late in the game to learn how to write well, but it isn't too late to learn how to write a high-scoring AP essay.

YOUR TEACHER KNOWS YOU

In school, you write essays for teachers who know you. They know what your writing looked like at the beginning of the year, they know that it has or has not improved, they know whether you do your homework assiduously, they know whether you contribute keen insights to class discussion, and they know that your real passion is for football, field hockey, dance, painting, physics, or reading. They may even know about special circumstances in your life that are affecting your work.

When you write your name on the first page of an essay, your teacher already knows much about your essay, and these are part of your teacher's reading. Inevitably, that familiarity has some effect on the grades that you receive.

The AP reader doesn't know you at all.

YOU KNOW YOUR TEACHER

Also, remember that you do not know anything about the reader of your AP essays. Who is he or she? In school, you know your teacher. You are accustomed to his or her demands; you know what that teacher wants to hear. Your AP essays will be written to a featureless face: Is it a kind face? Mean? Crazy? You will never know.

ALL ABOUT AP ESSAY SCORING

THE ZERO-TO-NINE SCALE

As we mentioned in Part I, each of your essays will be given a score between 0 and 9, with 0 being the worst score you can get, and 9 being the best. However, the scores are *not* spread out evenly over that range; the majority of essays receive a grade of 4 or 5. About 65 percent of the essays receive a score in the middle range: 4, 5, and 6. The high and low scores taper away pretty quickly. ETS does not *tell* its essay readers to bunch up the scores this way (in fact ETS often chastises the readers for this bulge in the middle), and they don't manipulate the results to make them produce this bell curve. It works out this way because most of the essays are, indeed, average. In fact, reading essays often becomes drudgery because there are so many middle-of-the-road essays. With this in mind, your goal is to have your essays stand out from the rest. Your goal should be to *at least* get a 6 or 7, and it's even realistic to expect at least one score of 8 if you practice enough before test day.

HOLISTIC SCORING

The essays are scored holistically. This means that the reader goes through your essay and gets an overall impression, which is translated into a single number (your score). There is no checklist of points; you won't receive 2 points for style, 2 points for grammar, 1 point for vocabulary, and 1 point for a clear thesis statement, for example.

About a week before the actual grading sessions, ETS goes through several essays to get a sense of how students did—this is the beginning of the calibration process. Next, the ETS table leaders comb through the student writing looking for representative essays: the perfect 9 essay, the average 5 essay, and so on. The table leaders use these sample essays to train (calibrate) the readers. For nearly an entire day, the table leader and readers—working on a single essay prompt—read essays together and discuss the grades that they would assign. Once the readers can grade sample essays the way the table leader can, the group is ready to embark on the grading process. ETS scrupulously applies certain control processes; for example, over time, a reader will end up rereading and correcting certain essays chosen at random, and the two sets of scores will be compared for consistency. To check consistency from one reader to another, every reader (without knowing it) grades essays that another reader has already graded. However, despite all this checking and rechecking, there is no way around one key fact: The readers are individuals who will make subjective judgments.

THE READER WANTS AN ESSAY THAT IS EASY TO SCORE

Readers are high school and college instructors who take a week out of their year to come to one site to grade essays. It's your job *not* to contribute to the monotony, but rather to make sure your essay stands out from the hundreds of ho-hum essays that each reader will score.

You need to strive to write an essay that's obviously better than average. The person who reads your test should feel confident about giving you at least a 6. Remember that three-quarters of the essays are average or worse, and readers are always hoping to come across something outstanding. Usually, the essays are generic and have no distinctive style to them, and often the essays barely address the prompt. If an essay starts out dull and poorly written, the reader may tune out and miss an excellent and well-written point later in the essay; likewise if an essay ends with a long, boring paragraph, the reader may forget some of the great points that were made earlier in the essay. But before we examine some basic tips for making it easy for the reader to give you a high score, let's look at the kind of scoring guide that the readers use.

A Typical Scoring Guide

As we discussed briefly, the readers receive a scoring guide for the essays that they will grade. The scoring guides for all of the AP essays are very similar. What follows is a combination of the various guides, without the details that are particular to any specific passage or prompt. As you look over the scoring guide, notice how little specific guidance ETS actually provides. The readers are actually given considerable leeway.

Scores 8–9

These are well-organized and well-written essays that clearly address the prompt. These essays include apt, specific examples to explain or argue a point. The argument is convincing, and the student successfully develops a position. While not flawless, these works demonstrate an understanding of the passage or concept, the techniques of composition, and the ability to control a wide range of elements. The writers of these essays express their ideas skillfully and clearly.

Scores 6–7

The content of these papers resembles that of the higher-scoring essays, but it is less precise and less aptly supported. These essays deal with elements such as rhetorical strategies, diction, imagery, and point of view, but they are less effective than the essays in the upper range. Essays that receive a score of 7 generally exhibit fewer mechanical errors and use slightly better specific examples than those that receive a score of 6.

Score 5

These essays are superficial. Although not seriously off topic or completely lacking in merit, they miss the complexity of the prompt or of the passage and offer only a perfunctory analysis. The treatment of elements such as rhetorical strategies, diction, imagery, and point of view is overly generalized. The writing adequately conveys the writer's thoughts, but the essays are limited, inconsistent, and uneven.

Scores 3–4

These essays attempt to address the prompt, but they reflect an incomplete understanding of the prompt or of the passage (or both); they do not address the prompt adequately. The discussion is oversimplified and misrepresented. The treatment of rhetorical elements is scanty or unconvincing, and there is little support for the writer's statements. Typically, these essays reveal marked weaknesses in the writer's ability to handle the mechanics of written English.

Scores 1–2

These essays contain the shortcomings found in the essays that are given a score of 3 and 4, but to a more pronounced degree. These essays either completely misunderstand the prompt or the passage (or both) or simply summarize the sources and prompt. Typically, these essays are incoherent, inchoate, or both. The writing evinces no control of written English, and the organization is poor.

Score 0

This is a response that fails to address the question. There may be a reference only to the task at hand.

Score "—"

This indicates that the response is completely off topic or that a response has not been made. The essay, of course, receives no points.

ANALYSIS OF THE SCORING GUIDE

The scoring guide should tell you two important things:

- First, that the high-scoring essays are *clear*. They are not perfect. They aren't moving and profound. They're simply clear. Practically every point made in the 8 to 9 score description is just another way of saying *clear*. "Well-organized" means clearly organized. "Apt, specific examples" is another way of saying that the writer has used clear examples. Clarity is your goal.

- Second, notice the jump that happens at the 5 score. Notice how the whole tone of the guide changes. Suddenly the guide is not talking about the fine points of addressing the prompt; it is talking about the life-choking drabness of it all. You can almost hear the guide's author muttering under his or her breath, "I wish we could give these essays an even lower score; they are so boring!" The 5 essay is just a trap; many 5 essays are written by good students, and most of these students probably think they wrote a pretty good essay. But in actuality they wrote only an adequate essay, a mechanical essay, a commonplace essay—a boring essay. After grading the fifty-fifth essay of the day, a reader writes down a 5 and picks up another essay from the pile, praying: "Please, not another drab, boring 5 essay!"

If you understand what you read and can write reasonably well, your goal should not be a 5. It should be at least a 6 or 7. You will almost certainly get better than even a 6 or 7 by following a few basic tips and familiarizing yourself with the types of essays you will be required to write.

HOW TO MAKE IT EASY FOR THE READER TO GIVE YOU A HIGH SCORE

About half the points you're given for your essay will come from its content, but the reader has to be able to get to that content. There are a few vital things that you must do to let your excellence shine through with full impact. These basic tips pertain to only the superficial aspects of your writing, but a clear surface is the first step toward getting a high score.

NEATNESS COUNTS

Do everything that's reasonably possible to make your essays readable. Your writing does not have to be pretty, but it needs to be legible. Think before you write! If your thoughts are clear before you write, you will express yourself more clearly in the essay; if your thoughts are a mess, your essay will be a mess too.

Some people will urge you to use cursive, rather than use print. This is bad advice, unless you ordinarily use cursive instead of printing when you write. Do not waste time by slowing down your writing or, worse, learning how to use cursive on the day of the test. Remember, unless you can also ace a test in penmanship, cursive is generally more difficult to read.

The general appearance of the essay is what's most important. An occasional scratch-out is perfectly fine; a scratch-out every third word is a sign that you don't know what you're doing. Messy essay writing is like a guy showing up for a job interview with his shoes untied, his fly unzipped, his belt skipping a few loops, ketchup all over his shirt, and his hair unwashed. First impressions count, and it is easy to dismiss a mess. Think, organize, and let your writing flow.

These days, using a word processor makes perfect sense for most writing that you do. Students like the auto-correct, spell-check, and auto-almost-everything functions that are part of word-processing programs; teachers like having fewer mistakes to correct—and the increased legibility. However, your teacher may have tried to prepare you by having you write essays in class and written by hand. Do *not* use your computer when you're writing the practice essays in this book. A significant part of your preparation for the exam should be to practice writing your essays by hand. Far too many students produce their only handwritten essays of the entire year on the day of the exam, and that's a huge handicap.

INDENT YOUR PARAGRAPHS

Your reader's first impressions are, indeed, crucial. The messy-looking character at the job interview has an uphill battle on his hands, if he hasn't lost his chance already. The overall look of your essay is a first impression. It is the smile on your face as you walk in the door. Your essay should look neat, organized, and clear. Make your paragraphs obvious. Indent twice as far as you normally would.

When in doubt, make a new paragraph. Have you ever opened a book and seen nothing but very long paragraphs? Your next thought is probably, "Do I really have to read this?" That's exactly what readers think when they see an essay without paragraphs. Make sure readers can see the paragraphs at first glance. Also, get in the habit of checking your essays for balance. All of the paragraphs should be approximately the same length, if possible.

Neat presentation, regular handwriting, and balanced paragraphs will put readers on your side before they even read a line.

WRITE PERFECTLY...FOR THE FIRST PARAGRAPH

Your first paragraph forms the reader's first impression, so put care into it. If you're unsure about the spelling of a word, don't use it. If you're unsure how to punctuate the sentence, rewrite it in a way that makes you feel confident. Don't make any mistakes in the first paragraph. Don't fret as much about the rest of the essay; the readers expect mistakes. But paragraph one has got to be strong. If you try to write the whole essay perfectly, you'll write so slowly, or fill up your brain with so much worry, that you'll probably run out of time.

All you need is a few sentences to convince the reader that you can write a good sentence when you want to. The glow of a good beginning carries over the whole essay. Mistakes later on look like minor errors not even worth bothering with. After all, the reader's already seen that you can write. Mistakes at the beginning look like just the opposite—they look like telling signs of inability and a weak grasp of fundamental English mechanics. Take extra care at the beginning of your essay; then relax and just write (*neatly*).

WRITE WITH PIZZAZZ

Take some risks when you write your essays; you may fall flat every once in a while, but the reader will appreciate your effort and reward it. Bored students write boring essays. Be decisive and let yourself go. For example, you may write, "The candidate's appearance was neat, and the boss gave him the job right away." That may be true, but the sentence is mundane at best. A better sentence would be something like, "The candidate's Armani suit and sleek silk tie captivated the boss, who slipped a contract across the table without comment or hesitation." Or, "The creases on the candidate's suit were as sharp as the pencil that the boss had tucked behind his ear, and, faster than a New York second, the wizened old man produced a contract and a pen." Over the top? Who cares! Nobody expects you to write like Toni Morrison or Neil Postman. In fact, the reader expects you to write like someone who is suffering through a tedious, nerve-racking exercise—because that's exactly how most of the other essays come across. If you write like someone who enjoys writing, the reader will enjoy reading your essay and reward you.

This does not mean that you should write tangled, complex sentences; in fact, you should try to avoid them. All you need to do is pay attention to diction (word choice). When you find yourself using a generic verb such as *look, see, says, walk, go, take,* or *give,* or a generic noun such as *street, house, car,* or *man,* ask yourself if there isn't a more precise, more colorful word that you could use instead. Why write "house" when you're referring to a mansion, shack, or cabin? Why write "car," when you really mean jalopy, Porsche, or limousine? A little bit goes a long way: You could even make it appear that writing the essay was fun, which may very well be the case.

Obviously, there can be too much of a good thing, so don't go overboard. Just try to let your writing flow naturally; from time to time, however, think about alternative diction.

Do not use contractions or shorthand symbols such as "&" or "w/" or "tho." Get in the habit of using a relatively high level of discourse when you write essays for class. The AP reader will not necessarily take off points if you neglect this advice, but you will not impress anyone with e-mail or instant messenger–style writing.

ANSWER THE QUESTION

If you write a great essay that does not address the prompt, you will get a lousy score. All three essays are directed essays, and, in the next chapter, you will study the types of prompts that you will encounter on the exam. It is extraordinarily easy to figure out how to address each prompt as long as you remain cool, read the prompt slowly, and follow the advice we give you. For now, know that every prompt has telltale signs that allow you to "answer the question"—even if you do not fully understand it.

BUDGET YOUR TIME

As we mentioned, you can take as much or as little time as you like to write each of the three essays, as long as the total time does not exceed two hours. Each essay is worth the same number of points, however, so it's essential that you allot about 40 minutes for each essay. A slightly better score on one essay will not make up for a bad score on another, and if you spend an hour on your first essay, you will not have enough time to write the other essays well.

With this in mind, when you approach the essays, you should definitely have a plan for budgeting your time. As we mentioned above, you have 2 hours of writing total or about 40 minutes for each essay. It is wise to use part of your 40 minutes for planning and jotting down an outline for the essay you're about to write; usually, 3 to 5 minutes is sufficient for this. In the next few chapters, you learn specific steps you can take to effectively plan your answers to all three types of essay prompts (synthesis, rhetorical analysis, and argumentative). Basically, you should first examine the question and circle key words and phrases, jot down a few notes (more on this in a bit), and begin to write your essay. It may also be helpful to write your thesis statement (or at least a key phrase) at the top of the page to keep you on track. Also, try to save a few minutes at the end for proofreading. You'll be surprised at the improvements you can make to your essay in the last minute or two, simply by correcting little mistakes in wording or grammar.

ORDERING THE SECTION

Just as with the reading passages in the multiple-choice section of the exam, you may write the essays in any order you like. However, you should probably not do this unless the first prompt makes you feel extremely uncomfortable. After all, you still have to write all three essays, and leaving the most difficult essay for the end (a common technique for many students), when you are tired and restless, isn't a great idea. In any event, once you learn how to identify the various kinds of prompts, there will be no such thing as a difficult essay. For most students, it is better to save time and tackle the essays in the order in which they are presented.

FOR AND AGAINST THE FIVE-PARAGRAPH ESSAY

One of the goals of the AP English Language and Composition course is to help students move beyond formulaic responses and to allow content, purpose, and audience to guide the organization of their writing. If you're a good writer, the standard five-paragraph essay will restrict you and prevent you from creating an essay that's as inspired as it may be otherwise. However, if you consider yourself a weak writer, you may want to rely on a safe method for writing your essay.

All writers should take the "five" in "five-paragraph essay" with a grain of salt. Your essay should have a brief introduction and a brief conclusion that isn't just a repetition of the introduction. Three body paragraphs often make sense, but you could also have only two, or four, depending on the prompt. Good writers should not restrict themselves to five paragraphs.

THE ORGANIZATION

The nice thing about the five-paragraph essay is that it provides you with a framework for organizing your ideas and achieving your goal—a high-scoring essay. Using this format, you will do the following:

1. State a thesis (often, the prompt does this for you).

2. Identify two to four—preferably three—ideas that will allow you to prove your thesis.

3. Wrap up your essay with some final thoughts that emphasize your overall points.

For example, consider the following prompt, which is typical of some of the real essay prompts:

> The statement "patience is a virtue" has become proverbial, but is
> it true? Is patience a virtue? Drawing from your readings or from your
> own experience, support, refute, or qualify the validity of the statement.

So, what are you going to do? Will you support, refute, or qualify?
First, simply think of whatever crosses your mind, pro or con.

- Patience helps you avoid making rash decisions, which are almost always bad. There was that time when you forgot your house key and, instead of waiting for your parents to come home, you broke a window to get into the house. The neighbors called the cops and... Patience is a virtue!

- Patience is a touchstone for love and friendship. Wow, there are lots of examples!

- Too much patience may prevent you from seizing an opportunity. Bill Gates lost patience with his university work and dropped out. I'll bet he's happy that he wasn't patient. Patience is not a virtue!

At this point, you could forget about the third idea, but why? You are set up to qualify the adage, and your thesis practically writes itself: *Patience is not an absolute virtue; while most often one does well to heed its voice, inevitably there are times when it is better to turn a deaf ear.*

You have already written half of the introduction and much of the essay.

THE OUTLINE

Do NOT waste time writing a formal outline! You need time to write and to write well, and your time is extremely limited. Solid organization is important, but quantity is also relatively important. Don't let anyone fool you into thinking that a wonderfully organized one-page essay will do the trick; it won't. Depending on the size of your handwriting, you should plan to fill two to three of the lined pages in the essay booklet. The test is not designed for the kind of carefully thought-out work that results from multiple drafts; this is a sprint, and you'd better get out of the starting blocks fast.

You should write down the main idea and a few notes (in your own code or shorthand) for each planned body paragraph. Although for purposes of clarity we used a few too many words in the bullet points above, they contain the basics of the outline. A more realistic version might be worded as below.

- Rash decisions; house key/cops
- Love/friendship; waiting for Jim; looking for lost notebook with Stephanie; time when Angela waited for me
- Bill Gates

Even this is a bit wordy. Write down only enough to remember what you want to include—for example, Bill Gates's name is enough to remind you about dropping out of college and going on to found Microsoft.

THE INTRODUCTION

Perhaps surprisingly, the introduction is usually the weakest part of an AP essay. Long introductions take up time that should instead be devoted to the essay, and they tend to leave the reader confused, bored, or both. You should write around three sentences in your introduction. The first will be your thesis statement, and the second and third will contain the enumeration of the main points that will substantiate your thesis. Basically, you will announce what you intend to explain or prove and give a road map to the rest of the essay. Here's what you could do with the information that you just came up with.

> Patience is not an absolute virtue; while most often one does well
> to heed its voice, inevitably there are times when it is better to turn
> a deaf ear. Patience impedes rash decisions, which are almost always
> bad; furthermore, it is the true touchstone for love and friendship.
> However, patience can also be an impediment to decisiveness, which is
> often an ingredient for greatness.

Is this a great introduction? No, but it isn't bad either. The student has already proven that he or she is addressing the prompt and, specifically, chosen to qualify the adage. Also, the reader knows that the writer has a plan; in fact, all that's lacking now is a good solution and presentation of examples drawn from his or her experience or readings.

A great writer could use the same material and write a more elegant introduction; a not-so-great writer could use the same material and lose it in a cloud of verbiage. If you are anything but an incredibly gifted writer, less is more when it comes to introductions.

THE BODY PARAGRAPHS

Present the body paragraphs of your essay in the order in which you presented the topics in the introduction. Begin each of the three body paragraphs with a sentence that is roughly equivalent to the appropriate phrase in the introduction; this will be your topic sentence. If possible, do not use identical wording. For example, you may begin your first body paragraph with the following:

> More often than not, when it comes to making decisions, patience is definitely a virtue.

Then you may use the example of the lost house key, and maybe you'd add more examples as they come to you (perhaps you jotted these down in your outline before beginning the essay). It could be fun to write about the lost key, the " break-in," the arrival of the police on the scene, and the ensuing arrival of your terrified parents. Good narration can earn you big points. What's so hard about narrating a humorous anecdote? However, don't get too carried away with your anecdotes; remember to stay on the topic.

End each paragraph with either a "clincher," which is a sentence that drives home your point, or a transitional sentence, which is one that leads the reader naturally into the next paragraph.

> (Clincher) One thing is for sure: Patience is a virtue that my parents expect me to practice in the future!

> (Transition) Although the police were not thrilled with my rash decision, my parents bore the event with patience; surely they proved their love for me that day.

That transition sentence gets you ready to start the next paragraph (about how patience is a touchstone for love and friendship). You write two more body paragraphs, and you're practically done!

THE CONCLUSION

Sometimes an essay will end suddenly, and the reader will be left staring at the blank lines, wondering if the student ran out of time, ran out of ideas, or ran out of the room. *Possibly* worse are the essays that end with a rambling, repetitive, boring rehashing of the introduction; this can erase some of the positive impressions earned in the body paragraphs.

Seldom will you have time to write a brilliant conclusion, so do the next best thing: Keep it short. If you can, invite the reader to reflect upon what you have written. As we mentioned in the planning stage, you may have a lot to say about what constitutes a virtue in the first place, so one possibility would be to end with something like the following:

> If patience is a virtue, like thrift, modesty, or generosity, it is not an absolute guide. Perhaps the only absolute virtue is the gift of knowing when to obey a virtue—like patience.

That's a lot of information to digest, but as you go through the next chapters you can always revisit this one to refresh your memory. For now, let's go through the major points of this chapter one more time before you move on.

SUMMARY

GENERAL ESSAY INFORMATION

- There are three essays; work on them as equally as possible.

- You have 2 hours total, or 40 minutes for each essay (not including the 15-minute reading period).

ESSAY SCORING

- Each essay is scored by a reader who grades only that particular type of essay.

- Each essay is given a score from 0 to 9.

- The essays are scored "holistically." There is no checklist of available points.

- The reader wants to read good essays that are easy to score.

- When in doubt, the reader will grade your essay in the middle range of scores.

- Clear essays earn high scores, generic and boring essays earn mid-range scores, and bad essays earn low scores.

PRESENTATION

- Do everything in your power to make the essay appear neat.

- Write confidently in the manner in which you feel most comfortable; there should be a regular flow to your writing.

- Make your paragraph indentations easy to spot.

- Your first paragraph should be grammatically perfect. Your reader will quickly make a judgment about your ability to write. Once the reader has decided that you can write clearly, he or she will cut you some slack later on.

- Vary your diction and sentence structure. A little extra effort when choosing verbs and nouns will pay great dividends.

- Do not use contractions or shorthand ("e.g." for "for example", "&" for "and").

- If you write a great essay that doesn't address the prompt, you'll get a lousy score.

- Do the questions in whatever order you feel comfortable with; however, reordering the prompts takes time. If at all possible, do the essays in the order in which they are presented.

- If you do not have a good organizational track record, use the "five-paragraph" form. It is always better to have too much organization than too little.

- Do not waste time crafting an outline; jot down just enough to capture the gist of a plan of attack for each body paragraph.

Now that you have a general idea of how the essay section is structured and scored, let's move on to a few more specifics about the different types of essays you'll see. The next three chapters outline how you should go about answering the three different kinds of prompts: synthesis, rhetorical analysis, and argumentative questions. To see real examples of each of these questions that have appeared on previous AP English Language and Composition Exams, visit **www.collegeboard.com/ student/testing/ap/english_lang/samp.html?englang**.

4

The Synthesis Essay

WHY ARE THEY DOING THIS TO ME?

The synthesis essay came about because college professors begged the AP English Language and Composition test writers to develop an essay that would test students' abilities to read and evaluate multiple sources and integrate appropriate ones into a coherent, cogent essay. In essence, professors wanted to know that students who use the AP English Language and Composition Exam for credit or placement out of freshman English know how to write a good research paper.

The good news is that, to allow enough time for students to both read the sources and write about them, the folks at ETS decided to allot a 15-minute reading period at the beginning of the essay section of the exam. We suggest you use at least part of this reading period to read all the sources given and start to plan how you will write the perfect synthesis essay.

SAMPLE ESSAY #1—HERE'S HOW IT'S DONE

On the synthesis essay, it's of utmost importance that you get a clear grasp of the prompt. Unless you know what you're looking for, you will not be able to deal with the mass of material that you must read and digest. If you know what to look for, then you can skim the parts that do not pertain to your thesis—and underline just the good stuff.

What follows is another sample question. Since these questions are so long, we'll break it into parts in this chapter.

The Directions

ENGLISH LANGUAGE AND COMPOSITION
SECTION II
Total time—2 hours

Question 1

(Suggested writing time—40 minutes. This question counts for one-third of the total essay section score.)

Throughout history, people have portrayed men and women differently, often requiring of the former masculinity and of the latter femininity. What does it mean to be a man, or masculine, and a woman, or feminine?

Carefully read the following six sources, including the introductory information for each source. Then synthesize information from at least three of the sources and incorporate it into a coherent, well-developed essay that defends, challenges, or qualifies the claim that men must be masculine and women must be feminine.

Make sure that your argument is central; use the sources to illustrate and support your reasoning. Avoid merely summarizing the sources. Indicate clearly which sources you are drawing from, whether through direct quotation, paraphrase, or summary. You may cite the sources as Source A, Source B, etc., or by using the descriptions in parentheses.

Source A (Kipling)
Source B (De Beauvoir)
Source C (Shakespeare)
Source D (Wollstonecraft)
Source E (David)
Source F (Angelou)

The First Time You Read the Prompt

As always, do your first reading of the prompt and underline key instructions and other terms. First, you should have underlined the phrase "Then synthesize information from at least three of the sources and incorporate it into a coherent, well-developed essay." Before you begin writing, you must double-check to make sure, in your outline, you planned to use *at least* the required number of sources. The number of sources will always be spelled out in the instructions; normally you will not be required to use all the sources provided (although there is nothing wrong with doing so, if each of the referenced sources helps advance your point). Finally, you should have underlined the key questions in the prompt: "What does it mean to be a man, or masculine, and a woman, or feminine?"

The Second Time You Read the Prompt

In this case, a second reading of the prompt probably won't help you much, unless you have already discussed gender roles and society in your classes. Even if you have, remember that your essay should primarily depend on the sources for support, not on what you know from outside.

It's Time to Read

As you read the passages for the first time, the amount of information you absorb will depend on how well you know the context of the topic. If you are not familiar with the topic at all, your first read will help you get your bearings on the topic; if you are familiar, you should read even more closely to ensure that you write about what is in the passages, rather than spending most of your essay writing about outside knowledge. In either case, you should have your pen in hand and be ready to underline anything that helps you answer the question. These passages will require some interpretation to determine what they say about masculinity and femininity. Once you've made up your mind about what position you will take in response to the question, you are free to underline only the points that substantiate your position.

As a general rule, you should carefully examine all the sources. Put a mark through the ones you do not intend to use. It is unlikely that you will use them all, but you should use as many as you can—and of course at least as many as the essay prompt requires.

As you plan your essay, remember your task. In this case, no one is asking you to document the historical progress of the development of masculinity and femininity. Your goal is simply to make a convincing case for what it means, in our culture, to be a man or a woman. Stick to your task.

If you can keep your head when all about you
Are losing theirs and blaming it on you;
If you can trust yourself when all men doubt you,
But make allowance for their doubting too;
If you can wait and not be tired by waiting,
Or, being lied about, don't deal in lies,
Or, being hated, don't give way to hating,
And yet don't look too good, nor talk too wise;

If you can dream—and not make dreams your master;
If you can think—and not make thoughts your aim;
If you can meet with triumph and disaster
And treat those two impostors just the same;
If you can bear to hear the truth you've spoken
Twisted by knaves to make a trap for fools,
Or watch the things you gave your life to broken,
And stoop and build 'em up with wornout tools;

If you can make one heap of all your winnings
And risk it on one turn of pitch-and-toss,
And lose, and start again at your beginnings
And never breath a word about your loss;
If you can force your heart and nerve and sinew
To serve your turn long after they are gone,
And so hold on when there is nothing in you
Except the Will which says to them: "Hold on";

If you can talk with crowds and keep your virtue,
Or walk with kings—nor lose the common touch;
If neither foes nor loving friends can hurt you;
If all men count with you, but none too much;
If you can fill the unforgiving minute
With sixty seconds' worth of distance run,
Yours is the Earth and everything that's in it,
And—which is more—you'll be a Man my son!

Source B

De Beauvoir, Simone. <u>The Second Sex</u>. Translated by H. M. Parshley. New York: Alfred A. Knopf, 1949.

The following passage is excerpted from a work of feminist philosophy.

The fact that I ask [the question, "What is a woman?"] is in itself significant. A man would never set out to write a book on the peculiar situation of the human male. But if I wish to define myself, I must first of all say: 'I am a woman'; on this truth must be based all further discussion. A man never begins by presenting himself as an individual of a certain sex; it goes without saying that he is a man. The terms masculine and feminine are used symmetrically only as a matter of form, as on legal papers. In actuality the relation of the two sexes is not quite like that of two electrical poles, for man represents both the positive and the neutral, as is indicated by the common use of man to designate human beings in general; whereas woman represents only the negative, defined by limiting criteria, without reciprocity. In the midst of an abstract discussion it is vexing to hear a man say: 'You think thus and so because you are a woman'; but I know that my only defense is to reply: 'I think thus and so because it is true,' thereby removing my subjective self from the argument. It would be out of the question to reply: 'And you think the contrary because you are a man', for it is understood that the fact of being a man is no peculiarity. A man is in the right in being a man; it is the woman who is in the wrong. It amounts to this: just as for the ancients there was an absolute vertical with reference to which the oblique was defined, so there is an absolute human type, the masculine. Woman has ovaries, a uterus: these peculiarities imprison her in her subjectivity, circumscribe her within the limits of her own nature. It is often said that she thinks with her glands. Man superbly ignores the fact that his anatomy also includes glands, such as the testicles, and that they secrete hormones. He thinks of his body as a direct and normal connection with the world, which he believes he apprehends objectively, whereas he regards the body of woman as a hindrance, a prison, weighed down by everything peculiar to it.

In the following dialogue, Henry the Fifth is speaking to one of his nobles, Lord Exeter. Exeter has just seen two of Henry's uncles, the Duke of York and the Earl of Suffolk, die in the tremendous battle with the French.

Exeter: The Duke of York commends him to your Majesty.

King: Lives he, good uncle? Thrice within the hour
I saw him down; thrice up again and fighting,
From helmet to the spur all blood he was.

Exeter: In which array, brave soldier, doth he lie,
Larding the plain; and by his bloody side,
Yoke-fellow to his honor-owing wounds,
The noble Earl of Suffolk also lies.
Suffolk first died; and York, all haggled over,
Comes to him, where in gore he lay insteeped,
And takes him by the beard, kisses the gashes
That bloodily did yawn upon his face.
He cries aloud, "Tarry, my cousin Suffolk!
My soul shall thine keep company to heaven.
Tarry, sweet soul, for mine, then fly abreast;
As in this glorious and well-foughten field
We kept together in our chivalry!"
Upon these words I came, and cheered him up;
He smiled me in the face, raught me his hand,
And, with a feeble gripe, says, "Dear my lord,
Commend my service to my Sovereign."
So did he turn, and over Suffolk's neck
He threw his wounded arm, and kissed his lips;
And so, espoused to death, with blood he sealed
A testament of noble-ending love.
The pretty and sweet manner of it forced
Those waters from me which I would have stopped;
But I had not so much of man in me,
And all my mother came into mine eyes
And gave me up to tears.

The following passage is excerpted from a treatise on women's rights.

To account for, and excuse the tyranny of man, many ingenious arguments have been brought forward to prove, that the two sexes, in the acquirement of virtue, ought to aim at attaining a very different character: or, to speak explicitly, women are not allowed to have sufficient strength of mind to acquire what really deserves the name of virtue. Yet it should seem, allowing them to have souls, that there is but one way appointed by Providence to lead mankind to either virtue or happiness.

If then women are not a swarm of ephemeron triflers, why should they be kept in ignorance under the specious name of innocence? Men complain, and with reason, of the follies and caprices of our sex, when they do not keenly satirize our headstrong passions and groveling vices. Behold, I should answer, the natural effect of ignorance! The mind will ever be unstable that has only prejudices to rest on, and the current will run with destructive fury when there are no barriers to break its force. Women are told from their infancy, and taught by the example of their mothers, that a little knowledge of human weakness, justly termed cunning, softness of temper, outward obedience, and a scrupulous attention to a puerile kind of propriety, will obtain for them the protection of man; and should they be beautiful, every thing else is needless, for, at least, twenty years of their lives....

How grossly do they insult us who thus advise us only to render ourselves gentle...

The following painting depicts a scene from Roman legend.

Source F

Angelou, Maya. "Phenomenal Woman." <u>And Still I Rise</u>. New York: Random House, 1978.

Pretty women wonder where my secret lies.
I'm not cute or built to suit a fashion model's
    size
But when I start to tell them,
They think I'm telling lies.
I say,
It's in the reach of my arms
The span of my hips,
The stride of my step,
The curl of my lips.
I'm a woman
Phenomenally.
Phenomenal woman,
That's me.

I walk into a room
Just as cool as you please,
And to a man,
The fellows stand or
Fall down on their knees.
Then they swarm around me,
A hive of honey bees.
I say,
It's the fire in my eyes,
And the flash of my teeth,
The swing in my waist,
And the joy in my feet.
I'm a woman
Phenomenally.
Phenomenal woman,
That's me.

Men themselves have wondered
What they see in me.
They try so much
But they can't touch
My inner mystery.
When I try to show them
They say they still can't see.
I say,
It's in the arch of my back,
The sun of my smile,
The ride of my breasts,
The grace of my style.
I'm a woman

Phenomenally.
Phenomenal woman,
That's me.

Now you understand
Just why my head's not bowed.
I don't shout or jump about
Or have to talk real loud.
When you see me passing
It ought to make you proud.
I say,
It's in the click of my heels,
The bend of my hair,
The palm of my hand,
The need of my care,
'Cause I'm a woman
Phenomenally.
Phenomenal woman,
That's me.

The Analysis

That's quite a lot of reading (not to mention some art history!). If you want to use your extra 15 minutes effectively, you must read selectively. You may have noticed that about half of the sources comment on manliness, and the other half comment on femininity. You may also have noticed that the women do not always seem pleased with the role given to them by society, while the men have many positive traits ascribed to them. You might even say that manliness is defined as courage, strength, and maturity, while being feminine is defined as being excluded from most of these virtues.

With that, you're ready to respond to the questions. Hopefully you underlined some great examples and jotted down a quick outline for how you'll go about using them. Now, it's time to write a strong synthesis essay.

When you're finished writing your essay, take a look at the essay on the following page. This is a sample of an essay that was written in the allotted 55 minutes. As you read it, evaluate how well it addresses the prompt and whether it integrates enough sources well.

A Student Essay

Every society tries to define what is masculine and what is feminine. In doing so, all societies assign certain traits to men, and others to women. In our own society, manhood is associated with bravery, stoicism, strength, and wisdom; the conventional (and insulting) view is that womanhood is the lack of those virtues. Instead, women are valued primarily because they are pleasing to men—even when they try to show themselves as powerful and strong on their own terms, they still look to male approval to measure their success. While one may wish to challenge these notions, men and women alike seem to agree with them—suggesting an inherent truth about men and women.

Our society's traditional view is that manhood is associated with bravery in battle, strength in the face of suffering, and level-headed rationality. Rudyard Kipling's poem, "If," provides a conclusive summary to manly virtues. For him, a boy becomes a man when he can wait patiently, endure the criticisms of lesser men and the reversals of fortune without complaint, and give his all by seeking success at every moment, neither proud in victory nor broken in defeat. These are admirable qualities in anyone—but Kipling assigns them specifically to men. Men are also stoic in the face of emotion: all the way back to Shakespeare's time, men were supposed to be strong enough to fight their own tears. Losing that battle is a feminine sign of weakness.

This cultural assumption has not gone unnoticed by women. Simone De Beauvoir notices that in discussions between men and women, the man's viewpoint is naturally considered to be "both the positive and the neutral" one. Men are the standard, the "absolute vertical," by which women are judged—and found wanting. An earlier feminist writer, Mary Wollstonecraft, also noticed (and objected to) the difference in social roles for men and women: in her view, men keep women in ignorance by denying them education and responsibility, but then say that women are not worthy of these things because it is their nature to be frivolous and overly emotional. Instead, women are to appeal to men for protection. Men are valuable in themselves; women cannot be, but must only be measured by their relationships with men.

It would be easy to dismiss the complaints of the feminist writers, except that both male and female creators reinforce those same complaints. Consider David's Oath of the Horatii. The scene shows a father stoically offering swords to his three sons, who are ready to go bravely off to war. Meanwhile, the women helplessly cry in the background, victim of their emotions and their own lack of courage. And in Maya Angelou's "Phenomenal Woman," for all the speaker's efforts to describe herself as a powerful, phenomenal woman, the measure of her quality is in the way "fellows…swarm around" her, wondering "what they see in" her. In the end, rightly or wrongly, both women and men have subconsciously agreed with the judgment: men are brave doers, while women are their accessories.

What did you think? Clearly, this is another strong essay—probably an 8. The introduction is very strong, but the conclusion is simply tacked on to the last body paragraph. The stance is clear: "[M]anhood is associated with bravery, stoicism, strength, and wisdom; the conventional (and insulting) view is that womanhood is the lack of those virtues." This sentence could be improved if it were more parallel in structure, but it is quite clear nonetheless. However, the thesis could be even more powerful if it were phrased more succinctly.

This essay uses appropriate sources and integrates them well, but using all six sources was probably too ambitious for the time and space allotted. Several of the sources make the same (or similar) points; it was not really necessary to discuss all of the Henry V passage, and the Kipling poem, and the David painting. Similarly, the essay did not strongly benefit from mentioning both De Beauvoir and Wollstonecraft. One extra source does not prove any kind of agreement among all the sources out there, but trying to introduce and use both of the sources meant that the author was not able to explore either one with much depth. It would be better to take a smaller number of sources, but interact with them in more detail.

Artistic works, in particular, are hard to use in these kinds of essays. In order to refer to the David painting in this essay, the author had to take valuable space and time to provide an explanation of the painting. But there is not necessarily solid textual evidence that there is any relationship among the men in the painting, or that the women in the background represent the reactions of all women everywhere to the events in the foreground. Also, the author depends on reading between the lines of the Angelou poem. This is an excellent critical skill that will be valued by the graders—but only if it is done well. It can be too easy to quote a passage and then make a tangential point.

Probably the best aspect of this essay is its use of language. The author uses strong vocabulary, but avoids the kind of long sentences that students often write when under time pressure. By writing in shorter sentences that still use high-level vocabulary, the author communicates his ideas clearly to the reader and shows solid command of language. The essay also benefits from a definite organizational pattern, even if it is not explicitly stated: The author begins by describing masculinity, then gives a critical perspective defining femininity, then shows that both male and female artists implicitly endorse the views that were explicitly stated above. This organizational plan could be improved and could be stated more clearly, but it is definitely noticeable to the reader.

This sample essay should get a score of at least 8. Like any essay written in such a limited time, it will not exhaustively explore the sources (and indeed, it was weaker for trying to touch on all the sources), but its clear organization, excellent use of language, and good thinking make it quite good. Remember, you don't need to be perfect. And to score high on the test overall, all you really need to do is keep all three of your essays in the 6 to 7 range—so an 8, or even a 9, would be fantastic. By following our strategies and using the essays that you've seen as models, you can do that.

Next, let's take a look at how to tackle the rhetorical analysis essay.

5

The
Rhetorical Analysis
Essay

IS THIS A RHETORICAL QUESTION?

The rhetorical analysis essay is a type of essay for which you will be asked to read between the lines of a text and discuss how the writer expresses himself or herself. Keep in mind that you are not expected to summarize the document; instead, you are pointing out what strategies the writer uses to effectively get his or her point across. Essays of this type will have prompts containing the words *analyze*, *explain*, and/or *point of view*.

SAMPLE ESSAY #1—HERE'S HOW IT'S DONE

Below is a sample rhetorical analysis prompt. Let's start by taking a quick look at the instructions for our first sample essay.

THE DIRECTIONS

Question 2

(Suggested time—40 minutes. This question counts for one-third of the total essay score.)

The passage below is extracted from Booker T. Washington's most famous speech, known as "The Atlanta Compromise Address." Washington presented the address to the Cotton States and International Exposition in 1895. Read the entire passage carefully. Then write an essay analyzing the rhetorical strategies that Washington uses to convey his point of view.

THE FIRST TIME YOU READ THE PROMPT

You should read the prompt twice, pen in hand. The first time, you should read only to identify the type of essay they're asking you to write and what you're supposed to do. Also underline any directions that the essay gives you. Your instructions should now look as follows:

The passage below is extracted from Booker T. Washington's most famous speech, known as "The Atlanta Compromise Address." Washington presented the address to the Cotton States and International Exposition in 1895. Read the entire passage carefully. Then write an essay <u>analyzing</u> the <u>rhetorical strategies</u> that Washington uses to convey his <u>point of view</u>.

For this question, you're expected to analyze Washington's rhetorical strategies. The prompts will not always have a marker to show that you are required to present your analysis in an *expository* essay, but it will be obvious that you are required to explain. Often, but not always, the prompt will contain the word *explain*. Basically, if the prompt doesn't instruct you to argue (or take a stand on an issue), then you'll be expected to explain something. Sometimes, the prompt will give you the point of view or position, but sometimes it won't. As you can see, this prompt does not give you the point of view. In this case, *What is his point of view?* amounts to *What is his position?*

Before reading the essay for the first time, you know that you have two main tasks. As you read the passage, you'll need to

1.   figure out Booker T. Washington's point of view, and

2.   identify the rhetorical strategies he uses.

By the way, almost all AP English Language and Composition Exams require that you identify or analyze rhetorical strategies, so it is essential that you spend a lot of time studying Chapters 9 through 11, which are devoted to rhetorical strategies.

The Second Time You Read the Prompt

The second time you read the prompt, you should circle clues or key elements that you know or need to figure out. For example, the first clue in this question is "Booker T. Washington." You may already know that he was a famous African American leader and scholar of the nineteenth century; many public schools in the United States are named after him. If you do not know that, then you would have to glean the information from the text. "Most famous" is another clue; this implies that this person gave several famous speeches, and this tells you something important about Booker T. Washington if you do not know about his fame to begin with. You should also note the date of the speech, for it gives a clue about the speech's historical context, which will be important. Washington delivered the speech in the South (Atlanta, Georgia) just 30 years after the Civil War. Finally, the audience is important. It is likely that the attendees of the Exposition were mostly white, and this is confirmed early in the reading passage—which you are ready to read.

One-third of the population of the South is of the Negro race. No enterprise seeking the material, civil, or moral welfare of this section
Line can disregard this element of our population
5 and reach the highest success. I but convey to you, Mr. President and Directors, the sentiment of the masses of my race when I say that in no way have the value and manhood of the American Negro been more fittingly and
10 generously recognized than by the managers of this magnificent Exposition at every stage of its progress. It is a recognition that will do more to cement the friendship of the two races than any occurrence since the dawn of our freedom.
15 Not only this, but the opportunity here afforded will awaken among us a new era of industrial progress. Ignorant and inexperienced, it is not strange that in the first years of our new life we began at the top instead of at the bottom;
20 that a seat in Congress or the state legislature was more sought than real estate or industrial skill; that the political convention or stump speaking had more attractions than starting a dairy farm or truck garden.
25 A ship lost at sea for many days suddenly sighted a friendly vessel. From the mast of the unfortunate vessel was seen a signal, "Water, water; we die of thirst!" The answer from the friendly vessel at once came back, "Cast down
30 your bucket where you are." A second time the signal, "Water, water; send us water!" ran up from the distressed vessel, and was answered, "Cast down your bucket where you are." And a third and fourth signal for water was answered,
35 "Cast down your bucket where you are." The captain of the distressed vessel, at last heeding the injunction, cast down his bucket, and it came up full of fresh, sparkling water from the mouth of the Amazon River. To those of my
40 race who depend on bettering their condition in a foreign land or who underestimate the importance of cultivating friendly relations with the Southern white man, who is their next-door neighbor, I would say: "Cast down your
45 bucket where you are"—cast it down in making friends in every manly way of the people of all races by whom we are surrounded.
Cast it down in agriculture, mechanics, in commerce, in domestic service, and in the
50 professions. And in this connection it is well to bear in mind that whatever other sins the South may be called to bear, when it comes to

business, pure and simple, it is in the South that the Negro is given a man's chance in
55 the commercial world, and in nothing is this Exposition more eloquent than in emphasizing this chance. Our greatest danger is that in the great leap from slavery to freedom we may overlook the fact that the masses of us are
60 to live by the productions of our hands, and fail to keep in mind that we shall prosper in proportion as we learn to dignify and glorify common labor, and put brains and skill into the common occupations of life; shall prosper
65 in proportion as we learn to draw the line between the superficial and the substantial, the ornamental gewgaws of life and the useful. No race can prosper till it learns that there is as much dignity in tilling a field as in writing a
70 poem. It is at the bottom of life we must begin, and not at the top. Nor should we permit our grievances to overshadow our opportunities.
To those of the white race who look to the incoming of those of foreign birth and strange
75 tongue and habits for the prosperity of the South, were I permitted I would repeat what I say to my own race, "Cast down your bucket where you are." Cast it down among the eight millions of Negroes whose habits you know,
80 whose fidelity and love you have tested in days when to have proved treacherous meant the ruin of your firesides. Cast down your bucket among these people who have, without strikes and labour wars, tilled your fields, cleared
85 your forests, built your railroads and cities, and brought forth treasures from the bowels of the earth, and helped make possible this magnificent representation of the progress of the South. Casting down your bucket among
90 my people, helping and encouraging them as you are doing on these grounds, and to education of head, hand, and heart, you will find that they will buy your surplus land, make blossom the waste places in your fields,
95 and run your factories. While doing this, you can be sure in the future, as in the past, that you and your families will be surrounded by the most patient, faithful, law-abiding, and unresentful people that the world has seen.
100 As we have proved our loyalty to you in the past, in nursing your children, watching by the sick-bed of your mothers and fathers, and often following them with tear-dimmed eyes to their graves, so in the future, in our humble way,

105 we shall stand by you with a devotion that no
foreigner can approach, ready to lay down our
lives, if need be, in defense of yours, interlacing
our industrial, commercial, civil, and religious
life with yours in a way that shall make the
110 interests of both races one. In all things that
are purely social we can be as separate as
the fingers, yet one as the hand in all things
essential to mutual progress.

The Analysis

What is Washington's point of view? Is he an angry man demanding change? Is he an outraged man warning of rebellion? Is he a timid man begging indulgence? No, he is none of these. Booker T. Washington's point of view is that of the inspirational Southern preacher who urges blacks and whites to rally round the same economic flag. He employs three principal rhetorical strategies in this part of his speech.

1. Throughout, there is an appeal to sentiment; this is particularly noteworthy in the first paragraph.

2. Next, there is the central image of the bucket, which could be considered part of either an extended metaphor or an allegory; this is first addressed to the black population, then to white people.

3. Finally, to support the imagery, Washington uses analogy (e.g., "there is as much dignity in tilling a field as in writing a poem"), scare tactics (e.g., the references to people of foreign birth), and interesting deductive reasoning. Washington purports that the continual loyalty and hard work of blacks in the past proves that they will be loyal, hard-working collaborators in the future. While the claim is reasonable, the logic is not; in the past that Washington is talking about, the blacks were slaves. For the most part, they had no choice but to be hard-working and loyal.

Now, keep all the above information in mind as you read the following sample essay, which was written in 40 minutes under actual test conditions.

A Student Essay

Born into slavery and liberated by the Emancipation Proclamation, Booker T. Washington is widely regarded as one of the most influential African American figures in the history of the United States. In 1881, he started the Tuskegee Normal and Industrial Institute, and soon became recognized, admired, and respected for his wisdom. Because a number of well-placed business leaders and political figures turned to him for advice, he delivered his most famous speech "The Atlanta Compromise Address" in 1895. It is an explication of his beliefs that his fellow African Americans and other former slaves should make the best of what they have and strive to excel in the positions and jobs they already occupy rather than continually fighting for something. Furthermore, he argues that the people of the white race also do not see what they have around them. A moving speech, the impact of the "Atlanta Compromise" was so powerful partially because of Washington's skill as an orator and partially because of his strong rhetorical strategies of appeal to ethos, allegory, and repetition, and style and tone.

One of the most memorable quotes from the "Atlanta Compromise" is "cast down your buckets where you are." In this short allegory about a lost ship without drinking water being found by another ship and saved by using what was around them, Washington conveys his central idea that African Americans can help themselves and save themselves by using what resources they already have. The lost ship, in thinking that it is surrounded by salty water, does not even attempt to try the water before the second ship suggests the idea. Similarly, Washington implies that simply because they do not think they have anything to work with, the African Americans who were once slaves do not try to see what can be done with what they have. The impact of the allegory of the two ships is strengthened by Washington's repetition of the phrase "cast down your bucket where you are." However, in repeating it, he applies it to not only the African Americans, but also to "those of the white race." In that context, he states that the white Americans could look to the African Americans for help with the "prosperity of the South" instead of looking to "those of foreign birth and strange tongue and habits." Again, he implores both sides to look around and make use of what is already present.

The idea of the speech is set up in the introductory paragraph, wherein Washington states that the recognition of the race of the "American Negro" at the Exposition will do much to "cement the friendship of the two races." It is in this paragraph and these phrases that Washington turns to the strategy of an appeal to ethos. By asserting that the Exposition will help further the friendship between the white Americans and the African Americans, he subtly suggests that this end, this friendship, is what the organizers of the exposition should want (a moral want). This appeal is utilized again in the final paragraph of the passage. In asking the white Americans to cast down their buckets, Washington also asks them to remember that the

African Americans "have proved [their] loyalty to [the white Americans] in the past." Thus, he seems to be saying it would be immoral for the white Americans to turn away from proved loyalty when they are in search of help and employees.

However, the most compelling element of Washington's speech is his tone and style. When reading the passage, one can almost imagine Washington delivering his oration. His tone and style are uplifting, optimistic, and emphatic, much like the tone of a passionate Southern preacher. His own emotions seem to be invested in every word. With phrases like "it is at the bottom of life that we must begin, and not at the top," or "there is as much dignity in tilling a field as in writing a poem," Washington lends nobility and a right to pride to the common labor that most African Americans performed at the time. When he speaks of casting down the bucket "in agriculture, in mechanics, in commerce, in domestic service, and in the professions," he assures both the African Americans and the white Americans that hard labor is not something to be looked down on. Neither, he implies, is the struggle to rise above your station a condemnable action. Nevertheless, he always comes back to the point that one must first make use of what is already present and readily available before searching for something else.

A wise and powerful man and speaker, Booker T. Washington often knew just what to say to convey his ideas and opinions. Even more important, he knew how to phrase and present what was important. In "The Atlanta Compromise Address," Washington successfully utilizes the strategies of appeal to ethos, repetition, allegory, style, and tone to impart his message of using what one had to improve oneself. In simplified terms, "The Atlanta Compromise" is a speech based on carpe diem, the idea of seizing what one has and using it to one's advantage.

What do you think? This essay would probably earn a score of 7 or 8; it's strong, but it isn't as clear as it could be. It's obvious from the outset that the student knows about Booker T. Washington and understands the historical context of the speech. The fact that both the introduction and the conclusion evince an attempt to go beyond the bare bones is probably what would make the reader lean toward the higher score.

However, there are two glaring problems in this essay. Although one of them would probably not affect the score, it is an unnecessary and entirely avoidable error; it has to do with the five-paragraph form. The last sentence of the introduction announces a road map for the essay: "strategies of appeal to ethos [sentiment], allegory and repetition, and style and tone." That's fine. However, the student goes on to address the three examples in a different order: First the student addresses allegory and repetition, then discusses appeal to sentiment, and, finally, gets to style and tone. Luckily, most AP readers would overlook this, but it's better to be safe than sorry—keep your organization consistent. There is another problem that readers would probably not overlook. Do you remember the two tasks that we set for our reading? One was to look for rhetorical strategies. The other was to establish a clear point of view. The student never addresses point of view in a coherent manner and in the only mention of it seems to confuse it with tone.

Let's look at another example of an analytical/expository essay, to get more practice.

SAMPLE ESSAY #2—GIVING IT ANOTHER TRY

For this one, make sure you try writing the essay on your own by hand before you read the student essay—you should get as much practice as you can before test day. Set your timer for 40 minutes and begin.

THE DIRECTIONS

Question 2

(Suggested time—40 minutes. This question counts for one-third of the total essay score.)

In 1676, Madame de Sévigné wrote the letter below. Read it carefully; then write an essay in which you identify the writer's purpose and analyze how she uses language to achieve that purpose. Pay particular attention to organization, point of view, and diction.

THE FIRST TIME YOU READ THE PROMPT

Write down the type of essay you'll need to write, and describe your "job" in writing this essay on the lines below.

_____

_____

_____

_____

_____

THE SECOND TIME YOU READ THE PROMPT

Next, circle the hints in the prompt.

There isn't much to circle, is there? There are only two items: the fact that the writer is a woman (Madame), and the historical context of the letter (seventeenth-century France under Louis XIV); if you know that "de" indicates nobility, then you have another clue to the point of view—the writer, indeed, belongs to the privileged nobility.

Here is the letter.

THE PASSAGE

The Brinvilliers Affair is still the only thing talked about in Paris. The Marquise confessed to having poisoned her father, her brothers, and one of her children. The Chevalier Duget had been one of those who had partaken of a poisoned dish of pigeon pie, and when the Brinvilliers woman was told three years later that he was still alive, her only remark was: "That man surely has an excellent constitution." It seems she fell deeply in love with Sainte Croix, an officer in the regiment of her husband, the Marquis, who lived in their house. Believing that Sainte Croix would marry her if she were free, she attempted to poison her husband. Sainte Croix, not reciprocating her desire, administered an antidote and, thus, saved the poor Marquis' life.

And now, all is over. The Brinvilliers woman is no more. Judgment was given yesterday, and this morning her sentence was read to her; she was to make a public confession in front of Notre Dame, after which she was to be executed, her body burned, and her ashes scattered to the winds. She was threatened with torture, but she said that it was unnecessary and that she would tell all. Accordingly, she recounted the history of her whole life, which was even more horrible than anyone had imagined, and I could not hear of it without shuddering.

At six in the morning she was led out, barefoot, and clad only in a loose garment, with a halter round her neck. From Notre Dame she was taken away in a wagon, in which I saw her lying on straw, with the doctor on one side of her and the executioner on the other; the sight of her struck me with horror. I am told that she mounted the scaffold with a firm step and died as she had lived, resolutely, and without fear or emotion.

She asked her confessor to place the executioner so that she need not gaze on Degrais, who, you will remember, tracked her to England and ultimately arrested her at Liège. After she had mounted the ladder to the scaffold, she was exposed to the public for a quarter of an hour, while the executioner prepared her for execution. This raised a murmur of disapproval among the people, and it was a great cruelty. It seems that some say she was a saint, and after her body had been burned, the people crowded near to search for bones as relics, but little was to be found, as her ashes were thrown into the fire. And, it may be supposed, that we now inhale what remains of her. It is to be hoped that we shall not inhale her murderous instincts also.

Line
5

10

15

20

25

30

35

40

45

50

55

List at least two, but no more than four, aspects of language that Madame de Sévigné's uses to serve her purpose.

_____

_____

_____

_____

_____

By the way, you are not expected to ascertain the "correct" purpose of the letter; the limited amount of text offered implies various points of view. Does Madame de Sévigné condemn the crime? Does she feel sorry for the criminal? The key is to point out that, above all else, the letter's purpose is to relate an event. Beyond that, you would only be conjecturing.

Here's a sample essay by the same student who wrote the previous one. This time there is no doubt: The essay falls clearly into the 8 to 9 range. The student addresses the difficult prompt well, follows the road map, provides relevant examples from the text, and supports it all with strong, organized writing.

A STUDENT ESSAY

In the 1600s, life was by no means easy for women. They were expected to cater to any whim their husband might have, and they were treated like property. Whenever a woman outstepped the boundaries society had established for her, and her crime was serious enough, she was humiliated and punished publicly. In her 1676 letter, Madame de Sévigné writes of the Brinvilliers affair and incites questions regarding the treatment of women in her time.

Society of the seventeenth century, especially the upper echelons of France, was mostly occupied with the scandalous doings of others in their class. Each affair was picked apart, discussed, and passed from ear to eager ear. Naturally, details tended to be embellished and exaggerated, and each individual's opinions and emotions wormed their way into the retelling. In her description of the Brinvilliers affair, Madame de Sévigné includes many of her own feelings upon witnessing and hearing of the fiasco. Watching the Marquise de Brinvilliers' be taken from Notre Dame to the scaffold, Sévigné declares that "the sight of [the Marquise] struck [her] with horror." Expressing her condemnation of the criminal, Sévigné writes that "it seems that some say [the Marquise] was a saint," implying that Sévigné herself does not share in that opinion. The Marquise's life story affected Madame de Sévigné in such a way that she shuddered. Further evidence of Sévigné disdain is evident in her hope that the Marquise's "murderous instincts" will not be inhaled by the people along with her ashes. Nevertheless, a certain reluctant admiration is evident in Sévigné's declaration that the Marquise "died as she had lived, resolutely, and without fear or emotion." Despite the Marquise's transgressions, one must respect a woman who displayed such strength in the face of the poor treatment they received from men, society, and even other women.

Though she has included some personal sentiments and observations, the majority of Sévigné's letter is dedicated to a fairly objective account of the proceedings of the Brinvilliers affair. She begins by explaining how the entire affair began—"The Marquis [...] poisoned her father, brothers [...] one of her children," and her husband because she believed that "Sainte Croix would marry her if she were free." Tracked to England by Degrais and arrested in Liege, the Marquise was brought back to France and sentenced. Her punishment included a public confession, an execution, and a cremation. Sévigné's narrative continues with details of the public punishment and humiliation of the Marquise. In a matter-of-fact manner, Sévigné relates the unfortunate end that the Marquise de Brinvilliers met with after her crimes against her family.

In the most obvious manner, Madame de Sévigné paints the Brinvilliers affair as a shocking event—she simply states that "the Brinvilliers affair is still the only thing talked about in Paris." The fact that the Marquise's proper first name is never mentioned lends the air and quality of an unmentionable scandal to the whole affair. One can imagine this straightforward letter being read in a shocked tone of voice, an underlying excitement and eagerness evident in the speaker's voice due to the very "deliciously scandalous" nature of the event. Her crime was so abominable that her persecutors even threatened her with torture to procure her confession. Sévigné's diction, quite candid, underscores the shocking quality of the Brinvilliers affair.

Madame de Sévigné effectively portrays society's treatment of women who have overstepped their limits in the seventeenth century. Her hinted-at emotions relay Sévigné's condemning opinion of the Marquise, while simultaneously they convey reluctant admiration. Both her narrative and her diction underline the fact that the Brinvilliers affair was a major scandal. However, overall, one is imparted with the sense that this treatment is ultimately unjust.

This essay is clear, precise, and well written. The student carefully grounds the letter's content in the world of the seventeenth century. The essay analyzes the subtext of Madame de Sévigné's words, pointing out that even though she does not see the woman as a saint, she perhaps harbors a secret admiration for her bravery under condemnation. Though the third paragraph includes some unnecessary summary, the fourth paragraph astutely analyzes useful details, such as Sévigné's decision to never mention the Marquise's first name, or the fact that Sévigné delights in being "deliciously scandalized." In the final paragraph, the student reiterates her insights to remind the graders of her strongest points. Is it perfect? No, but keep in mind that you do not have to write the perfect essay to earn a high score.

In this chapter, we talked about what goes into writing the analysis essay on the AP English Language and Composition Exam and looked at a couple of very well-written examples. Keep the method for approaching these essays that we outlined in this chapter in mind when you are doing the sample exams at the end of this book (and, of course, on the real exam).

In the next chapter, we move on to the argumentative essay.

6

The Argumentative Essay

FIRST, A WORD...

When you get to the argumentative essay on the AP English Language and Composition Exam, you will be asked to take a stand and present your point of view on a topic. This should be an essay that you look forward to! You are not only allowed to use the first person singular ("I"), but also required to use it. Plus, there is no correct position—all that matters is how effectively you argue and back up your position. If you like to debate, this is the part of the free-response section where you should really shine.

As you may recall from the last chapter, when you read the prompt for the first time, you should identify the type of essay you are required to write and figure out which tasks you're being asked to accomplish. Every argumentative essay prompt in recent history has contained the following phrase: "refute, support, or qualify." In other words, you should have no trouble distinguishing between a rhetorical analysis essay and an argumentative one.

SAMPLE ESSAY #1—HERE'S HOW IT'S DONE

Here's a sample argumentative essay prompt. The passage that follows this prompt is typical of argumentative essays you'll see on the test—they're much shorter than the analytical essays.

THE DIRECTIONS

Question 3

(Suggested time—40 minutes. This question counts for one-third of the total essay section score.)

Read and think carefully about the following quotation, taken from *Utilitarianism*, by John Stuart Mill. Then write an essay in which you refute, support, or qualify the author's claim. Make sure to use appropriate evidence from literary, historical, or personal sources to develop your argument.

THE FIRST TIME YOU READ THE PROMPT

Remember, as you read the prompt for the first time you should underline the directions it gives you. Your prompt should now look as follows:

Read and think carefully about the following quotation, taken from *Utilitarianism*, by John Stuart Mill. Then write an essay in which you <u>refute, support, or qualify the author's claim.</u> Make sure to use appropriate <u>evidence from literary, historical, or personal</u> sources to develop your argument.

Since you know that the argumentative essay prompt always contains the phrase "refute, support, or qualify," you know right away that this is an argumentative essay. Notice that we also underlined the phrase "evidence from literary, historical, or personal." When you read the passage for the first time and begin to formulate a response, the kind of evidence that pops into your mind should determine what stand you take on the argument. Remember that no reader knows or cares what you really think about an issue. This is an AP test, not a testimonial. You'll want to take the stand that's easiest for you to defend at that particular moment, based on the ideas that come to you.

The Second Time You Read the Prompt

Your second reading of the prompt can be fairly superficial; at this point there shouldn't be too much more information for you to glean. If you've taken a lot of history courses, then you may have studied John Stuart Mill, and this would give you some information about context. If not, then at least the title should be a tip-off about the content of the passage.

The Passage

> The creed which accepts as the foundation of morals, Utility, or the Greatest
> Happiness Principle, holds that actions are right in proportion as they tend to
> promote happiness, wrong as they tend to produce the reverse of happiness. By
> happiness is intended pleasure, and the absence of pain; by unhappiness, pain,
> and the privation of pleasure. To give a clear view of the moral standard set up by
> the theory, much more requires to be said; in particular, what things it includes
> in the ideas of pain and pleasure; and to what extent this is left an open question.
> But these supplementary explanations do not affect the theory of life on which this
> theory of morality is grounded—namely, that pleasure, and freedom from pain,
> are the only things desirable as ends; and that all desirable things (which are as
> numerous in the utilitarian as in any other scheme) are desirable either for the
> pleasure inherent in themselves, or as means to the promotion of pleasure and the
> prevention of pain.

The Analysis

In this case, the author's thesis is clearly stated in the topic sentence: "… actions are right in proportion as they tend to promote happiness, wrong as they tend to produce the reverse of happiness." In the next sentence, Mill defines happiness ("pleasure") and unhappiness ("pain or the privation of pleasure"). This is not a rhetorical analysis essay, so you do not have to take apart the entire passage; initially your goal is merely to identify the author's claim. After you do this, your next step is to refute, support, or qualify that claim.

If possible, you should refute the claim made by the author of the passage. If done well, essays that refute the author's claim will be the most interesting for the reader. However, if you take a clear, firm stand, in either direction—either for the author's claim or against it—you'll be off to a good start. The most important things are that you have clearly decided how you feel about the issue and that you have the examples to back up your claim.

In this passage, Mill has made an ethical claim: Good actions are those that give oneself pleasure (and, thus, happiness); bad actions are those that give oneself pain or deprive oneself of pleasure (causing unhappiness). What examples (from literary, historical, or personal sources) come to mind that either refute or support the thesis? Quickly jot down three to five of them on the lines below.

_____

_____

_____

_____

_____

Now review your ideas. Which are the easiest to develop? Which do you feel most strongly about? Do you have two or three that will allow you to refute the author's claim? If so, then go for it. If not, do you have two or three examples that will allow you to support the claim? Then go in that direction. In virtually all cases, you should be able to think of evidence for or against the claim. However, if you're caught without very strong evidence that points in either direction, then you'll have to qualify the author's claim. Whatever you decide to do, make your position perfectly clear in the introduction of your essay.

Let's look at an essay that was written by a student under actual testing conditions.

A STUDENT ESSAY

In John Stuart Mill's work <u>Utilitarianism,</u> the author advances a theory of morality that associates "the promotion of pleasure and the prevention of pain" with ethical correctness. While the pursuit of happiness can sometimes lead to a path of moral righteousness, Mill's claim is flawed in that it assumes hedonism will inherently bring positive results. By championing any action that produces pleasure, Mill condones humanity's greed, lust, and selfishness; three traits that are clearly immoral. As history and literature have demonstrated, pursuing goals motivated purely by self-interest does not lead to ethically responsible outcomes. Furthermore, the greatest achievements often arise when people readily eschew pleasure to attain a nobler end.

During the second half of the nineteenth century, a number of technological advances made the American economy blossom and helped to make the nation a world power. Eager to enjoy the pleasures made possible by great wealth, entrepreneurs and businessmen sought to increase profits and lower costs in any possible way. Workers were paid abysmally low wages, conditions were highly unsafe, and monopolies were commonplace. Though the heads of "Big Business" clearly adhered to Mill's "Greatest Happiness Principle," their actions were highly unethical. Their pleasure came at the expense of the poor and created a polarized society. In contrast, patriots seeking independence from England a century before, gladly relinquished the "absence of pain" afforded by accepting the status quo. Despite the great "privation of pleasure" brought about by the Revolutionary War, the patriots achieved their lofty goal of freedom, a morally desirable outcome. Evidently, seeking happiness does not necessarily entail finding "what is right and good."

F. Scott Fitzgerald's portrait of the Roaring Twenties, <u>The Great Gatsby</u>, examines hedonism and reaches a conclusion much different than Mill's. Jay Gatsby pursues pleasure in the form of rekindling a relationship with a former love, Daisy. Following utilitarian principles, seeking the desirable outcome should be an ethically sound choice. However, it instead leads Gatsby to engage in questionable business and to court a married woman, two clear violations of ethical standards. Clearly, morality based on pleasure is an unsound principle.

This essay is a little bit short—another example would have made it stronger—but it does the job remarkably well. It would most likely receive a score of 8. The introduction is slightly long, but notice how well this student addresses the two tasks set forth. Right away, the student states the author's claim: "…the author advances a theory of morality that associates the 'promotion of pleasure and the prevention of pain' with ethical correctness.…" Later in the paragraph, the student takes a clear stand that refutes Mill's claim: "As history and literature have demonstrated, pursuing goals motivated by mere self-interest does not lead to ethically responsible outcomes." The student gives the reader a road map for the rest of the essay; first the student uses a historical example (second half of the nineteenth century), and follows with a literary example (*The Great Gatsby*). Had a personal example been included, this essay would have scored a perfect 9.

DON'T FORGET TO WRITE IN THE PRESENT TENSE

Little things, such as underlining the title of the book, reinforce the impression that this writer knows how to write. As was the case in the two sample essays from the previous chapter, this writer does an excellent job of handling verb tenses. Particularly important is the use of the present tense when addressing the author, text, and claim: "the author advances," "it assumes," "achievements often arise," and so on. The student uses the past tense only when presenting historical facts in the second paragraph, with "advances made," "entrepreneurs and businessmen sought," and "monopolies were." One of the most common grammatical errors that students make in AP English essays is using improper verb-tense shifts. You should be writing in the present tense throughout the essay—and you should shift to the past tense only if you are relating historical facts.

SAMPLE ESSAY #2—GIVING IT ANOTHER TRY

Let's try another one. Again, now that you're comfortable with the process for writing the argumentative essay, try writing this one on your own before you look at the student's essay.

THE DIRECTIONS

Question 3

(Suggested time—40 minutes. This question counts for one-third of the total essay section score.)

Read carefully the passage below from "The Collective Wisdom," by Herbert Spencer (1820–1903). Then in a carefully written essay support, refute, or qualify Spencer's assertion that the House of Commons acted foolishly in denying the water rights.

THE FIRST TIME YOU READ THE PROMPT

Remember, as you read the prompt for the first time you should underline the directions it gives you. Your prompt should now look as follows:

Read carefully the passage below from "The Collective Wisdom," by Herbert Spencer (1820–1903). <u>Then in a carefully written essay support, refute, or qualify Spencer's assertion</u> that the House of Commons acted foolishly in denying the water rights.

THE SECOND TIME YOU READ THE PROMPT

Again, your second reading of the prompt can be fairly superficial; at this point there shouldn't be too much more information for you to glean. Circle the dates that Herbert Spencer lived, circle the House of Commons, and get right to the passage.

THE PASSAGE

On the edge of the Cotswolds, overhanging the valley of the Severn, occur certain springs, which, as they happen to be at the end of the longest of the hundred streams which join to form the Thames, have been called by poetical fiction "the sources of the Thames." Names, even when poetical fictions, suggest conclusions; and conclusions drawn from words instead of facts are equally apt to influence conduct. Thus it happened that, when, recently, there was formed a company for supplying Cheltenham and some other places from these springs, great opposition arose. The Times published a paragraph headed, "Threatened Absorption of the Thames," stating that the application of this company to Parliament had "caused some little consternation in the city of Oxford, and will, doubtless, throughout the valley of the Thames;" and that "such a measure, if carried out, will diminish the water of that noble river a million of gallons per day." A million is an alarming word—suggests something necessarily vast. Translating words into thoughts, however, would have calmed the fears of the Times paragraphist. Considering that a million gallons would be contained by a room fifty-six feet cube, the nobility of the Thames would not be much endangered by the deduction. The simple fact is that the current of the Thames, above the point at which the tides influence it, discharges in twenty-four hours eight hundred times this amount.

When the bill of this proposed water company was brought before the House of Commons for second reading it became manifest that the imaginations of members were affected by such expressions as the "sources of the Thames," and "a million gallons daily," in much the same way as the imaginations of the ignorant. Though the quantity of water proposed to be taken bears to the quantity which runs over Teddington were about the same ratio that a yard bears to a half a mile, it was thought by many members that its loss would be a serious evil. No method of measurement would be accurate enough to detect the difference between the Thames as it now is, and the Thames minus the Cerney springs; and yet it was gravely stated in the House that, were the Thames diminished in the proposed way, "the proportion of sewage to pure water would be seriously increased." Taking a minute out of twelve hours would be taking as large a proportion as the Cheltenham people with to take from the Thames. Nevertheless, it was contended that to let Cheltenham have this quantity would be "to rob the towns along the banks of the Thames of their rights." Though, of the Thames flowing by each of these towns, some 999 parts out of 1,000 pass by unused, it was held that a great injustice would be committed were one or two of these 999 parts appropriated by the inhabitants of a town who can now obtain daily but four gallons of foul water per head.

But the apparent inability thus shown to think of causes and effects in something like their true quantitative relations was still more conspicuously shown. It was stated by several members that the Thames Navigation Commissioners would have opposed the bill if the commission had not been bankrupt, and this hypothetical opposition appeared to have weight. If we may trust the reports, the House of Commons listened with gravity to the assertion of one of its members, that, if the Cerney springs were diverted, "shoals and flats would be created." Not a laugh nor a cry of "Oh! oh," appears to have been produced by the prophecy that the volume and scouring power of the Thames would be seriously affected by taking away from it twelve gallons per second! The whole quantity which these springs supply would be delivered by a current moving through a pipe one foot in diameter at the rate of less than two miles per hour. Yet, when it was said that the navigability of the Thames would be injuriously affected by this deduction, there were no shouts of derision. On the contrary, the House rejected the Cheltenham Water Bill by a majority of one hundred and eighteen to eighty-eight.

Phew! After writing your own essay, take a look at the essay below, which was written by a student under actual time constraints.

A Student Essay

In "The Collective Wisdom," Herbert Spencer suggests that "conclusions drawn from words instead of facts are equally apt to influence conduct." Under this premise, Spencer goes on to examine a decision made by the House of Commons to reject the Cheltenham Bill that granted water rights to several towns along the so-called "source springs" of the Thames. In his essay, Spencer correctly asserts that the House of Commons' opposition to the bill was quite foolish by taking a closer look at the "facts" (or rather, "words") that were presented to the members of the committee.

First, the House of Commons voted against the water rights bill based on some deceiving information about its impact on the Thames' water volume. The Times published an article that cited a million gallon loss of water per day, were the bill to be passed in the House. To most people, including the members of the House of Commons, a million gallons per day sounds like quite a lot of water. However, Spencer provides the reader with some comparison to make the situation clearer. Apparently, a million gallons is not much of a problem for the Thames since it discharges at about 800 times this amount in a single day. In fact, Spencer also notes that there would be methods accurate enough to measure the difference in volume between the river with and without its "source springs." In this case, the House of Commons was influenced by the seemingly large quantity of "a million gallons per day," which was not presented in an appropriate context.

Second, the House of Commons was given another set of misleading statistics regarding the bill's supposed impact on the purity of the Thames. A report in the House stated that "the proportion of sewage to pure water would be seriously increased" if the springs were tapped by the surrounding towns. Again, Spencer helps the reader to see the ignorance of the House's decision by shedding some light on the situation with a more logical comparison. The towns in question only use about one part out of 1,000 parts of water each day from the springs, so 999 out of 1,000 parts pass by unused. Therefore, the ratio of sewage to pure water is quite insignificant and definitely not as dangerous as the report makes it seem.

The central idea of Spencer's essay is that the House of Commons acted with ignorance when they rejected the Cheltenham Water Bill without seeking the appropriate context for certain facts and figures. Spencer qualifies this as acting "foolishly" since the members of the committee did not consider the whole picture when making their decisions. One assumes that members of the House of Commons would have acted with the intelligence of a legislative body instead of the ignorance of the general public; however, Spencer's essay suggests that this is not always the case, especially when "words" instead of facts are the basis for judgment.

This student essay is strong enough for a distinguished mark—probably a 7—but certainly not an 8 or a 9. The student takes a clear stand and writes strongly. The only snafu comes in the following thesis statement:

In his essay, Spencer correctly asserts that the House of Commons' opposition to the bill was quite foolish by taking a closer look at the "facts" (or rather, "words") that were presented to the members of the committee.

The phrase "Spencer correctly asserts" is clear and appropriate, but note the ambiguity caused by the position of the prepositional phrase (underlined). Was the opposition quite foolish because the House took a closer look at the facts? Clearly, this is not what the student means. By placing the prepositional phrase close to the noun it modifies (Spencer), the introduction would gain clarity—and clarity translates into points.

By taking a closer look at the "facts" (or rather, "words") that were presented to the members of the committee, Spencer correctly asserts that the House of Commons' opposition to the bill was quite foolish.

Also notice that we have eliminated the phrase "in his essay." Don't get into the habit of including superfluous words in the introduction, such as: "in the novel *Pride and Prejudice*," "in the play *A Doll's House*," "in the novella *Heart of Darkness*," and so on. The reader knows that the student is talking about Spencer's essay, so does the phrase add anything? No. If words do not add, then they subtract. Sometimes, students make even worse errors by using phrases such as "in the novel *A Doll's House*" or "in the play, *A Doll's House*." The first is an egregious error that calls into question the student's knowledge of either the work in particular or literature in general, and the second is an error in usage.

The rest of the sample essay is very good, but the reader would probably like to see the student bring more original thought to bear on the subject. First and foremost, the student makes the mistake of limiting proof to Spencer's thoughts without providing personal thoughts. Essentially, Spencer is taking a stand on what we consider a modern issue: ecology. The student should have brought this issue to the fore and integrated it into the essay.

It would also have been helpful if the student had highlighted some of the rhetorical fallacies used by Spencer in his essay. For example, on the one hand Spencer accuses the *Times* of using scare tactics, and a supporter of Spencer's free use stand could compare this with current radical ecologists' ploys. On the other hand, one could argue that Spencer himself is guilty of using straw man arguments by simplifying the conservationists' position, or that his *ad hominem* attack on the *Times* reporter ("the paragraphist") reveals that Spencer is not limiting himself to facts. A student writing against Spencer's stand could bring in a rhetorical fallacy of his or her own: the slippery slope argument—if one begins by permitting the diversion of the Cerney Springs, then one is opening the door to the kind of ecological rape of watersheds that, in fact, occurred in England over the course of the next hundred years.

By taking a "personal" stand (not necessarily what the student truly believes, by the way) on this ecological dispute, and even without explicitly naming the rhetorical fallacies, this student would have improved the grade by at least one point.

MOVING ON...

In this and the two preceding chapters, you've seen some pretty solid examples of essays. In the next parts of this book, you learn (or review) the important aspects of formal training in rhetoric and composition that will prepare you to craft essays that equal—or exceed—the ones that you've examined so far.

PART IV

AP English Language

7

Words and Their Use

THE GOOD NEWS AND THE BAD NEWS ABOUT THE AP ENGLISH LANGUAGE AND COMPOSITION EXAM

THE GOOD NEWS

While the title of this exam allows people to differentiate between this test and the AP English *Literature* Exam, it's still somewhat misleading. The AP English *Language* Exam is not a language exam—at least not in the sense that you may think. For example, it is possible not to know the difference between a gerund and a present participle—or even a gerund and a giraffe—and still score a 5 on this exam.

In the multiple-choice section of the exam, test writers will attempt to evaluate your ability to analyze how writers use language to explain or to argue; in the free-response, or essay, section they will expect *you* to use language to explain or to argue. Naturally, you'll want to avoid making egregious errors in grammar or usage on the test, but as you study don't get hung up on the rules of language. If you're considering taking the AP exam, your language skills are probably sufficient for the task. Now, you may be wondering what *is* tested on the exam. The answer is *composition,* and we'll spend Part V of this book reviewing all you need to know about composition to be fully prepared for the test.

THE BAD NEWS

Now for the bad news. Despite the test's lack of emphasis on the rules of language, there are some aspects of language that we must examine here to make sure you're ready for test day. We'll start by discussing diction, style, tone, and point of view. We'll move on to circumlocution and euphemism, and discuss irony and satire. Finally, we will review the many types of figurative language and go through some drills that will prepare you for the types of questions you'll see on all of these topics. Let's begin!

DICTION

The basic definition of **diction** is "word choice." Generally, the diction questions you'll see on the test will ask you to evaluate why an author's choice of words is particularly effective, apt, or clear. However, as we explained in Part II, in the multiple-choice section, more often than not it is the test writer's diction that you have to crack. While knowledge of grammar and usage is almost irrelevant for this exam, a broad vocabulary is a necessity.

After common sense, vocabulary is the most important tool that you can use on the multiple-choice section of the exam. For this reason, we've included a Hit Parade in Part VI of this book—a list of terms and their definitions that you should know cold before you sit down to take the test, and lists of key terms at the end of every content chapter. To ensure that you'll remember these terms for the exam, you may want to make flashcards as you work through this book.

Let's look at a question that emphasizes the importance of studying vocabulary as you prepare for the test.

1. The style of the first paragraph on the previous page
   can best be described as

   (A) pedantic
   (B) lyrical
   (C) terse
   (D) ludic
   (E) edifying

While it's possible that none of the answers stands out to you as the correct choice, you could rule out *pedantic* if you knew that it meant "narrowly, stodgily, and often ostentatiously learned,"—it isn't possible that you could think that of the writing in this book! Likewise, a Princeton Review book and lyricism (intense, intimate display of emotion) make for an unlikely pair, so you can use Process of Elimination and get rid of that choice too. The test writers slipped *ludic* (pertaining to game, playful) in there in case you wanted to misremember some Latin (*ludus*); and finally *terse* (concise, without superfluous detail) shows up regularly on this exam but probably doesn't describe the writing in this book very well. Given that the last choice can mean both enlightening and informative, (E) is the best answer.

But as you can see, if you knew none of these words, the question may as well have read as follows:

2. The style of the paragraph above can best be
   described as

   (A) pompom
   (B) banana
   (C) dog
   (D) tire iron
   (E) Susan

And then which would seem like the correct answer? Obviously, vocabulary is important, so study the Hit Parade in the next chapter.

Let's try another question that illustrates the importance of a relatively wide vocabulary to scoring well on this exam.

> If survival is an art, then mangroves are artists of the
> beautiful: not only that they exist at all—smooth-barked,
> glossy-leaved, thickets of lapped mystery—but that they
> *Line* can and do exist as floating islands, as trees upright and
> 5 loose, alive and homeless on the water.
> I have seen mangroves, always on tropical ocean
> shores, in Florida and in the Galapagos. There is the
> red mangrove, the yellow, the button, and the black.
> They are all short, messy trees, waxy-leaved, laced all
> 10 over with aerial roots, woody arching buttresses, and
> weird leathery berry pods. All this tangles from a black
> muck soil, a black muck matted like a mud-sopped rag,
> a muck without any other plants, shaded, cool to the
> touch, tracked at the water's edge by herons and nosed
> 15 by sharks.

3. The style of the passage on the previous page is characterized by

   (A) extended metaphors
   (B) historical allusions
   (C) vividness of diction
   (D) technical language
   (E) colloquial expressions

The best answer is (C); vividness of diction. The speaker's language is very descriptive and paints a very clear picture of the mangrove. Here's a list of the vocabulary you needed to know to answer this question: metaphor, allusion, diction, and colloquial.

As we explained in Part II, if you understand the passage but don't know the meaning of any of the answers, it's still possible to get the right answer. However, it's easier and faster to get the right answer if you do know the meanings of the words that make up the answer choices. Let's continue our review of important language terms.

SYNTAX

Another language term that you should be familiar with for the AP English Language Exam is *syntax*. **Syntax** is the ordering of words in a sentence; it describes sentence structure. Syntax is not a topic that excites many high school students—or teachers—and therefore is not discussed very much. However, *syntax* is a word that finds it way onto AP English Language Exams on a regular basis. Don't worry: You don't need to be an expert on this subject, but you should know how manipulating syntax can enhance an author's meaning, tone, or point of view. Let's look at an example from *Candide,* from the famous opening of Chapter 3.

> Never was anything so gallant, so well outfitted, so brilliant, and so finely disposed as the two armies. The trumpets, fifes, reeds, drums, and cannon made such harmony as never was heard in Hell.

The first sentence poses as a fairly simple sketch of a glorious battle scene. The second begins in the same fashion, but its words are arranged in a way that maximizes the effect of surprise that comes at the end of the sentence. The cannons are slipped in as the final member of a list of military musical instruments; the formation of the list creates an expectation that the final element will fit nicely into the set. It doesn't, but we don't have time to register our surprise because we're immediately distracted by a new setup with the phrase "such harmony as never was heard…." We expect harmony to be something beautiful, and we already begin to supply the final word (Earth? Heaven?) when—surprise—we are jolted by the word that Voltaire chose instead: hell. The syntax in this sentence is brilliant.

Here's another slightly different example. In the following example, Candide through his servant and sidekick, Cacambo, is asking about the proper etiquette for greeting the King of Eldorado.

> When they drew near to the royal chamber, Cacambo asked one of the officers in what manner they were to pay their respects to His Majesty; whether it was the custom to fall upon their knees, or to prostrate themselves upon the ground; whether they were to put their hands upon their heads, or behind their backs; whether they were to lick the dust off the floor; in short, what was the usual ceremony for such occasions.

The syntax of this long sentence is very carefully constructed; Voltaire uses all of the parallel clauses that begin with "whether" to achieve great comic effect. At first, the text is fairly straightforward—after all, going down on one's knees before a king would have been fairly standard for a European reader of the eighteenth century; however, with each clause, the groveling etiquette becomes more extreme, and the final image—of licking the dust off the floor—pushes the concept beyond the believable. The syntax of this sentence is structured in a way that allows us to see the absurdity of *all* forms of ceremonial deference. In fact, in this story the enlightened King of Eldorado simply embraces both Cacambo and Candide.

Related to syntax are style, tone, and point of view. As you will read in the next section, these elements work together with syntax to create a "profile" of the speaker that tells us how the speaker or author feels about the subject at hand.

STYLE, TONE, AND POINT OF VIEW

You can count on seeing some combination of the terms *style, tone,* and *point of view* in both multiple-choice and essay questions on this exam, so let's make sure you're familiar with their definitions.

Style is the manner of expression. It describes how the author uses language to get his or her point across (e.g., pedantic, scientific, and emotive).

Tone is the attitude, mood, or sentiments revealed by the style. Tone describes how the author seems to be feeling (e.g., optimistic, ironic, and playful).

Point of view is the stance revealed by the style and the tone of the writing. The author's point of view expresses his or her position on the topic discussed. Point of view can be tricky—sometimes, especially in works of fiction, it is difficult to determine point of view, and, thus, you may be left with nothing more to say than "first-person narrator" or "third-person omniscient narrator."

Consider this passage.

> Our left fielder couldn't hit the floor if he fell out
> of bed! After striking out twice (once with the bases
> loaded!), he grounded into a double-play. My grand-
> *Line* mother runs faster than he does! In the eighth inning,
> 5 he misjudged a routine fly ball, which brought in the
> winning run. What a jerk! Why didn't the club trade him
> last week when it was still possible? What's wrong with
> you guys?

The *style* is simple, direct, unsophisticated, truculent, and even crass. The style helps evoke a simple sentiment: anger. The *tone* is angry, brash, emotional, and even virulent.

The *point of view* is clear; the author appears to be a disgruntled spectator who doesn't like the player at all and wants the team to get rid of him.

Okay. You may not have needed any help with that passage, but let's take a look at another that's more like something you'd see on test day.

So what was the big argument all about in the time of
Columbus? The sages of Salamanca had, in fact, made
calculations more precise than his, and they held that
Line the earth, while assuredly round, was far more vast than
5   the Genoese navigator believed, and therefore it was
mad for him to attempt to circumnavigate it in order to
reach the Orient by way of the Occident. Columbus, on
the contrary, burning with a sacred fire, good navigator
but bad astronomer, thought the earth smaller than it
10   was. Naturally, neither he nor the learned men of Salamanca suspected that between Europe and Asia there
lay another continent. And so you see how complicated
life is, and how fragile are the boundaries between truth
and error, right and wrong. Though they were right, the
15   sages of Salamanca were wrong, and Columbus, while
he was wrong, pursued faithfully his error and proved to
be right—thanks to serendipity.

Serendipities by Umberto Eco

Style: What can you say about the style of this passage? At the beginning, the writing is scholarly, but toward the end the author addresses the reader personally ("And so you see…"), and the passage takes on a looser, more personal style.

Tone: The tone is ambiguous. For example, why does the writer assiduously avoid using the term "professors"? We have "the sages of [the University of] Salamanca" and "the learned men of [the University of] Salamanca"—is there a reason for this *periphrasis* (circumlocution)? Is the author being respectful, or, rather, is he using a tone of mocking condescension? Also consider the phrase "burning with a sacred fire, good navigator but bad astronomer." Although the words appear innocent and "factual" enough, what's behind the trite cliché of the first part and the humor lurking in the second part? And doesn't the title, *Serendipities,* call forth a light, playful tone? Perhaps—but it is difficult to pin down the author; it's almost as if he were deliberately playing a scholarly game of hide and seek.

Point of view: Style and tone provide us with clues about the point of view of the author. He appears to be questioning the "truths" of the past, and cautioning us against believing too much in the "truths" of the present. The point of view appears to be that of an erudite man who is considering history with a critical eye and is suggesting that serendipity (chance) might play as great a role as any other force in shaping history.

As we've said before, the questions on the AP English Language and Composition Exam will test your ability to analyze writing as we analyzed the passage above. More often than not, identifying elements of style and tone will help you uncover what the test writers might call "the purpose of the writer" or "the author's attitude," and in some cases, get you one step closer to choosing the right answer on a test question.

Now that you're comfortable using these terms, let's try a sample question with an excerpt from Fyodor Dostoyevsky's *Notes from Underground.*

The long and the short of it is, gentlemen, that it is better to do nothing! Better conscious inertia!

4.   The tone of the speaker is best characterized as

    (A) ironic
    (B) nihilistic
    (C) reflective
    (D) optimistic
    (E) accusatory

You probably immediately eliminated (C) and (D) because the passage did not sound particularly reflective or optimistic. The author is not accusatory (E) either. Choice (B) may have confused you a bit; nihilism refers to a belief in nothing. (Again notice the importance of vocabulary!) The speaker's tone can indeed by described as "nihilistic," so the correct choice is (B).

RHETORIC AND FIGURATIVE LANGUAGE

Rhetoric is the art of speaking or writing effectively. **Figurative language** is strictly defined as speech or writing that departs from literal meaning to achieve a special effect or meaning. The terms covered later in this section are terms you should know cold before taking the exam. Multiple-choice questions may use them in answer choices, and you are certainly expected to use them in your free-response essays.

RHETORIC

First of all, what *is* rhetoric? It is often referred to as the stylistic devices an author uses to appeal successfully to a specific audience and is usually persuasive in nature. Before we get into the nitty gritty of figurative language and how it's used, let's review the three classical rhetorical appeals—methods of persuasion—you should know for the exam.

Classical Appeals

Aristotle identified three methods of appealing to an audience in order to persuade them to your point of view: *logos*, *pathos*, and *ethos*.

Logos is an appeal to reason and logic. An argument that uses logos to persuade needs to provide things like objective evidence, hard facts, statistics, or logical strategies such as "cause and effect" to back up its claim. (*Logos* is the root of our word "logic," which is a good way to remember which of the appeals this is!)

Ethos is an appeal to the speaker's credibility—whether she is to be believed on the basis of her character and expertise. For example, the prosecution in a murder trial might put a renowned psychiatrist on the stand to testify that the defendant is able to identify right and wrong and is thus capable of standing trial. Their argument would be using an appeal to *ethos* to persuade the jury (their audience) that the testimony of this expert is to be trusted. (*Ethos* is related to our word "ethics"—the principles of conduct that govern people and organizations and give them the authority to speak on certain topics.)

Pathos is an appeal to the emotions, values, or desires of the audience. Aristotle felt that, although ideally people would be persuaded by appeals to logic (*logos*, remember?), they would probably most often be persuaded by their emotions and beliefs instead. This is why, in that same murder trial, a defense attorney might tell the jury about the lonely childhood and difficult life of the defendant— he would be appealing to the *pathos* of the audience to convince them that his client should not be convicted. (*Pathos* is also the root of "pathetic," a word we use to describe something that is, shall we say, *suffering* from inferiority.)

FIGURATIVE LANGUAGE

As we stated at the beginning of this chapter, you don't need to be an expert in rhetoric to ace the AP English Language and Composition Exam; however, you do need to have some understanding of how language works. With the exception of technical manuals (like the one that helped you assemble your entertainment center), few texts are written such that all of their language is meant to be taken literally. Take, for example, the end of one of Abraham Lincoln's inaugural speeches.

> With malice toward none, with charity for all, with
> firmness in the right as God gives us to see the right, let
> us strive on to finish the work we are in, to bind up the
> *Line* nation's wounds, to care for him who shall have borne
> 5 the battle and for his widow and his orphan, to do all
> which may achieve and cherish a just and lasting peace
> among ourselves and with all nations.

Are we supposed to take "to bind up the nation's wounds" literally? Of course not. Lincoln has personified our country to make the suffering of particular individuals relatable to all the people of the nation. And what about "him who shall have borne the battle"? Clearly, Lincoln is using the singular (a man) to represent the collective mass of soldiers, and when he adds "his widow and his orphan," we understand that "shall have borne the battle" really means "shall have died in battle." Lincoln personalizes the suffering of this group of people by instead speaking of individual sacrifice, which he knows is far more likely to strike a profound emotional chord in his listeners.

Despite the effectiveness of Lincoln's speech, you should keep in mind that many other perfectly convincing arguments and explanations are conveyed primarily through literal language. On this exam, there's no need for you to strain yourself attempting to use figurative language in the free-response section. But it will be very helpful for you to review the common terms associated with figurative language that we've listed below because you will be obliged to analyze texts that contain figurative language on this test.

With all this in mind, here is a list of some common terms related to figurative language; we've put them in order of their decreasing relevance to the test.

Imagery

For the purposes of this exam, you may consider **imagery** to be synonymous with figurative language. However, in a more restricted sense, imagery is figurative language that is used to convey a sensory perception (visual, auditory, olfactory, tactile, or gustatory).

Hyperbole

Hyperbole is overstatement or exaggeration; it is the use of figurative language that significantly exaggerates the facts for effect. In many instances, but certainly not all, hyperbole is employed for comic effect.

> Example: If you use too much figurative language in your free-response essays, the AP readers will crucify you!

Clearly, this statement is a gross exaggeration; while the readers may give you a poor grade if you use figurative language that doesn't suit the purposes of your essay, they will not kill you.

Understatement

Understatement is figurative language that presents the facts in a way that makes them appear much less significant than they really are. Understatement is almost always used for comic effect.

Example: After dinner, they came and took into custody Doctor Pangloss and his pupil Candide, the one for speaking his mind and the other for appearing to approve what he heard. They were conducted to separate apartments, which were extremely cool and where they were never bothered by the sun.

Taking the last sentence literally would lead you astray. The understatement in this case ("They were conducted to separate apartments, which were extremely cool and where they were never bothered by the sun") should be taken to mean that the poor men were thrown into horribly dark, dank, and cold prison cells.

Simile

A **simile** is a comparison between two unlike objects, in which the two parts are connected with a term such as *like* or *as*.

Example: The birds are like black arrows flying across the sky.

You can easily identify a simile—and distinguish it from a metaphor—because of the use of *like* or *as*.

Metaphor

A **metaphor** is a simile without a connecting term such as *like* or *as*. Here's an example of a metaphor.

Example: The birds are black arrows flying across the sky.

Birds are not arrows, but the commonalities (both are long and sleek, and they travel swiftly through the air—and both have feathers) allow us to easily grasp the image.

Extended Metaphor

An **extended metaphor** is precisely what it sounds like—it is a metaphor that lasts for longer than just one phrase or sentence. A word of caution for the exam, however; do not use extended metaphors in your own AP essays, for many scholars (and many AP graders) believe that the extended metaphor is a poor expository or argumentative technique.

Example: During the time I have voyaged on this ship, I have avoided the cabin; rather, I have remained on deck, battered by wind and rain, but able to see moonlight on the water. I do not wish to go below decks now.

As surprising as this may seem, this passage is not about nautical navigation. The ship's voyage is the central metaphor (representing the course of life); the writer extends the metaphor by relating elements of figurative language: cabin, deck, wind and rain, moonlight, water, and decks. The cabin is a safe place, but it's a place where you can't experience much; on deck, you're exposed to the elements, but you can experience beauteous sights. Having made the difficult, dangerous, but rewarding choice of staying on deck, it would be a personal defeat, a kind of surrender to wish for the safety, comfort, and limited horizons of the cabin later in life.

Symbol

A **symbol** is a word that represents something other than itself.

Example: The Christian soldiers paused to remember the lamb.

In this case, the rough, tough soldiers did not stop to think about the actual animal; the lamb is a traditional Christian symbol for Jesus Christ.

Sometimes, it is difficult to distinguish between metaphor and symbol. Remember that a metaphor always contains an implied comparison between two elements. Recall the metaphorical image of the birds and the arrows: The birds remain birds, and the arrows remain arrows—the metaphor serves to give us an image of the flight of the birds by suggesting a visualization of arrows. However, in the case of a symbol, the named object really doesn't count. There is no lamb; *lamb* is merely an object that's meant to conjure up another object or element.

Denotation and Connotation

Denotation refers to a word's primary or literal significance, while **connotation** refers to the vast range of other meanings that a word suggests. Context (and at times, author's intent) determines which connotations may be appropriate for a word. An author will carefully pick a particular word for its connotations, knowing or hoping a reader will make an additional inference as a result. Some literary critics argue that it is impossible to distinguish between denotation and connotation. Who, they ask, is to determine which meaning to assign as a primary significance? Let's move on and look at an example.

> Example: I am looking at the sky.

The denotation of the underlined word should be as clear as a cloudless sky (the space, often blue, above the earth's surface). However, there can be connotations associated with the word. The sky is often associated with heaven; it can also evoke the idea of freedom or vast openness. Because of connotation, one can't help but believe that the sky evokes in the writer a sense of longing for freedom from work, the computer, or the AP English Language and Composition Exam.

Oxymoron

An **oxymoron** is an apparent contradiction of terms.

> Example: I advise you to make haste slowly.

What would you do if someone said this to you? At first, you might think that this is simply a foolish, contradictory statement, and you might ignore the advice. However, it is possible to make sense of the apparent contradiction, which is in fact an oxymoron. In essence, the sentence advises you to go as fast as you can, while going slowly enough to do things right.

Paradox

The **paradox** is an apparent contradiction of ideas or statements and, therefore, is closely related to the oxymoron. Think of a paradox as an oxymoron on a larger scale.

> Example: The only way to overcome death is to die.

This paradox pops up in various contexts; it is not a contradiction, for some would say that only after death is it possible to pass on to eternal life (in heaven, for instance), and *eternal* life precludes (another) death. Thus, one dies (physically) but then lives (spiritually) forever.

It is possible to have a paradox that offers no real hope of resolution. For instance, there is the Cretan Liar Paradox (dating from Greek times), which goes like this: "All Cretans are liars; I am a Cretan."

Personification

Personification is the figurative device in which inanimate objects or concepts are given human qualities. It can enhance our emotional response because we usually attribute more emotional significance to other humans than to things or concepts.

> Example: He had been wrestling with lethargy for days, and every time that he
> thought that he was close to victory, his adversary escaped his hold.

This figurative wrestling match, in which lethargy is personified as the opponent to the author of this sentence, brings the struggle to life—human life. If you don't believe this, think about the literal alternative: He tried to stop being lethargic, but he was not successful. This doesn't sound very lively.

Rhetorical Question

A **rhetorical question** is a question whose answer is obvious; these types of questions do not need to be answered—and usually aren't. Rhetorical questions attempt to prove something without actually presenting an argument; sometimes they're used as a form of irony, in which something is stated, but its opposite is meant.

> Example (no irony): With all the violence on TV today, is it any wonder kids bring guns to school?

Since it has already been determined that you agree (even if you don't), the writer need not substantiate this remark.

> Example (with irony): Aren't AP exams great fun?

Here, there is an assumption that you would answer in the negative, although there is no way for you to respond—unless you write a letter. Rhetorical questions allow a writer to make a point without further support, whether it's a straightforward remark or one with a touch of irony.

Bombast

Bombast (adjective = bombastic) is language that is overly rhetorical (pompous), especially when considered in context. Generally speaking, graduation speeches contain bombast; pedantic people (those who use their learning ostentatiously) tend to use bombast. Occasionally, a passage on the AP English Language and Composition Exam will contain bombast.

> We are here in these hallowed halls, accompanied by
> genial kin and erudite mentors, surrounded by Corin-
> thian columns and the three wisdoms of the ages, to
> *Line* celebrate the conjunction of fare thee well and many
> 5 happy returns and to proffer advice worthy of Athena
> to these prodigal sons and daughters as they depart our
> august institution. You happy survivors are not gradu-
> ates, but champions who have been assailed on all sides
> by demons of mathematics, dragons of science, and
> 10 inhuman beasts of humanities, but who have emerged
> victorious from each and every battle. In this respect, one
> is reminded of Thucydides, who writes: "So long as a
> vessel was coming up to charge another boat, the men on
> the decks rained darts, arrows and stones upon her, but
> 15 once alongside, the heavy infantry tried to board each
> other's vessel, fighting hand to hand. In many quarters
> it happened, because of the restricted space, that a vessel
> was charging an enemy on one side and being charged
> herself on another, and that two or even more ships
> 20 were entangled all around one, obliging the helmsmen
> to attend to defense here, offense there, not to one thing
> at a time, but to many things on all sides, while the huge
> commotion caused by the number of ships crashing
> together not only spread terror, but also made the orders
> 25 of the boatswains inaudible." I urge you to remember
> Attica, and to remember the Spartan way, for…

The passage above is marked by pretentious and inflated speech; it is a perfect example of bombast.

Pun

A **pun** is a play on words. In general, a pun either plays on the multiple meanings of a word or replaces one word with another that is similar in sound but very different in meaning. Puns are almost always used for comic effect.

> Example: In *Star Wars*, why did the Evil Empire leave the Catholic nuns alone? Force of habit.

If you know anything about *Star Wars*, you know that the "force" is the power of good, and you'll get the play on words here.

Metonymy and Synecdoche

Both *metonymy* and *synecdoche* are terms that mean the use of figurative language in which characteristics are substituted for the things with which they are associated.

In **metonymy,** one term is substituted for another term with which it is closely associated.

> Example: The sailors drank a glass of hearty red.

Red is a color; sailors cannot drink it. However, metonymically, the color represents wine (red wine), which sailors over the age of twenty-one may drink.

Synecdoche is a form of metonymy that's restricted to cases where a part is used to signify the whole.

> Example: All hands on deck!

The hands (part of each sailor) represent the sailors (the whole).

If you have an aversion for learning rhetorical terms, then for the purposes of this exam you can feel free to forget the definition of synecdoche; you can get away with using the term *metonymy* for any situation in which a characteristic of a certain thing is used to represent the thing.

Theme

A **theme** is a general idea contained in a text; the theme may be stated explicitly or only suggested. A theme is not just an idea; it is *an idea that is developed,* often over the course of a chapter or an entire book. Usually, one can identify a central theme and several minor ones. Sometimes both are overtly stated, as in the example that follows:

> Many scholars agree that the central theme in *Huckleberry Finn* is the conflict between nature and civilization. But clearly, the book contains other themes, such as the worth of honor and the voyage of self-discovery.

Read the following passage, and see if you can identify a central theme.

> We now touch on civilization's most sensitive spot; it is
> an unpleasant task to raise one's voice against the folly of
> the day, against chimeras that have caused a downright
> *Line* epidemic.
> 5   To speak against the absurdities of trade today means
> to expose oneself to anathemas, just as much as if one
> had spoken against the tyranny of the popes and the bar-
> ons in the twelfth century. If it were a matter of choosing
> between two dangerous roles, I think it would be

10 less dangerous to offend a sovereign with bitter truths
    than to offend the mercantile spirit that now rules like a
    despot over civilization—and even over sovereigns!
        And yet a superficial analysis will prove that our
    commercial systems defile and disorganize civilization
15 and that in trade, as in all other things, we are being led
    further and further astray.
        The controversy on trade is barely half a century old
    and has already produced thousands of books, and yet
    the participants in the controversy have not seen that the
20 trade mechanism is organized in such a way that it is a
    slap in the face to all common sense. It has subordinated
    the whole of society to one class of parasitic and unpro-
    ductive persons: the merchants. All the essential classes
    of society—the proprietor, the farmer, the manufacturer,
25 and even the government—find themselves dominated
    by a non-essential, contingent class, the merchant, who
    should be their subordinate, their employed agent, re-
    movable and accountable, and who, nevertheless, directs
    and obstructs at will all the avenues of circulation.

It should not surprise you that the title of the essay that this passage is excerpted from is "On Trade." In his essay, the French socialist Charles Fourier develops a central theme: Merchants, through trade, have both corrupted society and become its tyrant.

Many of the passages in the multiple-choice and free-response sections of the AP exam are long enough to permit you to identify at least one central theme, and you will almost certainly be asked to do so.

Aphorism
An **aphorism** is a concise, pithy statement of an opinion or a general truth.

> Example: Life is short, the art [of medicine] is long, opportunity fleeting, experimen-
> tation dangerous, reasoning difficult.

That aphorism is attributed to Hippocrates, the "Father of Medicine." Note that his statement is more sophisticated than the "commonplace wisdom" of a saying like "Haste makes waste."

Malapropism
Malapropism is the unintentional use of a word that resembles the word intended but that has a very different meaning.

> Example: He was a man of great statue.

The AP English Language and Composition readers often collect malapropisms to share with friends and colleagues as they read through the free-response essays; it isn't in your best interest to provide them with any good laughs, so try to avoid them.

Circumlocution and Euphemism
Circumlocution has two meanings, and you should be familiar with both of them. For the purposes of this exam, we'll say that one meaning of circumlocution is "talking around a subject" and that the other is "talking around a word." Now let's take a closer look at some examples of circumlocution.

It is entirely possible that you have used circumlocution when addressing your parents. For instance, instead of simply asking them straight out if you may borrow the car, have you ever said something such as, "I understand that you guys are going to stay in tonight and watch a DVD, right?

If so, since I've already seen that movie, I was thinking about maybe going downtown. It's a nice summer evening and all that, but it's still too far to walk, and I'll be with Nina, anyway, and she'd never agree to walk downtown. We were thinking that she could drive, but, unfortunately, Nina's parents are going out, so she can't take their car. I know that I forgot to put gas in your car the last time that I drove to the mountains, but I learned my lesson. That won't happen again." You may even have gone on speaking for longer. You might never have gotten to the point where you actually asked to borrow the car, but your parents understood what you wanted and put you out of your misery by saying something such as, "We already told your sister that she could use the car tonight."

That kind of circumlocution is an example of the first meaning of circumlocution—"talking around the subject."

On the AP English Language and Composition Exam, you're more likely to encounter the second type of circumlocution—"talking around a word"—that is, using several words or a phrase in place of a specific word (or specific words). You may have noticed that sometimes it is more effective to be wordy than to be precise. For example, some people consider their automobiles cars, and, not surprisingly, they refer to these objects just as cars. Other people, however, use evocative circumlocutions when referring to their heap of metal—one of which is "cruisin' machine" (and the other of which is "heap of metal.") The point is that circumlocution is often an effective means for communicating points of view. Take a look at the following sentence.

> Candide was court-martialed, and he was asked which he liked better, to run the
> gauntlet six and thirty times through the whole regiment, or to have his brains
> blown out with a dozen musket-balls.

In this sentence, we read that in a spirit of compassion and justice, the military court is giving Candide a choice: He may choose to be either beaten to death or executed by firing squad. The wording of the second choice, in particular, provides a wonderful example of the evocative power of well-used circumlocution. While using the phrase "execution by firing squad" would have allowed both the author and the reader to remain distant from the event and dispassionate, the circumlocution that the author employed with "to have his brains blown out with a dozen musket-balls" vividly describes the horror and brutality of the event. In this sentence, Voltaire succeeds in relating his feelings about the court-martial without commenting on it.

A **euphemism** is a word or words that are used to avoid employing an unpleasant or offensive term. Again, you probably (hopefully) use euphemisms all the time. In both fiction and nonfiction, the most common euphemisms have to do with sex. In these cases, the author knows what he or she means, you know what he or she means, and the author knows that you know what he or she means. Let's look at another example from Voltaire's *Candide*. In this passage, Voltaire uses euphemism for comic effect.

> One day when Mademoiselle Cunégonde went to
> take a walk in a little neighboring wood that was called
> a park, she saw—through the bushes—the sage Doctor
> *Line* Pangloss giving a lecture in experimental philosophy to
> 5 her mother's chambermaid, a little brown wench, very
> pretty and very accommodating.

Voltaire knows that his readers know what is really going on here. This particular example of euphemism is used for comic effect rather than direct avoidance of the word *sex*. One may expect Pangloss to limit his sagacity to philosophical matters, but clearly his "lecture in experimental philosophy" is most prosaic.

IRONY AND SATIRE

When reading the passages on the AP English Language Exam, you cannot always take what you see at face value; in fact, when reading you must always be on the lookout for slightly or very veiled meanings behind the words.

ISN'T IT IRONIC?

Irony: Most people use the term without really knowing its definition. Alanis Morissette's 1996 song about irony didn't help the situation. If you don't believe this, ask one of your friends to define irony and see what kind of answer you receive. The two basic types of irony that you'll need to be familiar with for this test are verbal irony and situational irony.

VERBAL IRONY

Verbal irony refers to the process of stating something but *meaning* the opposite of what is stated. Verbal irony can refer to irony that's used in spoken language as well as in print. In spoken language, intonation is often a clue to ironic intent; however, in writing, it is not possible to imply things through intonation, so there's always a danger that the irony may be missed; in essence, the writer who employs irony risks communicating the exact opposite of what is intended. For example, let's say that you write, "This Princeton Review book is really interesting." Unless your listener or reader hears your remark in context, he or she won't know if this is high praise for this book, or if you're bored silly and have chosen to express your sentiment more forcefully by using verbal irony.

Consider the following passage. The philosopher Pangloss has just given a rather personalized history of venereal disease, a veritable uncontrollable—and uncontrolled—plague in eighteenth-century Europe.

> "O sage Pangloss," cried Candide, "what a strange
> genealogy is this! Is not the devil at the root of it all?"
> "Not at all," replied the great man, "it was unavoidable, a necessary ingredient in the best of worlds."

The student Candide shows sincere respect for Pangloss when he addresses him as "sage Pangloss;" Candide has no ironic intent. However, the same cannot be said of the narrator—who for all intents and purposes is Voltaire. In *Candide,* one of Voltaire's principal aims is to excoriate (to censure scathingly) the "philosophers of optimism," of whom Pangloss is a caricature. He does this through the frequent use of verbal irony; in the passage above, his use of "great man" is ironic—even though Candide's tone is not. After all, neither the narrator nor the careful reader views Pangloss as a great man—he is just the opposite.

In essence, to fully appreciate the passage, we must read in stereo, simultaneously picking up on Candide's serious tone and the narrator's ironic tone. This is a pretty complicated case of verbal irony.

Sarcasm is simply verbal irony used with the intent to injure. It's often impossible to discern between irony and sarcasm, and, more often than not, sarcasm is in the mind of the beholder. Let's say that your close friend and soccer teammate missed a wide-open goal from ten feet away, and you smiled and shouted, "Nice shot!" Presumably your friend, used to your jests, would interpret your quip as playful irony. If the opposing team's goalie said the same words, however, it is far more likely that your friend would take the remark as sarcasm—and reply with a not-so-kind word or two. In written form, irony and sarcasm can be considered to be fairly synonymous—but just think of sarcasm as malicious. Here is an example from Heinrich Ibsen's *Hedda Gabbler*.

> Brack: There's a possibility that the appointment may
> be decided by competition—
> Tesman: Competition! By Jove, Hedda, fancy that!
> Hedda: [*motionless in her chair*] How exciting, Tesman.

Of course, it is easier to see the sarcasm when you are familiar with the play, but it is sufficient for you to know that Tesman is the rather boring, plodding husband and that Hedda is an unfulfilled wife. The stage direction ("motionless in her chair") helps us see that her words are at least full of irony; if you add the bitter, malignant intent, which the husband misses but we do not, then you have sarcasm.

SITUATIONAL IRONY

Situational irony refers to a situation that runs contrary to what was expected.

Suppose you live in Seattle during the rainy season and plan a vacation to sunny Phoenix. While you are in Phoenix, it rains every day there, but is sunny the entire week in Seattle. This is situational irony.

SATIRE

In **satire**, something is portrayed in a way that's deliberately distorted to achieve comic effect. Implicit in most satire is the author's desire to critique what is being mocked. Voltaire's *Candide* is principally a satire of optimism, the philosophy that, given that the first "cause" was perfect (God's creation of the world), all causes and effects must naturally be part of this original perfect plan. The French satirist takes on many other causes, however, and one of his favorite targets is the part of religion that he considers no more than fanatical superstition. Here is what happens after Candide and Pangloss are caught in the infamous earthquake of Lisbon, Portugal.

> After the earthquake, which had destroyed three-
> fourths of the city of Lisbon, the sages of that country
> could think of no better manner to preserve the kingdom
> *Line* from complete ruin than to entertain the people with an
> 5 *auto-da-fe*, it having been decided by the University of
> Coimbra that burning a few people alive over low heat
> and with great ceremony is an infallible way to prevent
> earthquakes.
>
> In consequence, they had seized a Biscayan for marry-
> 10 ing his godmother and two Portuguese for taking out the
> bacon of a larded chicken they were eating; after dinner,
> they came and took into custody Doctor Pangloss and
> his pupil Candide, the one for speaking his mind and
> the other for appearing to approve what he heard. They
> 15 were conducted to separate apartments, which were
> extremely cool and where they were never bothered
> by the sun. Eight days later, they were each dressed in
> a *sanbenito* and their heads were adorned with paper
> *mitres*. The *mitre* and *sanbenito* worn by Candide were
> 20 painted with upside down flames and with devils that
> had neither tails nor claws, but Doctor Pangloss's devils
> had both tails and claws, and his flames were right side
> up. In these clothes they marched in the procession and
> heard a very pathetic sermon, which was followed by an
> 25 anthem accompanied by bagpipes. Candide was flogged
> to the beat of the music while the anthem was being
> sung; the Biscayan and the two men who would not eat
> bacon were burned, and Pangloss was hanged, which is
> not a common custom at these solemnities. The same day
> 30 there was another earthquake, which created the most
> dreadful havoc.

After the real earthquake of 1755, there were real *auto-da-fes* ("acts of faith"), where "evil" inhabitants of Lisbon were sacrificed to appease God, who, ostensibly (to all outward appearances), had provoked the earthquake to punish the city. The "evils" that are being punished say more about the ridiculous prejudices of the persecutors than they do about the so-called evil victims. The two Portuguese who refrained from eating the bacon are guilty of nothing—but they are taken for Jews; the man who married his godmother, who, presumably, is not tied to him by blood, is guilty of no more than infringing on a technicality of the religious code (Catholicism, in this case).

Note that the satire is heightened by Voltaire's use of verbal irony ("the sages"), situational irony (right after the ceremony there is a second earthquake), and a comical circumlocution ("burning a few people alive over low heat and with great ceremony" is a circumlocution for *auto-da-fe*). Satire can be effective in both fiction and nonfiction, and *Candide*, a philosophical story that combines both, is thought to be one of the most brilliant satires of all.

Most critics, however, relegate satire—and satirists—to a secondary sphere in the universe of writing; satire makes for good entertainment, but mocking others does not measure up to the conviction of cogent writing. Had Voltaire been nothing more than a satirist, he would not have been remembered as a brilliant *philosophe*, but as a clever joker—if he were remembered at all. Although Voltaire's satire in *Candide* is quite brilliant, some other examples of satire are a little easier to figure out. Let's look at a sample question based on a passage from Jonathan Swift's *Gulliver's Travels*.

For about seventy moons past there have been two struggling parties in this empire, under the names of *Tramecksan* and *Slamecksan*, from the high and low heels
Line of their shoes, by which they distinguish themselves. It
5 is alleged, indeed, that the high heels are most agreeable to our ancient constitution; but, however this be, his majesty has determined to make use only of low heels in the administration of the government, and all offices in the gift of the crown, as you cannot but observe; and particu-
10 larly that his majesty's imperial heels are lower at least by a *drurr* than any of his court (*drurr* is a measure about the fourteenth part of an inch). The animosities between these two parties run so high, that they will neither eat, nor drink, nor talk with each other. We compute the *Tra-*
15 *mecksan*, or high heels, to exceed us in number; but the power is wholly on our side. We apprehend his imperial highness, the heir to the crown, to have some tendency towards the high heels; at least we can plainly discover that one of his heels is higher than the other, which gives
20 him a hobble in his gait.

5. The above passage is an example of

  (A) an analysis of court customs
  (B) a satire of British footwear
  (C) a study of British eccentricities
  (D) a satire of the British court
  (E) a nonsensical account of life at court

Well, the correct answer must be either (B) or (D) because this section is all about satire. The correct answer is (D). The passage serves to satirize the Whig-Tory discord (the Whigs dominated politics during much of the eighteenth century) and the relationship of the "parties" (the Whigs and Tories were not really political parties as we know them today) and the King. Unless you recognize that the passage is satirical, you will not have a good grasp of what is going on—which will lead to major problems with all of the multiple-choice questions on that passage.

KEY TERMS

diction

syntax

style

tone

point of view

rhetoric

figurative language

logos

ethos

pathos

imagery

hyperbole

understatement

simile

metaphor

extended metaphor

symbol

denotation

connotation

oxymoron

paradox

personification

rhetorical question

bombast

pun

metonymy

synecdoche

theme

aphorism

malapropism

circumlocution

euphemism

irony

verbal irony

sarcasm

situational irony

satire

8

The Hit Parade—
Words, Words, Words

A great way to improve your reading and essay-writing skills is to improve your vocabulary. The more words you know on the day of the test, the easier it will be. It's as simple as that. For this reason, it's important that you get to work on your vocabulary immediately. We suggest that you mark any words you don't know in the chapter and make flashcards for yourself.

THE HIT PARADE

The Hit Parade list consists of the words that show up most often on the AP English Language and Composition Exam. Each word on the list is accompanied by its definition, a pronunciation guide, and a sentence that uses the word. Your vocabulary-building program should start with these words.

LEARN THE WORDS IN GROUPS

This Hit Parade has been arranged into groups of related words. Learning groups of related words can help you better remember each word's meaning. After all, even if you don't remember the exact meaning of a word, you may remember what group it's from. This will give you an idea of the word's meaning, which can help you use POE to get to an answer.

Make each group of words a part of your life. Rip out one of the group lists, carry it around with you, and use the words throughout your day. For example, on Monday you may feel like using words of *disdain* (see the "If you can't say anything nice" list), but on Friday you may wish to be more *affable* (see the "Friendly" list).

DON'T MEMORIZE THE DICTIONARY

Only a tiny percentage of all the words in the English language are ever used on the exam. Generally speaking, it tests the kinds of words that an educated adult—your English teacher, for example—would know without having to look up. It tests the sorts of words that you encounter in your daily reading, from a novel in English class to the newspaper.

HOW TO MEMORIZE NEW WORDS

Here are three effective methods for learning new words.

- **Flashcards:** You can make your own flashcards out of 3 x 5 index cards. Write the word on one side and its definition on the other. It is also quite useful to write a memorable sentence under the definition. Then quiz yourself on the words, or practice with a friend. You can carry a few cards around with you every day and work on them in spare moments, like when you're riding on the bus.

- **The Image Approach:** The image approach involves letting each new word suggest a wild image to you, then using that image to help you remember the word. For example, the word *enfranchise* means, "to give the right to vote." Women did not become enfranchised in the United States until 1920, when the Nineteenth Amendment to the Constitution guaranteed them the right to vote in state and federal elections. The word *franchise* may suggest to you a McDonald's franchise. You could remember the new word by imagining people lined up to vote at a McDonald's. The weirder the image, the better you'll remember the word.

- **Mnemonics:** Speaking of "the weirder, the better," another way to learn words is to use mnemonics. A mnemonic is a device or trick, such as a rhyme or song, that helps you remember something. "In fourteen hundred ninety-two Columbus sailed the ocean blue" is a mnemonic that helps you remember a date in history. The funnier or stranger you make your mnemonic, the more likely you are to remember it. Write down your mnemonics (your flashcards are a great place for these).

Although you may not be able to think of a mnemonic for every Hit Parade term, sometimes you'll end up learning the word just by thinking about the definition and a suitable mnemonic long enough.

LOOK IT UP

Well-written general publications—such as *The New Yorker* and *The Economist*—are good sources of vocabulary. You should read them on a regular basis. When you come across a new word, write it down, look it up, and remember it. You can make flashcards for these words as well.

Before you can memorize the definition of a word you come across in your reading, you have to find out what it means. You'll need a real dictionary for that. ETS uses two dictionaries in writing the AP English Language and Composition Exam: the *American Heritage Dictionary* and the *Webster's New Collegiate Dictionary*. You should own a copy of one or the other. (You'll use it in college too—it's a good investment.)

Keep in mind that most words have more than one definition. The dictionary will list these in order from the most to least common meanings of the word. ETS will also often trip you up by testing the second, third, or even fourth definition of a familiar-sounding word. For example, the word *pedestrian* shows up repeatedly on the exam. When ETS uses it, however, it never means a person on foot—the definition of *pedestrian* you're probably most familiar with. ETS uses it to mean common, ordinary, banal—a *secondary* definition.

Very often, when you see easy words on hard AP English Language and Composition Exam questions, ETS is testing a second, third, or fourth definition that you may not be familiar with.

Here we go!

ARE YOU TALKIN' TO ME?

assertion   uh SUR shun
a declaration or statement
We could not believe John's assertion that he had never seen *Star Wars*.

cogent   KOH jent
convincing; reasonable
Christina's argument was so cogent that even her opponents had to agree with her.

coherent   koh HEER ent
logically connected
The old prospector's story was not coherent; he rambled on about different things that had nothing to do with one another.

cohesive   koh HEE siv
condition of sticking together
Eric's essay was cohesive because each point flowed nicely into the next point.

didactic   dye DAK tik
intended to instruct
The tapes were entertaining and didactic because they amused and instructed the children.

discourse   DIS kors
verbal expression or exchange; conversation
Their discourse varied widely; they discussed everything from Chaucer to ice fishing.

eloquence   EH lo kwens
the ability to speak vividly or persuasively
Cicero's eloquence is legendary; his speeches were well-crafted and convincing.

fluid   FLOO id
easily flowing
The two old friends' conversation was fluid; each of them was able to respond quickly and easily to what the other had to say.

implication   im pli KAY shun
the act of suggesting or hinting
When your mother asks, "Were you raised in a barn?" the implication is that you should close the door.

lucid   LOO sid
easily understood; clear
Our teacher does a good job because he provides lucid explanations of difficult concepts.

rhetoric   RET uh rik
the art of using language effectively and persuasively
Because they are expected to make speeches, most politicians and lawyers are well versed in the art of rhetoric.

I'LL BE THE JUDGE OF THAT

arbiter   AHR bih ter
a judge who decides a disputed issue
An arbiter was hired to settle the Major League Baseball strike because the owners and players could not come to an agreement.

biased   BYE ist
prejudiced
Judges should not be biased but should rather weigh the evidence fairly before making up their minds.

exculpate   EKS kul payt
to free from guilt or blame
When the gold coins discovered in his closet were found to be fake, Dr. Rideau was exculpated and the search for the real thief continued.

impartial   im PAR shul
not in favor of one side or the other, unbiased
The umpire had a hard time remaining impartial; his son was pitching for the home team, and this made it difficult to call the game fairly.

incontrovertible   in kahn truh VERT uh bul
not able to be denied or disputed
The videotape of the robbery provided incontrovertible evidence against the suspect—he was obviously guilty.

integrity   in TEG rit ee
trustworthiness; completeness
The integrity of the witness was called into question when her dislike for the defendant was revealed—some jurors suspected that she was not being entirely truthful.

objectivity   ahb jek TIV ih tee
treating facts without influence from personal feelings or prejudices
It is important that judges hear all cases with objectivity, so that their personal feelings do not affect their decision.

plausible   PLAWZ ih bul
seemingly valid or acceptable; credible
Keith's excuse that he missed school yesterday because he was captured by space aliens was not very plausible.

substantiated   sub STAN shee ay tid
supported with proof or evidence; verified
The fingerprint evidence substantiated the detective's claim that the suspect had been at the scene of the crime.

vindicated   VIN duh kayt id
freed from blame
Mrs. Layton was finally vindicated after her husband admitted to the crime.

You're so Vain

condescending   kahn de SEND ing
treating people as weak or inferior
Robert always looked down on his sister and treated her in a condescending manner.

contemptuous   kun TEMP choo us
feeling hatred; scornful
She was so contemptuous of people who wore fur that she sprayed red paint on them.

despotic   des PAHT ik
exercising absolute power; tyrannical
He was a despotic ruler whose every law was enforced with threats of violence or death.

dictatorial   dik tuh TOR ee ul
domineering; oppressively overbearing
The coach had a dictatorial manner and expected people to do whatever he demanded.

disdain   dis DAYN
(n.) contempt, scorn, (v.) to regard or treat with contempt; to look down on
(n.) I felt nothing but disdain for the person who stole my lunch—what a jerk!
(v.) A self-proclaimed gourmand, he disdains to eat any meal that comes in a box.

haughty   HAW tee
arrogant; vainly proud
His haughty manner made it clear that he thought he was better than everyone else.

imperious   im PEER ee us
arrogantly domineering or overbearing
She had a very imperious way about her; she was bossy and treated everyone as if they were beneath her.

patronizing   PAY truh ny zing
treating in a condescending manner
Patrick had such a patronizing attitude that he treated everyone around him like a bunch of little kids.

WHEN THE GOING GETS TOUGH

convoluted   kahn vuh LOO tid
intricate; complex
The directions were so convoluted that we drove all around the city and got lost.

cryptic   KRIP tik
difficult to comprehend
The writing on the walls of the crypt was cryptic; none of the scientists understood it.

futile   FEW tul
having no useful purpose; pointless
It is futile to try to explain the difference between right and wrong to your pet.

impede   im PEED
to slow the progress of
The retreating army constructed barbed-wire fences and destroyed bridges to impede the advance of the enemy.

obscure   ahb SKYUR
(adj.) relatively unknown, (v.) to conceal or make indistinct
Scott constantly makes references to obscure cult films, and no one ever gets his jokes.
The man in front of me was so tall that his head obscured my view of the movie.

quandary   KWAHN dree
a state of uncertainty or perplexity
Ann was in a quandary because she had no soap with which to do her laundry.

I'M A LOSER, BABY

indolent   IN duh lunt
lazy
Mr. Lan said his students were indolent because they had not done their homework.

insipid   in SIP id
uninteresting; unchallenging
That insipid movie was so boring and predictable.

lament   luh MENT
express grief for; mourn
After Beowulf was killed by the dragon, the Geats wept and lamented his fate.

listless   LIST luss
lacking energy
Because he is accustomed to an active lifestyle, Mark feels listless when he has nothing to do.

melancholy   MEL un kaw lee
sadness; depression
Joy fell into a state of melancholy when her Arcade Fire CD got scratched.

torpor   TOR per
laziness; inactivity; dullness
The hot and humid day filled everyone with an activity-halting torpor.

REVOLUTION

alliance   uh LIE uhns
a union of two or more groups
The two countries formed an alliance to stand against their common enemy.

disparity   dis PAR uh tee

inequality in age, rank, or degree; difference

There is a great disparity between rich and poor in many nations.

impinge   im PINJ

hinder; interfere with

By not allowing the students to publish a newspaper, the school was impinging upon their right to free speech.

sanction   SANK shun

an economic or military measure put in place to punish another country

In 1962, the United States imposed economic sanctions on Cuba to protest Fidel Castro's dictatorship; travel and trade between the countries are severely restricted to this day.

servile   SER vile

submissive; like a servant

Cameron's servile behavior finally ended when he decided to stand up to his older brother.

suppressed   suh PREST

subdued; kept from being circulated

The author's book was suppressed because the dictator thought it was too critical of his regime.

You Are So Beautiful

embellish   em BELL ish

to make beautiful by ornamenting; to decorate

We embellished the account of our vacation by including descriptions of the many colorful people and places we visited.

florid   FLOHR id

describing flowery or elaborate speech

The candidate's speech was so florid that although no one could understand what he was talking about, they all agreed that he sounded good saying it.

opulent   AHP yuh lunt

exhibiting a display of great wealth

Dances at the king's palace are always very opulent affairs because no expense is spared.

ornate   or NAYT

elaborately decorated

The carved wood was so ornate that you could examine it several times and still notice things you had not seen before.

ostentatious   ah sten TAY shus

describing a showy or pretentious display

Whenever the millionaire gave a party, the elaborate decorations and enormous amounts of food were always part of his ostentatious display of wealth.

poignant　POYN yunt
profoundly moving; touching
The most poignant part of the movie was when the father finally made peace with his son.

OVERKILL

ebullience　ih BULL yuns
intense enthusiasm
A sense of ebullience swept over the crowd when the matador defeated the bull.

effusive　eh FYOO siv
emotionally unrestrained; gushy
Halle Berry was effusive in her thanks after winning the Oscar; she even burst into tears.

egregious　uh GREE jus
conspicuously bad or offensive
Forgetting to sterilize surgical tools before an operation would be an egregious error.

flagrant　FLAY grunt
extremely or deliberately shocking or noticeable
His throwing the pie at his teacher was a flagrant sign of disrespect.

frenetic　freh NEH tik
wildly excited or active
The pace at the busy office was frenetic; Megan never had a moment to catch her breath.

gratuitous　gruh TOO ih tus
given freely; unearned; unwarranted
The film was full of gratuitous sex and violence that was not essential to the story.

superfluous　soo PER floo us
extra; unnecessary
If there is sugar in your tea, adding honey would be superfluous.

IT GETS BETTER

alleviate　uh LEEV ee ayt
to ease a pain or burden
John took aspirin to alleviate the pain from the headache he got after taking the SAT.

asylum　uh SY lum
a place of retreat or security
The soldiers sought asylum from the bombs in the underground shelter.

auspicious　aw SPISH us
favorable; promising
Our trip to the beach had an auspicious start; the rain stopped just as we started the car.

benevolent   buh NEH vuh lunt
well-meaning; generous
She was a kind and benevolent queen who was concerned about her subjects' well-being.

benign   buh NINE
kind and gentle
Uncle Charlie is a benign and friendly man who is always willing to help.

mollify   MAHL uh fye
to calm or soothe
Anna's apology for scaring her brother did not mollify him; he was mad at her all day.

reclamation   rek luh MAY shun
the act of making something useful again
Thanks to the reclamation project, the once unusable land became a productive farm.

sanction   SANK shun
to give official authorization or approval
The students were happy when the principal agreed to sanction the use of calculators in math classes.

LIAR, LIAR, PANTS ON FIRE

dubious   DOO bee us
doubtful; of unlikely authenticity
Jerry's claim that he could fly like Superman seemed dubious—we didn't believe it.

fabricated   FAB ruh kay tid
made; concocted to deceive
Fabio fabricated the story that he used to play drums for Metallica; he had never actually held drumsticks in his life.

hypocrisy   hih PAHK ruh see
the practice of pretending to be something one is not; insincerity
People who claim to be vegetarian but eat chicken and fish are guilty of hypocrisy.

slander   SLAN der
false charges and malicious oral statements about someone
After the radio host stated that Monica was a space alien, she sued him for slander.

spurious   SPUR ee us
not genuine
The sportscaster made a spurious claim when he said that the San Antonio Spurs were undefeated.

SHE'S CRAFTY

astute   uh STOOT
shrewd; clever
Kevin is financially astute; he never falls for the tricks that credit card companies play.

clandestine   klan DES tin
secretive
The spies planned a clandestine maneuver that depended on its secrecy to work.

coup   KOO
a brilliantly executed plan
It was quite a coup when I talked the salesperson into selling me this valuable cuckoo clock for five dollars.

disingenuous   dis in JEN yoo us
not straightforward; crafty
Mr. Gelman was rather disingenuous; although he seemed to be simply asking about your health, he was really trying to figure out why you'd been absent.

ruse   ROOZ
a crafty tick
The offer of a free cruise was merely a ruse to get people to listen to their sales pitch.

stratagem   STRAT uh jem
a clever trick used to deceive or outwit
Planting microphones in the gangster's home was a clever, but illegal, stratagem.

surreptitiously   sur ep TISH us lee
done by secretive means
Matt drank the cough syrup surreptitiously because he didn't want anyone to know that he was sick.

wary   WAIR ee
on guard
My father becomes wary whenever a salesman calls him on the phone; he knows that many crooks use the phone so that they can't be charged with mail fraud.

wily   WYE lee
cunning
Each year, a new batch of wily campers devised ways to torture the cabin leader.

Sittin' on the Fence

ambiguous   am BIG yoo us
open to more than one interpretation
His eyes were an ambiguous color: Some thought they were brown, and some thought they were green.

ambivalent   am BIH vuh lunt
simultaneously having opposing feelings; uncertain
She had ambivalent feelings about her dance class: On one hand, she enjoyed the exercise, but on the other hand, she thought the choice of dances could be more interesting.

apathetic   a puh THEH tik
feeling or showing little emotion
When the defendant was found guilty on all charges, her face remained expressionless and she appeared to be entirely apathetic.

arbitrary   AR bih trayr ee
determined by impulse rather than reason
The principal made the arbitrary decision that students could not wear hats in school without offering any logical reason for the rule.

capricious   kuh PREE shus
impulsive and unpredictable
The referee's capricious behavior angered the players because he was inconsistent with his calls; he would call foul for minor contact, but ignore elbowing and kicking.

equivocate   eh KWI vuh kayt
to avoid making a definite statement
On critical reading questions, I choose answers that equivocate; they use words such as *could* or *may* that make them difficult to disprove.

indifferent   in DIF rent
not caring one way or the other
The old fisherman was completely indifferent to the pain and hunger he felt; his only concern was catching the enormous marlin he had hooked.

spontaneous   spahn TAY nee us
unplanned; naturally occurring
Dave is such a good musician that he can create a song spontaneously, without having to stop and think about it.

whimsical   WIM zuh kul
subject to erratic behavior; unpredictable
Egbert rarely behaved as expected; indeed, he was a whimsical soul whose every decision was anybody's guess.

Just a Little Bit

inconsequential   in kahn suh KWEN shul
unimportant
The cost of the meal was inconsequential to Quentin because he wasn't paying for it.

superficial   soo per FISH ul
concerned only with what is on the surface or obvious; shallow
The wound on his leg was only superficial, even though it looked like a deep cut.

tenuous   TEN yoo us
having little substance or strength; shaky; unsure, weak
Her grasp on reality is tenuous at best; she's not even sure what year it is.

trivial   TRIH vee ul
of little importance or significance
Alex says he doesn't like trivia games because the knowledge they test is trivial; he prefers to spend his time learning more important things.

I Will Survive

assiduous   uh SID yoo us
hard-working
Spending hours in the hot sun digging out every tiny weed, Sidney tended her garden with assiduous attention.

compelling   kuhm PEL ing
forceful; urgently demanding attention
By ignoring the problems in the city, the mayor gave people a very compelling reason to vote him out of office.

diligent   DIL uh jent
marked by painstaking effort; hard-working
With a lot of diligent effort, they were able to finish the model airplane in record time.

dogged   DOG id
stubbornly persevering
Her first attempts resulted in failure, but her dogged efforts ultimately ended in success.

endure   en DUR
to put up with; to survive a hardship
It was difficult to endure the incredibly boring lecture given in class the other day.

intrepid   in TREH pid
courageous; fearless
The intrepid young soldier scaled the wall and attacked the enemy forces despite being outnumbered 50 to 1.

maverick   MAV uh rik
one who is independent and resists adherence to a group
In the movie *Top Gun*, Tom Cruise was a maverick; he often broke the rules and did things his own way.

obdurate   AHB dur ut
stubborn; inflexible
Leanna was so obdurate that she was unable to change her way of thinking on even the most minor issues.

obstinate   AHB stin ut
stubbornly adhering to an opinion or a course of action
Even though he begged them constantly, Jeremy's parents were obstinate in their refusal to buy him a Wii.

proliferate   pro LIF er ayt
to grow or increase rapidly
Because the number of cell phones has proliferated in recent years, many new area codes have been created to handle the demand for phone numbers.

tenacity   ten ASS uh tee
persistence
With his overwhelming tenacity, Clark was finally able to interview Zac Efron for the school newspaper.

vitality   vy TA lih tee
energy; power to survive
After a few days of rest, the exhausted mountain climber regained his usual vitality.

GO WITH THE FLOW

assimilation   uh sim il AY shun
to absorb; to make similar
The unique blend of Mexican culture was formed by the assimilation of the cultures of the Native Americans and the Spanish.

consensus   kun SEN sus
general agreement
After much debate, the committee came to a consensus, although they differed on minor points.

context   KAHN tekst
circumstances of a situation; environment
The senator complained that his statements had been taken out of context and were therefore misleading; he said that if the newspaper had printed the rest of his speech, it would have explained the statements in question.

derived   de RYVD
copied or adapted from a source
Many AP English Language and Composition questions are derived from older questions—the details may have been changed, but the same basic concept is being tested.

incumbent   in KUM bunt
imposed as a duty; obligatory
Since you are the host, it is incumbent upon you to see that everyone is having fun.

inevitable   in EV ih tuh bul
certain to happen, unavoidable
Gaining a little extra weight during the wintertime is inevitable, especially after the holidays.

malleable   MAL ee uh bul
easily shaped or formed; easily influenced
Gold is malleable; it is easy to work with and can be hammered into very thin sheets.

subdue   sub DOO
to restrain; to hold back
It took four officers to subdue the fugitive because he fought like a madman.

Ways of Knowing

acquired   uh KWY erd
developed or learned; not naturally occurring
A love of opera is an acquired taste; almost nobody likes it the first time he or she hears it.

conception   kun SEP shun
the ability to form or understand an idea
Most people have no conception of the enormous amount of genetic information present in a single living cell.

conviction   kun VIK shun
a fixed or strong belief
Although he privately held onto his convictions, threats by the church caused Galileo to publicly denounce his theory that the Earth orbited the sun.

dogmatic   dog MAT ik
stubbornly adhering to unproved beliefs
Doug was dogmatic in his belief that exercising frequently boosts one's immune system.

enlightening   en LITE uh ning
informative; contributing to one's awareness
The Rosetta Stone was enlightening because it allowed linguists to begin to translate Egyptian hieroglyphs, which had previously been a mystery.

impression   im PREH shun
a feeling or understanding resulting from an experience
It was my impression that I was supposed to throw a curve ball, but I must have been wrong because the catcher didn't expect it.

intuition   in too ISH un
the power of knowing things without thinking; sharp insight
It is said that some people have intuition about future events that allows them to predict the future.

misconception   mis kun SEP shun
an incorrect understanding or interpretation
His belief that storks bring babies was just one of his many misconceptions.

perception   per SEP shun
awareness; insight
The detective's perception of people's hidden feelings makes it easy for him to catch liars.

perspective   per SPEK tiv
point of view
People from the North and South viewed the Civil War from different perspectives—each side's circumstances made it difficult for them to understand the other side.

profound   pro FOWND
having great depth or seriousness
There was a profound silence during the ceremony in honor of those who died during World War II.

FEELING AT HOME

inherent   in HER ent
inborn; built-in
One of the inherent weaknesses of the AP English Language and Composition Exam is that a multiple-choice test, by definition, cannot allow students to be creative in their answers.

innate   in AYT
possessed from birth; inborn
Cats have an innate ability to see well in the dark; they are born with this skill and do not need to develop it.

inveterate   in VET uh rit
long established; deep-rooted; habitual
Stan has always had trouble telling the truth; in fact, he's an inveterate liar.

omnipotent   om NIP uh tent
all-powerful
He liked to think that he was an omnipotent manager, but he really had very little control over anything.

proximity   prahk SIM ih tee
closeness
I try to sit far away from Roxy—I don't like sitting in proximity to her because she wears too much perfume.

ON THE ROAD AGAIN

elusive   il OO siv
difficult to capture, as in something actually fleeting
The girl's expression was elusive; the painter had a hard time recreating it on the canvas.

emigrate   EM ih grayt
to leave one country or region and settle in another
Many Jews left Russia and emigrated to Israel after it was founded in 1948.

transient   TRAN zhi unt
passing away with time; passing from one place to another
Jack Dawson enjoyed his transient lifestyle; with nothing but the clothes on his back and the air in his lungs, he was free to travel wherever he wanted.

transitory   TRAN zih tor ee
short-lived or temporary
The sadness she felt was only transitory; the next day her mood improved.

FRIENDLY

affable   AF uh bul
easy-going; friendly
We enjoyed spending time with Mr. Lee because he was such a pleasant, affable man.

amenable   uh MEN uh bul
responsive; agreeable
Because we had been working hard all day, the group seemed amenable to my suggestion that we all go home early.

camaraderie   kahm RAH duh ree
good will between friends
There was great camaraderie among the members of the team; they were friends both on and off the field.

cordial   KOR jul
friendly; sincere
Upon my arrival at camp, I received a warm and cordial greeting from the counselors.

facetious   fuh SEE shus
playfully humorous
Although the teacher pretended to be insulting his favorite student, he was just being facetious.

I Write the Songs

aesthetic   es THET ik
having to do with the appreciation of beauty
The arrangement of paintings in the museum was due to aesthetic considerations; as long as the paintings looked good together, it didn't matter who painted them or when they were painted.

anthology   an THAH luh jee
a collection of literary pieces
This anthology contains all of William Shakespeare's sonnets, but none of his plays.

contemporary   kun TEM puh rer ee
current, modern; from the same time
Contemporary music is very different from the music of the 1920s.
Pocahontas and William Shakespeare were contemporaries; they lived during the same time, though not in the same place.

dilettante   dih luh TAHNT
one with an amateurish or superficial understanding of a field of knowledge
You can't trust Betsy's opinion because she's just a dilettante who doesn't understand the subtleties of the painting.

eclectic   uh KLEK tik
made up of a variety of sources or styles
Lou's taste in music is eclectic; he listens to everything from rap to polka.

excerpt   EK serpt
a selected part of a passage or scene
We read an excerpt from *Romeo and Juliet* in which Juliet says, "Romeo, Romeo, wherefore art thou Romeo?"

genre   ZHAHN ruh
describing a category or artistic endeavor
Gene enjoyed only science-fiction movies; in fact, he never went to see anything that was not in that genre.

medley   MED lee
an assortment or a mixture, especially of musical pieces
At the concert, the band played a medley of songs from its first album, cutting an hour's worth of music down to five minutes.

mural   MYUR ul
a large painting applied directly to a wall or ceiling surface
The mural on the wall of the library showed the signing of the Declaration of Independence.

narrative   NAR uh tiv
(adj.) characterized by the telling of a story, (n.) a story
Tony gave us a running narrative of the game, since he was the only one who could see over the fence.

parody   PAR uh dee
an artistic work that imitates the style of another work for comic effect
The Onion is a satirical publication that is a parody of other, nonsatirical newspapers that give real, true news.

realism   REE uh liz um
artistic representation that aims for visual accuracy
His photographs have a stark realism that conveys the true horror of the war.

virtuoso   ver choo OH so
a tremendously skilled artist
Some people say that Jason Loewenstein is a guitar virtuoso because of his amazing work in Sebadoh—others say that his music is just noise.

COOL IT NOW

decorous   DEK er us
proper; marked by good taste
The class was well-behaved and the substitute was grateful for their decorous conduct.

equanimity   ee kwuh NIH muh tee
the quality of being calm and even-tempered; composure
She showed great equanimity; she did not panic even in the face of catastrophe.

modest   MAH dist
quiet or humble in manner or appearance
Although Mr. Phillips is well-off financially, he lives in a modest, simple home.

propriety   pruh PRY uh tee
appropriateness of behavior
Anyone who blows his nose on the tablecloth has no sense of propriety.

prudent   PROO dunt
exercising good judgment or common sense
It wouldn't be prudent to act until you've considered every possible outcome.

serene   suh REEN
calm
The quiet seaside resort provided a much-needed vacation in a serene locale.

staid   STAYD
unemotional; serious
Mr. Carver had such a staid demeanor that he remained calm while everyone else celebrated the team's amazing victory.

stoic   STOH ihk
indifferent to pleasure or pain; impassive
Not one to complain, Jason was stoic in accepting his punishment.

IF YOU CAN'T SAY ANYTHING NICE

condemn   kun DEM
to express strong disapproval of; denounce
Homer Simpson condemned Mayor Quimby for allowing the schoolchildren to drink spoiled milk; he was outraged and let the mayor know it.

discredit   dis CRED it
to cause to be doubted
The claim that pi is exactly equal to 3 can be discredited simply by careful measurement.

disparage   dis PAR uj
to speak of in a slighting way or negatively; to belittle
Glen disparaged Wanda's work as being careless and unoriginal.

pejorative   puh JOR uh tiv
describing words or phrases that belittle or speak negatively of someone
Teachers should refrain from using such pejorative terms as *numbskull* when dealing with students who need encouragement.

plagiarism   PLAY juh riz um
the act of passing off the ideas or writing of another as one's own
The author was accused of plagiarism when an older manuscript was discovered that contained passages that she had used, word for word, in her own book.

vilify   VIL uh fye
to make vicious statements about
Chad issued a series of pamphlets that did nothing but vilify his opponent, but his cruel accusations were not enough to win him the election.

Nasty Boys

brusque   BRUSK
rudely abrupt
Mr. Weird was a brusque teacher who didn't take time to talk to or listen to his students.

caustic   KAW stik
bitingly sarcastic or witty
He had a very caustic wit, and he seldom told a joke without offending someone.

fractious   FRAK shus
quarrelsome; unruly
Leonard was a fractious child who disagreed with everything and refused to listen.

incorrigible   in KOR ij uh bul
unable to be reformed
She is absolutely incorrigible; no matter how many times you punish her, she goes right ahead and misbehaves.

ingrate   IN grayt
an ungrateful person
It is a true ingrate who can accept favor after favor and never offer any thanks.

insolent   IN suh lunt
insulting in manner or speech
It was extremely insolent of him to stick his tongue out at the principal.

notorious   noh TOR ee us
known widely and usually unfavorably; infamous
Al Capone was a notorious gangster in the 1930s; he was feared throughout America.

pugnacious   pug NAY shus
combative; belligerent
Lorenzo was a pugnacious child who settled his differences by fighting with people.

reprehensible   rep ree HEN si bul
worthy of blame
It was reprehensible of the girls to spit their gum in their teacher's water bottle; they had detention for a week.

Pure Evil

deleterious   del uh TEER ee us
having a harmful effect; injurious
Although it may seem unlikely, taking too many vitamins can actually have a deleterious effect on your health.

enmity   EN muh tee
mutual hatred or ill-will
There was a great enmity between the opposing generals, and each wanted to destroy the other.

heinous   HAY nus
hatefully evil; abominable
To murder someone in cold blood is a heinous crime.

malfeasance   mal FEEZ uns
wrongdoing, misconduct
The senator was accused of malfeasance after he was caught sneaking out of a local brothel.

malice   MAL is
extreme ill-will or spite
It was clear that he was acting with malice when he disconnected the brakes in his business partner's car.

putrid   PYOO trid
rotten
He threw his lunch in the bottom of his locker every day and it was a putrid mess by the end of the year—rotten bananas, moldy sandwiches, and curdled milk were some of the more disgusting ingredients.

rancorous   RANK er us
hateful; marked by deep-seated ill-will
They had such a rancorous relationship that no one could believe that they had ever gotten along.

toxic   TAHK sik
poisonous
Since many chemicals are toxic, drinking from random flasks in the chemistry lab could be hazardous to your health.

OLD SCHOOL

archaic   ar KAY ik
characteristic of an earlier period; old-fashioned
"How dost thou?" is an archaic way of saying, "How are you?"

hackneyed   HACK need
worn out through overuse; trite
All my mom could offer in the way of advice were these hackneyed old phrases that I'd heard a hundred times before.

medieval   med EE vul
referring to the Middle Ages; old-fashioned
His ideas about fashion were positively medieval; he thought that a man should always wear a coat and tie and a woman should always wear a dress.

obsolete   ahb suh LEET
no longer in use; old-fashioned
Eight-track tape players are obsolete because music isn't recorded in that format anymore.

Bo-o-o-ring

austere   aw STEER
without decoration; strict
The gray walls and bare floors provided a very austere setting.

mediocrity   mee dee AH krih tee
the state or quality of being average; of moderate to low quality
Salieri said that he was the patron saint of mediocrity because his work could never measure up to Mozart's.

mundane   mun DAYN
commonplace; ordinary
We hated going to class every day because it was so mundane; we never did anything interesting.

ponderous   PAHN duh rus
extremely dull
The 700-page book on the anatomy of the flea was so ponderous that I could not read more than one paragraph.

prosaic   pro ZAY ik
unimaginative; dull
Rebecca made a prosaic mosaic—it consisted of only one tile.

sedentary   SEH dun tair ee
not migratory; settled
Galatea led a sedentary existence; she never even left her home unless she had to.

Who Can It Be Now?

apprehension   a preh HEN shun
anxiety or fear about the future
My grandmother felt apprehension about nuclear war in the 1960s, so my grandfather built a bomb shelter in the backyard to calm her fears.

harbinger   HAR bin jer
something that indicates what is to come; a forerunner
When it is going to rain, insects fly lower, so cows lie down to get away from the insects; therefore, the sight of cows lying down is a harbinger of rain.

ominous   AH min us

menacing; threatening

The rattling under the hood sounded ominous because we were miles from the nearest town and would have been stranded if the car had broken down.

premonition   prem uh NISH un

a feeling about the future

Luckily, my premonition that I would break my neck skiing was unfounded; unluckily, I broke my leg.

timorous   TIM uh rus

timid; fearful about the future

Tiny Tim was timorous; he was afraid that one day he would be crushed by a giant.

trepidation   trep uh DAY shun

uncertainty; apprehension

We approached Mrs. Fielding with trepidation because we didn't know how she would react to our request for a field trip.

New Sensation

innovative   IN no vay tiv

introducing something new

The shop on the corner has become known for its innovative use of fruit on its pizzas.

naive   nah YEEV

lacking sophistication

It was naive of him to think that he could write a novel in one afternoon.

nascent   NAY sunt

coming into existence; emerging

If you study Coldplay's first album, you can see their nascent abilities that were brought to maturity by their second album.

novel   NAH vul

strikingly new or unusual

Sharon's novel approach to the problem stunned the scientific community; no one had ever thought to apply game theory to genetics.

novice   NAH vis

a beginner

Having only played chess a couple of times, Barry was a novice compared with the contestants who had been playing all their lives.

STRAIGHT UP

candor   KAN der
sincerity; openness
It's refreshing to hear Lora's honesty and candor—when asked about her English teacher, she says, "I can't stand her!"

frank   FRANK
open and sincere in expression; straightforward
When Jim lost my calculator, he was frank with me; he admitted to losing it without trying to make up some excuse.

EARTH, WIND, AND FIRE

arid   AYR id
describing a dry, rainless climate
Since they receive little rain, deserts are known for their arid climates.

conflagration   kahn fluh GRAY shun
a widespread fire
The protesters burned flags, accidentally starting a fire that developed into a conflagration that raged out of control.

nocturnal   nok TER nul
of or occurring in the night
Owls are nocturnal animals because they sleep during the day and hunt at night.

sonorous   SAH nuh rus
producing a deep or full sound
My father's sonorous snoring keeps me up all night unless I close my door and wear earplugs.

FULL ON

ample   AM pul
describing a large amount of something
Because no one else wanted to try the new soda, Andy was able to have an ample sample.

comprehensive   kahm prih HEN siv
large in scope or content
The final exam was comprehensive, covering everything that we had learned that year.

copious   KOH pee us
plentiful; having a large quantity
She had taken copious notes during class, using up five large notebooks.

permeated   PER mee ay tid
spread or flowing throughout
After Kathryn had her hair professionally curled, the scent of chemicals permeated the air.

pervasive   per VAY siv
dispersed throughout
In this part of town, graffiti is pervasive—it's everywhere.

prodigious   pruh DIJ us
enormous
The shattered vase required a prodigious amount of glue to repair.

replete   ruh PLEET
abundantly supplied; filled to capacity
After a successful night of trick-or-treating, Dee's bag was replete with Halloween candy.

R-E-S-P-E-C-T

exemplary   eg ZEM pluh ree
commendable; worthy of imitation
Jay's behavior was exemplary; his parents wished that his brother, Al, were more like him.

idealize   eye DEE uh lyze
to consider perfect
The fans had idealized the new star pitcher; they had such unrealistically high expectations that they were bound to be disappointed.

laudatory   LAW duh tor ee
giving praise
The principal's speech was laudatory, congratulating the students on their AP exam scores.

paramount   PAR uh mount
of chief concern or importance
The workers had many minor complaints, but the paramount reason for their unhappiness was the low pay.

venerated   VEN er ay tid
highly respected
Princess Diana was venerated for her dedication to banning land mines around the world; people today still sing her praises.

catalog   KAT uh log
(v.) to make an itemized list of
He decided to catalog his expenses for the week, hoping that this list would show him where he could cut back his spending.

facile   FAS ul
done or achieved with little effort; easy
Last night's math homework was such a facile task that I was done in ten minutes.

fastidious   fas TID ee us
possessing careful attention to detail; difficult to please
Because Kelly was so fastidious, we tried to keep her out of our group.

hierarchy   HY er ar kee
a group organized by rank
With each promotion raising him higher, Archie moved up in his company's hierarchy.

meticulous   muh TIK yuh lus
extremely careful and precise
The plastic surgeon was meticulous; he didn't want to leave any scars.

pragmatic   prag MAT ik
practical
Never one for wild and unrealistic schemes, Amy took a pragmatic approach to research.

solvent   SAHL vunt
able to pay one's debts
After five years of losing money, the business has finally solved its financial problems and become solvent.

A Little Bit of Everything

alienated   AY lee en ay tid
removed or disassociated from (friends, family, or homeland)
Rudolph felt alienated from the other reindeer because they never let him join in their reindeer games.

abstract   ab STRAKT
not applied to actual objects
"Justice" is an abstract concept because it is merely an idea.

anachronism   an A krun ism
something out of place in time or sequence
Jill was something of an anachronism; she insisted on carrying a parasol when going out in the sun and believed that a woman's place was at home in the kitchen and with the children.

anthropomorphism   an thrah puh MOR fizm
the attribution of humanlike characteristics to inanimate objects, animals, or forces of nature
Beatrix Potter is known for her children's books filled with anthropomorphism; Peter Rabbit, Squirrel Nutkin, and Samuel Whiskers were all animal characters with very human qualities.

apology   uh PAWL uh gee
defense of an idea
Du Bellay wrote an apology in which he justified the use of French in place of Latin.

apparatus   ap uh RAT us
equipment; a group of machines
The storeroom behind the physics lab was filled with a cumbersome apparatus that has since been replaced by a much smaller and more accurate piece of equipment.

apposition   app uh ZIH shun
a grammar construction in which a noun (or noun phrase) is placed with another as an explanation
My grandmother, a fine woman of 83, enjoys riding her motorcycle at high speeds in heavy traffic on Highway 280.

archetype   AR keh type
a perfect example; an original pattern or model
Steve enjoyed stealing candy from babies, tripping elderly women in crosswalks, and pilfering money from the Save the Children charity jar; he was the archetype of pure evil.

brittle   BRIT ul
easily broken when subjected to pressure
That antique vase is so brittle that it may break at any moment.

chiasmus   ky AZ muss
an inversion in the second of two parallel phrases
John F. Kennedy's "Ask not what your country can do for you, but what you can do for your country" is an example of chiasmus.

gesticulating   jes TIK yeh lay ting
making gestures while speaking
The commencement speaker's gesticulating hands were quite distracting; the students had stopped listening to her words and were now counting the number of times she made awkward gestures.

hypothetical   hye puh THET ih kul
existing only as an assumption or speculation
Heather wondered why her class had to study hypothetical cases when they had actual case histories they could look at.

lexicon   LEKS uh kahn
a word book describing language with definitions; a dictionary
When his teacher wrote that his essay was "abysmal," Eddie decided to look it up in his lexicon and found that this was quite insulting.

metonymy   meh TAHN uh mee

a type of figurative language in which one term is substituted for another term with which it is closely associated

"Today, Capitol Hill (U.S. Congress) voted on the Internet Privacy bill" is an example of metonymy.

oxymoron   ahk see MORE on

an apparent contradiction of terms

Angela spent her lazy summer afternoon contemplating oxymorons: "freezer burn," "plastic glasses," and "deafening silence" were among her favorites.

panegyric   pan eh JIR ik

statement of high praise

For his senior essay, Boris wrote an eloquent panegyric to his high school; he had truly enjoyed the last four years, and he wanted his teachers to know how much he appreciated them.

paradigm   PAR a dym

an example or model

The current educational paradigm has students engaged in discovery-based learning, whereas the older model had teachers lecturing and students merely taking notes.

parallelism   PARE uh lell izm

a grammar construction in which two identical syntactic constructions are used

On Mondays, Ms. Smith spends her time *baking cakes* for local charities and *knitting socks* for the homeless.

penitent   PEN ih tunt

expressing remorse for one's misdeeds

His desire to make amends to the people he had wronged indicated that he was truly penitent, so the parole board let him out of the penitentiary.

period (periodic sentence)   PEER ee uhd

long, complex, grammatically correct sentence

While writing his essay, Sam thought he was being very articulate with his long, complex sentences. However, his English teacher disagreed; those lengthy sentences weren't periods; they were simply rambling run-ons.

pernicious   per NIH shus

causing great harm

In *Mean Girls*, the Plastics loved to spread pernicious rumors about their classmates; they effectively ruined the social lives of several students with their nasty gossip.

phenomenon   feh NAH meh nahn

an unusual, observable event

The phenomenon of lightning remained unexplained until scientists discovered electricity.

propitious   pruh PIH shus
presenting favorable circumstances; auspicious
In Chinese culture, the color red is seen as sort of propitious omen; red is thought to bring luck.

rational   RASH un ul
logical; motivated by reason rather than feeling
While Joe is more impulsive, Frank is more rational because he thinks things through rather than acting on his feelings.

sardonic   sar DAH nik
disdainfully or ironically humorous; harsh, bitter, or caustic
In Rachel's group of friends, Estelle was known as the sardonic one; sometimes her sarcastic comments really hurt the other girls.

syllogism (syllogistic reasoning)   SIH luh jih zum
a form of deductive reasoning: a major premise, a minor premise, and a conclusion
Humans are mortal (major premise); Seth is human (minor premise); Seth is mortal (conclusion).

synecdoche   sin ECK duh kee
a form of metonymy that's restricted to cases where a part is used to signify the whole
"A thousand swords came charging toward us from the nearby mountain range; we could hear the angry army as it marched closer and closer" is an example of synecdoche.

theoretical   thee oh RET ih kul
lacking application or practical application
Theoretical physics is concerned with ideas, whereas applied physics is concerned with using ideas.

truncated   TRUN kay tid
shortened; cut off
The file Chris downloaded from the Internet was truncated; the end of it was missing.

PART V

AP English Composition

9

Rhetorical Fallacies

AVOIDING THE FATAL FALLACY

A **fallacy** is strictly defined as guile or trickery or a false or mistaken idea. Fallacies have the appearance of truth but are erroneous. Let's say that you really want to attend a famous university in Cambridge, Massachusetts, and you've heard that the acceptance rate for the institution is 25 percent higher for early decision applicants than for regular applicants. However, it is a fallacy that applying early would increase your chances of being accepted. But why? Because if you have a 2.8 GPA, then that university isn't going to accept you regardless of when you apply.

Does this sound more like logic and rhetoric than language to you? What is it doing on the AP English Language and Composition Exam? Well, as we mentioned earlier, although "language" is contained in the title of this exam, the exam primarily tests rhetoric and composition. In other words, this exam tests how language works.

In this chapter we provide you with an overview of some common rhetorical fallacies. You should be familiar with *all* of these for the exam. Rhetorical fallacies may appear as answers on the multiple-choice sections. In addition, they may be relevant to your essays in the free-response questions.

COMMON RHETORICAL FALLACIES

Oftentimes, when writers have trouble making convincing "honest" arguments with the facts that they have in hand, they resort to using rhetorical fallacies. As you may expect, when you begin to write your essays in the free-response section of the exam, you shouldn't resort to these tactics. However, you should be able to recognize the use of these common fallacies in the reasoning of others; this will help you substantially on test day.

Ad Hominem Argument

An *ad hominem* (in Latin, "to the man") **argument** is any kind of fallacious argument that criticizes an idea by pointing something out about the person who holds the idea, rather than directly addressing the actual merit of the idea. There are people who learn this form of rhetorical fallacy at a very tender age and may argue thusly: "You're wrong because you're a jerk." But there are plenty of mature examples of *ad hominem* arguments, too.

> Example: Of course the writer supports tax cuts; She's rich!

The attack shifts from the issue (tax cuts) to the wealth of the writer.

Argument from Authority (or Argument from False Authority)

An **argument from authority** tempts us to agree with the writer's assumptions based on the authority of a famous person or entity or on his or her own character (when the writers are well-known).

> Example: It is absurd to believe that professional baseball players have used steroids because the most famous slugger of our time has repeatedly asserted that such a claim is false.

You see how it works? Or how about this: If The Princeton Review put the following quotation on the back cover of a book, how impressed would you be?

"This is absolutely awesome—it's the best review book ever written."—John Schiff

Would that convince you? Probably not. How about this quote?

"This is absolutely awesome—it's the best review book ever written."—Shakira

Even though the rock star didn't have to take AP exams in her native Colombia, her fame may give her the authority necessary to get some students to buy the book.

APPEAL TO IGNORANCE

Appeal to ignorance is based on the assumption that whatever has not been proven false must be true (or, similarly, whatever has not been proven true must be false).

Example #1: No one can prove that the Loch Ness monster does not exist; therefore the Loch Ness monster exists.

Example #2: No one can prove that the Loch Ness monster exists; therefore the Loch Ness monster does not exist.

This is a fairly common form of rhetorical fallacy.

BEGGING THE QUESTION

Begging the question is a fallacious form of argument in which someone assumes that parts (or all) of what the person claims to be proving are proven facts. (Keep in mind that this does not refer to incomplete or illogical statements that actually would prompt someone to ask a question.) This circular form of reasoning is easier to grasp by example than explanation.

Example #1: The Loch Ness monster spoke to me in my dreams, so it must exist.

Well, wouldn't you want me to prove to you *first* that the Loch Ness monster really did speak to me in my dreams before you would accept my conclusion? I hope so. It may have been the pepperoni pizza that was speaking to me in my dreams.

Example #2: Examine the following scenario.

Interviewer: Your resume looks impressive, but I need another reference.

Brendan: Heidi can give me a good reference.

Interviewer: Good, but how do I know that Heidi is trustworthy?

Brendan: I can vouch for her.

HASTY GENERALIZATION

Sometimes a writer will deliberately lead you to a conclusion by providing insufficient, selective evidence. This is called a **hasty generalization.**

> Example: Ping-pong is an extremely dangerous sport; last year, my friend got hit in the eye with a ping-pong ball and almost lost his vision in that eye.

This rhetorical fallacy can be used very effectively. In the case of hasty generalization, often statistics that are "good"—meaning empirically true—are used to "prove" things that aren't true.

NON SEQUITUR

In Latin, *non sequitur* means "It doesn't follow." In English, a *non sequitur* is a statement that does not relate logically to what comes before it.

> Example: If you really wanted to earn a 5 on the AP English Language and Composition Exam, you wouldn't spend so much time reading Isabel Allende's novels.

Wait a second. First of all, reading novels may help you prepare for the exam. Second, who says that you don't have plenty of time for preparing for the exam and reading—especially now that you've stopped wasting time in front of the computer? In a *non sequitur*, there is no logical connection between the initial phrase and the one that follows it, so you shouldn't try to make one.

FALSE DICHOTOMY

False dichotomy consists of a consideration of only the two extremes when there are one or more intermediate possibilities.

> Example: AP Calculus BC class is impossible; either you get it or you don't.

This statement sounds like a great way to explain to your parents why you just earned a less-than-stellar grade on your last calculus test, but it sets up a false dichotomy. In fact, there are various levels of understanding and thus various degrees of success in AP Calculus, and as is the case in many fields, success is a direct result of effort.

SLIPPERY SLOPE

Slippery slope arguments suggest dire consequences from relatively minor causes.

> Example: If we stop requiring men to wear coats and ties in the dining room, pretty soon they'll start coming in dressed in beachwear.

Another way that the slippery slope fallacy can be expressed is by the phrase "give 'em an inch, and they'll take a mile."

FAULTY CAUSALITY

Faulty causality refers to the (sometimes unintentional) setting up of a cause-and-effect relationship when none exists. In faulty causality, one event can happen after another without the first necessarily being the direct cause of the second.

> Example: Violent crime among adolescents has risen in the past decade, and that is the result of increased sales of violent video games.

As is the case with all examples of faulty causality, there is no proof for the video game argument, and it is possible to think of a dozen other convincing reasons for the rise of violent crime—a trend that we just made up.

STRAW MAN ARGUMENT

The **straw man argument** consists of an oversimplification of an opponent's argument to make it easier to attack.

Here's an example of how this works.

> Example: Students who want to eliminate the school uniform are exhibitionists who want to show off bare midriffs.

In fact, students who are arguing against having to wear a school uniform may be interested only in expressing their individuality; it's even possible that they would be happy in conservative clothing. However, if the author of this sentence attributes a simplistic argument to the students, who had, in reality, a more substantive motivation (individuality), it is easier to attack their position.

SENTIMENTAL APPEALS

A **sentimental appeal** is a tactic that attempts to appeal to the *hearts* of readers (or, of course, listeners) so that they forget to use their *minds*.

> Example: "The assignment that I gave you last night was much too long, but just think how pleased your parents and I will be when you score a 5 on the AP exam. Think about the pride you'll feel when tears of joy stream down our faces!"

Here, the teacher knew that arguing that the assignment was an important intellectual exercise wouldn't convince his students, even though that may have been a more valid argument. So in this case, he decided to use a sentimental appeal. Sentimental appeals are generally not valid arguments, but they work sometimes!

RED HERRING

A **red herring** attempts to shift attention away from an important issue by introducing an issue that has no logical connection to the discussion at hand.

> Example: "My opponent talks about the poor quality of military intelligence, but this is a time for decisiveness, not for weakness. We must stick together and present a common front as the other nations look on. If we do not, we could jeopardize our position as a global leader."

As you can see, this is very similar to a sentimental appeal, although the political speaker is (apparently) still appealing to minds, rather than sentiments. In this case, the speaker shifts the discussion from the topic under debate (military intelligence) to a different issue (our role as a super power).

SCARE TACTICS

The aptly named **scare tactic** is used to frighten readers or listeners into agreeing with the speaker; often, when scare tactics are used, the speaker has no logical argument on which to fall back.

Example: "My opponent talks about the need to explore stem cell research, but this would bring about an end to ethical uses of technology, and, before long, scientists will be creating superraces—the Nazi dream of an Aryan Nation will ensue!"

Here the speaker mentions Nazis to frighten the listeners; there is no logical (or at least, logically presented) link between exploring stem cell research and the creation of an Aryan Nation. The example may seem to you like a combination of scare tactics and slippery slope; this combination is sometimes seen when a slippery slope argument is used to scare readers or listeners.

BANDWAGON APPEALS

Bandwagon appeals have a different name in school settings; there, they are known as "peer pressure." A bandwagon appeal encourages the listener to agree with a position because everyone else does. The logic goes something like this: If everybody else is doing it, it must be all right.

Example: It's time for our county to repeal the ban on strip mining—every other county in the state has already done so!

Notice that the speaker (or writer) avoids having to explain the merits of the issue and explain why the ban is inappropriate.

DOGMATISM

Dogmatism does not allow for discussion because the speaker presumes that his or her beliefs are beyond question; essentially, the "logic" runs thusly: I'm correct because I'm correct.

Example: We are members of the Wombat Party and, as such, know that we are right when we assert that Wombats are the best!

There is no way to rebut the claim.

EQUIVOCATION

Equivocation is telling part of the truth, while deliberately hiding the entire truth; typically, this is similar to lying by omission.

Example: There is a Pink Panther movie in which Inspector Clouseau enters a quaint European hotel and, upon spying a cute little dog, asks the owner, "Does your dog bite?" The manager responds, "No," and Clouseau attempts to pet the dog, which growls and bites him. "You told me that your dog does not bite!" exclaims Clouseau. "That's not my dog," responds the owner.

Setting the comedy aside for a moment, the owner of the chalet gave an equivocal answer. Presumably, he was telling the truth when he responded that his dog does not bite, but that truth hid the more relevant truth—the dog he was with at the time does, in fact, bite. It is possible that you have indulged in equivocation. Let's say that you're about to leave the house, but your mom stops you and says, "You're not going to Marina's party tonight, are you? I heard that her parents are out of town and there's not going to be any supervision." "No, Mom, I'm not going there." Your mom smiles in relief and lets you go. You're relieved too because you are going to Dave's party, where there will be no supervision because his parents are out of town. You did not exactly lie because you truly are not going to Marina's party; however, you did lie because you are going to the same kind of party somewhere else, and it is the *kind* of party that your mom objects to, not its specific location.

FAULTY ANALOGY

A **faulty analogy** is an illogical, misleading comparison between two things.

> Example: Why should we invade that country? Let me explain it to you like this. What if you looked out the window and saw a 20-dollar bill in the street? Wouldn't you go outside and take it?

This analogy is *really* faulty! A better analogy would be: What if you saw a person in the street with a 20-dollar bill? Wouldn't you go outside and try to steal it from the person? Analogy is always a weak form of argumentation; a faulty analogy exploits this weakness to mislead listeners (or readers), when true logic may not convince them.

As we mentioned earlier, make sure you have memorized all of these rhetorical fallacies before test day. After you've studied them carefully (make flashcards if you need to, using the examples we gave you), try the following questions.

SAMPLE QUESTIONS

In each question, choose the most fitting rhetorical fallacy.

1. If such actions were not illegal, then they would not be prohibited by law.

   (A) faulty causality
   (B) begging the question
   (C) appeal to ignorance
   (D) argument from authority
   (E) *ad hominem*

2. We all knew he would think abortion is wrong! He's a priest!

   (A) faulty causality
   (B) hasty generalization
   (C) *ad hominem*
   (D) false dichotomy
   (E) dogmatism

3. "Recently, I've been thinking that there is some merit in the Republicans' tax-cut plan. I suggest that we come up with something like it because if we Democrats are going to survive as a party, we have got to show the people that we are as tough-minded as the Republicans, because that is what the public wants."

   (A) red herring
   (B) straw man argument
   (C) slippery slope
   (D) equivocation
   (E) *non sequitur*

4. "We should have a car wash to raise money for Senior Prom. The three classes before us have all done it!"

   (A) begging the question
   (B) bandwagon appeal
   (C) red herring
   (D) scare tactics
   (E) dogmatism

5. The mill must be polluting the river because there has been a recent increase in bird deaths around there.

   (A) straw man argument
   (B) appeal to ignorance
   (C) faulty analogy
   (D) *non sequitur*
   (E) slippery slope

Rhetorical fallacies, when used with savvy, can be very convincing. It is worth knowing about them to do well on the AP English Language and Composition Exam and to become a critical reader and listener—and not to become the victim of clever rhetorical tactics.

In the next chapter, we will discuss rhetorical modes, or patterns of exposition. This is an important topic because it will outline ready-made tactics and methods for writing your free-response essays.

The answers to the above questions are: (B), (C), (A), (B), and (D). If you didn't get them right, go back and review those rhetorical terms.

KEY TERMS

fallacy

ad hominem argument

argument from authority

appeal to ignorance

begging the question

hasty generalization

non sequitur

false dichotomy

slippery slope

faulty causality

straw man argument

sentimental appeals

red herring

scare tactic

bandwagon appeals

dogmatism

equivocation

faulty analogy

10

Basic Rhetorical Modes

WHAT ARE RHETORICAL MODES?

The rhetorical modes (or patterns) contained in this chapter are worth studying for two reasons. First, they will provide you with ready-made approaches for writing your essays on the exam, and second, the multiple-choice questions on the test also often include some of the rhetorical mode terminology.

As you prepare for the exam by taking practice tests, you'll see that 40 minutes is not much time in which to write a sophisticated essay, and the shortcuts you'll learn in this chapter will be invaluable in helping you write a great essay in the allotted time. However, you do not need to cram and memorize all the material in this section. If you read and understand the explanations and just make sure you retain the basics, you'll be comfortable enough with the process to do well on the exam.

Another important point to remember is that, more often than not, rhetorical modes are used in combination. Breaking them up into individual components is a somewhat arbitrary process—but for our purposes, it makes the material easier to understand. Let's begin.

EXAMPLE OR ILLUSTRATION

Our first rhetorical mode consists of using specific examples to illustrate an idea. Now, this may seem like a pretty simple idea, but one of the most common mistakes students make when writing their AP English Language and Composition essays is to use poor examples. Remember that all examples are not created equal. If you use poor illustrative examples, your ideas will be communicated much less clearly and effectively than if you'd used solid, appropriate ones. In writing these essays, your principal goal is clarity.

Read the following passage based on *Candide*, and as you do so, evaluate the effectiveness of the examples that it uses.

> Pangloss is correct when he claims that everything is for the best in the best of all possible worlds. First of all, we are seeing more and more technological innovation every year. Computer technology, in particular, has helped us in many ways, and breakthroughs in medicine have helped raise the life expectancy significantly. Furthermore, in most cities, there are bustling restaurants and great nightlife. Finally, travel has become affordable for most people, and paradises like Aruba and Hawaii await us all!

Surely you agree that the examples are not convincing, but you should also understand that they are not even relevant. Implicit in the examples chosen is the reduction of the best of all possible worlds to the writer's own tiny corner. A better approach would be something as follows:

> Pangloss is correct when he claims that everything is for the best in the best of all possible worlds. First of all, the challenges that we have faced or are facing have inspired some of our most important scientific advances. Great famines have led scientists to exciting new agricultural discoveries, such as drought-resistant crops; great droughts have inspired engineers to develop cost-effective desalination plants. In essence, the evils in the world have been necessary stimulants for

changes for the better. Furthermore, advances in medicine are no longer restricted to the wealthy nations of the world, and there is reason to hope that coordinated efforts to help developing countries will become more effective; take, for example, the international relief efforts to help the people whose homes were destroyed by the recent tsunami. Not only will the victims have better and safer homes now, but also the cooperation among the developed nations will translate into a better, safer world. Indeed, everything is for the best.

While the second essay may be naive, at least it does its best to substantiate an untenable position. Without any doubt, the examples in the second passage are much more appropriate for the argument than those that were used in the first passage.

Just as it is important to choose relevant, convincing examples to substantiate your own ideas, it is essential to constantly evaluate the examples that others use in their attempts to explain or to convince.

Tricksters, dogmatists, and charlatans usually illustrate their positions with scanty, inappropriate details. Be critical.

Laundry List for Example (Illustration)

- Use examples that your reader (the person who reads your essays) will identify with and understand. Do not assume that the AP reader has seen the latest teen cult film or knows any pop culture icons younger than Britney Spears.

- Draw your examples from "real life," "real" culture (literature, art, classical music, and so on), and well-known folklore.

- Make sure the example really does illustrate your point. Don't use a fancy example just to show off your knowledge; find ones that really work!

- Introduce your examples using transitions, such as, *for example, for instance, case in point,* and *consider the case of.*

- A single example that is perfectly representative can serve to illustrate your point.

- A series of short, less-perfect (but still relevant) examples, can, by their accumulation, serve to illustrate your point.

- The ideal approach is to construct a well-developed, representative example supported by several shorter examples.

- Remember that you are in control of what you write. As you brainstorm, discard examples that may disprove your point. Your AP essays will have little or nothing to do with your beliefs or with a balanced examination of an issue. You will be defending a point of view (argumentative essay) or explaining something (expository essay)—don't feel like you have to be fair to all sides of an argument; your aim is to get your point across.

- Quality is more important than quantity; poorly chosen examples detract significantly from your presentation.

SAMPLE QUESTION

Write a thoughtful and carefully constructed essay in which you use specific examples to defend, challenge, or qualify the assertion that Hollywood movies are a reflection of a decaying society.

DRILL: REFLECT ON HOW YOU COULD USE EXAMPLES TO ADDRESS THE FOLLOWING TOPICS

As you read each of the topics listed below, make a list of five examples you could use to support them. Are your examples all relevant? Do they support just this side of the argument? Treat each as the basis for your thesis statement in a practice free-response question.

TOPIC 1: High schools unwittingly encourage students to cheat.

TOPIC 2: Studying the humanities is important.

TOPIC 3: Respecting diversity reveals much about a person.

CLASSIFICATION

How do you classify things? Well, you probably start by dividing up whatever you have into groups according to certain characteristics. For example, if you wanted to explain "new music" to someone, you might divide the artists into groups by type (female vocalists, male vocalists, and bands) and classify the groups by genre (heavy metal, punk rock, alternative, and so on). This would make the material easier for someone to understand because it would be organized. In other words: *We classify to more easily analyze and explain.*

There is almost always more than one way to classify things. Right now, you may group your teachers as being either cool or uncool. Later, it's more likely that you'll classify them according to what they helped you learn: The new categories may be teachers who inspired you, teachers who taught you the most, teachers who taught you about life, and teachers who should not have been teachers.

When you place things into categories on the AP English Language and Composition Exam, avoid creating classifications that overlap. For example, it would not make sense to classify your favorite foods in the following way: sweets, barbecued meats, vegetables, and chocolates; logically, the last group is a smaller subset of the first group.

All of this boils down to the following: Classification is nearly the same thing as organization. And organization is important. As you know by now, the directions in the Free-Response section of the AP English Language and Composition Exam request that you write "a well-organized essay." It may seem obvious that the test writers would request this of you—but then you'd be surprised how poorly organized many of the AP essays that students write are. Classify before you write.

Aristotle liked to classify, and he did so quite often. Some of classifications have stood the test of time, including the one you see below, which is the beginning of Part 6 of an essay entitled "Categories."

> Quantity is either discrete or continuous (…). Instances of discrete quantities are number and speech; instances of continuous quantities are lines, surfaces, solids, and, *Line* besides these, time and place.
>
> 5 In the case of the parts of a number, there is no common boundary at which they join. For example: two fives make ten, but the two fives have no common boundary,

but are separate; the parts three and seven also do not join at any boundary. Nor, to generalize, would it ever
10 be possible in the case of number that there should be a common boundary among the parts; they are always separate. Number, therefore, is a discrete quantity.

The same is true of speech. That speech is a quantity is evident: for it is measured in long and short syllables.
15 I mean here that speech which is vocal. Moreover, it is a discrete quantity for its parts have no common boundary. There is no common boundary at which the syllables join, but each is separate and distinct from the rest.

A line, on the other hand, is a continuous quantity, for
20 it is possible to find a common boundary at which its parts join. In the case of the line, this common boundary is the point; in the case of the plane, it is the line, for the parts of the plane have also a common boundary. Similarly you can find a common boundary in the case of the
25 parts of a solid, namely either a line or a plane.

Space and time also belong to this class of quantities. Time, past, present, and future, forms a continuous whole. Space, likewise, is a continuous quantity; for the parts of a solid occupy a certain space, and these have a
30 common boundary; it follows that the parts of space also, which are occupied by the parts of the solid, have the same common boundary as the parts of the solid. Thus, not only time, but space also, is a continuous quantity, for its parts have a common boundary.

Here, Aristotle's division of quantity into two categories (discrete and continuous) makes sense. The examples that he uses to illustrate the nature of his categories reveal a great deal about his interests: time, space, language, and mathematics. This is a well-organized passage; the categories are well-defined and Aristotle has clearly explained why the members of each category have been put in their categories.

LAUNDRY LIST FOR CLASSIFICATION

- Remember that when you're asked to analyze and explain something, classification will be very useful.

- Make sure you have a central idea (thesis).

- Sort your information into meaningful groups. Are there enough elements in each group to allow you to write a convincing, useful paragraph? Sometimes you'll find that you need to combine categories.

- Make sure you have a manageable number of categories—three or four. Remember that you have only about 40 minutes to plan and execute each essay.

- Make sure the categories (or the elements in the categories) do not overlap.

- Before writing, make sure the categories and central idea (thesis) are a good fit. Sometimes you'll want to modify your thesis statement based on the categories that you've found.

- As you write, do not justify your classification unless this is somehow necessary to address a very bizarre free-response question. Justify your thesis, not your categories.

SAMPLE QUESTION

Write a short essay in which you analyze the different methods a teacher uses to convey information to his or her class.

DRILL: REFLECT ON HOW YOU COULD USE
CLASSIFICATION TO ADDRESS THE FOLLOWING TOPICS

As you read each of the topics, think about how you would organize your essay in terms of classification. Come up with a possible thesis (central idea), and plan how you could categorize the information you have on these topics into three or four meaningful divisions.

TOPIC 1: Television commercials

TOPIC 2: Movies

TOPIC 3: Students

TOPIC 4: Cars

COMPARISON AND CONTRAST

You compare and contrast every day. When you note similarities between objects, people, characteristics, and even actions, you're making comparisons. When you note the differences, you're using a rhetorical mode called contrast.

It is very likely that you will have to use comparison and contrast when writing at least one of your essays for the free-response section of the AP test. Sometimes you'll use this mode merely *to explain*—especially when you're comparing something unfamiliar with something well known; other times, you will use comparison and contrast *to argue* in favor of one of the two elements.

Keep in mind that to compare and contrast two elements, they need to have enough commonalities to justify comparison or contrast. It may be interesting to compare and contrast a baseball team from the National League and another from the American League, but it would be less pertinent (although potentially very entertaining) to compare and contrast one of those baseball teams with your neighbor's poker club.

To write a successful compare-and-contrast essay for the AP English Language and Composition Exam, you must first select the points of comparison (and contrast) and present them. Does this sound familiar? In other words, you must start by *classifying* them.

The most common mistake people make when comparing and contrasting is to present a discussion of one of the elements first (in one paragraph), and then discuss the other element afterward (in a second paragraph). Do not do this. Instead, we'll show you an example of a good method for comparing and contrasting:

Comparison and contrast of my favorite classes	
AP English	**AP Art History**
Involves essay writing, which I love Teacher writes intriguing questions Most writing done in class	Involves essay writing Teacher writes intriguing questions Most writing done out of class
Interesting reading A variety of books No pictures in books	Interesting reading A textbook Lots of pictures in book
Teacher is old Teacher tells bad jokes Teacher is grumpy	Teacher is young Teacher is funny Teacher is good-natured

Ideally, when you turned this into an essay you would not write the first half of your essay about AP English, and the second half about AP Art History. Using the information you collected in the outline above, ideally you would spend your first paragraph discussing the role of writing in both classes, spend your second paragraph discussing aspects of the reading in the two classes, and spend your third paragraph discussing the teachers. Integration is key in comparison and contrast.

Here is a real example, taken from Charles Darwin's *The Descent of Man*, of a passage that uses comparison and contrast.

My object in this chapter is to show that there is no
fundamental difference between man and the higher
mammals in their mental faculties. Each division of the
Line subject might have been extended into a separate essay
5 but must here be treated briefly. As no classification of
the mental powers has been universally accepted, I shall
arrange my remarks in the order most convenient for my
purpose; and will select those facts which have struck me
most, with the hope that they may produce some effect
10 on the reader (…).

As man possesses the same senses as the lower animals, his fundamental intuitions must be the same. Man
has also some few instincts in common, as that of self-
preservation, sexual love, the love of the mother for her
15 new-born offspring, the desire possessed by the latter
to suck, and so forth. But man, perhaps, has somewhat
fewer instincts than those possessed by the animals
which come next to him in the series. The orangutan in
the Eastern islands and the chimpanzee in Africa, build
20 platforms on which they sleep; and, as both species follow the same habit, it might be argued that this was due
to instinct, but we cannot feel sure that it is not the result
of both animals having similar wants, and possessing
similar powers of reasoning (…).

25   The lower animals, like man, manifestly feel pleasure
and pain, happiness and misery. Happiness is never
better exhibited than by young animals, such as puppies, kittens, lambs, etc., when playing together, like our
own children. Even insects play together, as has been
30   described by that excellent observer, P. Huber, who
saw ants chasing and pretending to bite each other, like
so many puppies. The fact that the lower animals are
excited by the same emotions as ourselves is so well
established, that it will not be necessary to weary the
35   reader by many details. Terror acts in the same manner
on them as on us, causing the muscles to tremble, the
heart to palpitate, the sphincters to be relaxed, and the
hair to stand on end. Suspicion, the offspring of fear, is
eminently characteristic of most wild animals (…).

Interestingly, Darwin extends this rhetorical mode of comparison and contrast over entire chapters of his famous work. Notice the rhetorical statements of comparison he uses (for example, "the lower animals, like man" or "like our own children"); Darwin does not leave it up to us to draw compari-sons—he points out virtually all of them with examples. Speaking of examples (the first rhetorical mode that we discussed), notice that in the case of this passage, the two rhetorical modes of examples and comparison/contrast are used together.

LAUNDRY LIST FOR COMPARISON AND CONTRAST

- When comparing and contrasting A and B, find common elements (which will be-come your examples) from both.

- Do not write about A in one paragraph and B in another.

- Do your best to combine common elements into a limited number of groups—three, if possible—and write a paragraph about each group.

- Do not attempt to justify your groups or your examples; simply present them.

SAMPLE QUESTION

Write an essay in which you compare and contrast the careers and lifestyles of professional musicians and doctors. Be sure to include examples.

DRILL: REFLECT ON HOW YOU COULD USE COMPARISON
AND CONTRAST TO ADDRESS THE FOLLOWING TOPICS

For each topic, make a list like the one above (AP English versus AP Art History). First, write down several similarities and differences. Then organize these similarities and differences in a logical man-ner; try to sort them out so that you have about three or four central ideas, which would translate into about three or four separate compare and contrast paragraphs. Do not attempt to answer the question by addressing one choice and then the other in separate paragraphs.

TOPIC 1:   Two of your friends

TOPIC 2:   Two teachers at your school

TOPIC 3:   Two singers or bands

TOPIC 4:   New York and Los Angeles (even if you haven't been to either)

TOPIC 5:   The experience of traveling to the mountains and the experience of
                traveling to the ocean

ANALOGY

Although analogies are not that useful in argumentative writing, they *are* useful in expository writing—this means that analogies will be useful when you write your expository essay for this test.

Think of an **analogy** as a comparison used to explain something.

Analogies are sometimes used to explain things that are difficult to understand by comparing them with things that are easier to understand. Let's say that you want to explain how a well-run corporation works. You might explain that it functions like a football team. In both cases there are owners or stockholders. In the corporation, there's a CEO, who is similar to the coach of a football team. The CEO directs the managers (or vice presidents), just as the coach directs the assistant coaches; these work directly with the employees—the players. When an employee doesn't heed directions, the success of the enterprise is put at risk, just like when a player fails to execute a block or a tackle. The most important thing about using analogies is that you choose one that will be readily understood by your audience. In this case, if the reader knows nothing about football, this analogy may do more harm than good.

You can also use an analogy to explain something that's abstract by comparing it with something that's concrete. Throughout history, people have used analogies to explain their god or gods. Christians explain their god, for example, through analogy. They say that their god is like a father who loves his children and, thus, both punishes and rewards them. The only difference is that they consider their god's judgment to be perfect. They believe that their god is like a father in that both are good, but that the difference is that their god is *perfectly* good.

The most famous philosophical analogy serves as the basis for Plato's "allegory of the cave." The analogy purportedly evolved from a conversation between Socrates and Glaucon.

> Imagine human beings living in an underground cave;
> here they have been from their childhood, and they
> have their legs and necks chained so that they cannot
> Line move and can only see before them, being prevented by
> 5 the chains from turning round their heads. Above and
> behind them, a fire is blazing at a distance, and between
> the fire and the prisoners there is a raised way; and there
> is a low wall built along the way, like the screen which
> marionette players have to hide them and over which
> 10 they show the puppets.
>
> Men are passing along the wall (and screened by the
> wall) and are carrying all sorts of things and animals
> made of wood and stone and various materials that ap-
> pear over the wall. Some of them are talking, others are
> 15 silent.
>
> Like ourselves, they see only their own shadows, or
> the shadows of one another, or the shadows of the things
> and animals, which the fire throws on the opposite wall
> of the cave.
>
> 20 And if the human beings were able to converse with
> one another, would they not suppose that they were
> naming what was actually before them (even though
> they were seeing only shadows of those things)?
>
> And suppose further that the prison had an echo
> 25 which came from the other side, would they not be sure
> to fancy when one of the passers-by spoke that the voice
> which they heard came from the passing shadow?
>
> To them, I said, the truth would be literally nothing
> but the shadows of the images.

This is only part of the analogy, but you probably get the idea. Socrates uses this analogy to explain that we think that we see things just as they really are in our world, but that we are seeing only reflections of a greater truth, an abstraction that we fail to grasp. The cave is our world; the shadows are the objects and people that we "see." We are like the prisoners, for we are not free to see what creates the shadows; the truth, made up of ideal forms, is out in the light.

LAUNDRY LIST FOR ANALOGY

- Use analogy for expository writing (explanation).

- Do not use analogy for argumentative writing (argumentation).

- Use analogy to explain something difficult to understand or that is abstract.

- Make sure your audience will readily understand your "simple" or concrete subject.

SAMPLE QUESTION

Write an essay in which you explain the process of applying to college. Use analogy when appropriate.

DRILL: REFLECT ON HOW YOU COULD USE ANALOGY TO ADDRESS THE FOLLOWING TOPICS

As you read each topic, think of it as the basis for the thesis of an expository essay. Come up with a simpler subject that you can use as an analogy for this more complex topic. Write down a basic plan for an essay.

TOPIC 1: The way your school functions

TOPIC 2: The benefits of honesty

MOVING ON...

In this chapter we discussed three rhetorical modes: example, classification, and comparison and contrast (analogy falls under this last category). Make sure you are familiar with the laundry lists in this chapter. If you get into good habits now when using these rhetorical modes, you'll be much better off on test day!

Further proving how useful these modes will be, we guarantee that both your expository and argumentative essay questions will fit into some combination of these modes.

Of course, remember to plan your essay before you begin writing. It often helps to write your thesis statement along with this plan so that you can keep in mind whether the parts of your plan are relevant to your central idea. This will ensure that you write the best organized, most coherent essay you can.

Now that we've covered the three basic rhetorical modes, let's move on to review a few complex modes in the next chapter.

KEY TERMS

basic rhetorical modes

example (illustration)

classification

compare and contrast

analogy

11

Complex Rhetorical Modes

In this chapter, we'll discuss a few more—and more complex—rhetorical modes, including process analysis, cause-and-effect, definition, description, narration, and induction and deduction. As was the case with the rhetorical modes you learned about in the last chapter, it will be extremely beneficial to you to know all you can about these modes on test day. It will not only help you recognize when these modes are used in the sample passages, but also enable you to use them in your essays.

So let's jump right in.

PROCESS ANALYSIS

Process analysis is a rhetorical mode that's used by writers when they want to explain either how to do something or how something was done. When your science teacher hands you instructions for a lab, she is giving you a rather dry sheet of process analysis that says, "first do this; then do that; then examine the data; then explain such-and-such." When you write your lab report, you're also indulging in process analysis, saying, "first we did this; then we did that; then we examined the data; then we determined such-and-such." If you like to follow recipes when you cook, then you've already been exposed to process analysis. However, process analyses used in writing generally aren't as dry as recipes or how-to manuals; they usually have a few examples to spice them up a little.

Process analysis can be an effective way of relating an experience. Take, for example, this now famous passage about "dumpster diving."

> I learned to scavenge gradually, on my own. Since
> then I have initiated several companions into the trade. I
> have learned that there is a predictable series of stages a
> person goes through in learning to scavenge.
>
> *Line*
> 5   At first the new scavenger is filled with disgust and
> self-loathing. He is ashamed of being seen and may lurk
> around, trying to duck behind things, or he may try to
> dive at night. (In fact, most people instinctively look
> away from a scavenger. By skulking around, the novice
> 10 calls attention to himself and arouses suspicion. Diving
> at night is ineffective and needlessly messy.)
>
> Every grain of rice seems to be a maggot. Everything
> seems to stink. He can wipe the egg yolk off the found
> can, but he cannot erase the stigma of eating garbage out
> 15 of his mind.
>
> That stage passes with experience. The scavenger finds
> a pair of running shoes that fit and look and smell brand
> new. He finds a pocket calculator in perfect working
> order. He finds pristine ice cream, still frozen, more than
> 20 he can eat or keep. He begins to understand: people do
> throw away perfectly good stuff, a lot of perfectly good
> stuff.
>
> At this stage, Dumpster shyness begins to dissipate.
> The diver, after all, has the last laugh. He is finding all
> 25 manner of good things which are his for the taking.
> Those who disparage his profession are the fools, not he.

He may begin to hang onto some perfectly good things
for which he has neither a use nor a market. Then he
begins to take note of the things which are not perfectly
30 good but are nearly so. He mates a Walkman with broken earphones and one that is missing a battery cover.
He picks up things which he can repair.

At this stage he may become lost and never recover.
Dumpsters are full of things of some potential value
35 to someone and also of things which never have much
intrinsic value but are interesting. All the Dumpster div-
ers I have known come to the point of trying to acquire
everything they touch. Why not take it, they reason,
since it is all free.

Excerpt from "On Dumpster Diving" by Lars Eighner from
TRAVELS WITH LIZBETH (St. Martin's Press)

Here's a good example of process analysis in writing. Although the material is organized in chronological stages, the author inserts explanatory examples and personal commentary that make the passage more lively. In this passage, the author is not instructing the reader on how to scavenge for food in Dumpsters; rather, he is explaining the psychological evolution of a homeless scavenger—based on his own experience—and illustrating the excesses of a consumerist society.

Remember that process analysis is a rhetorical mode that serves to organize something in a step-by-step manner, and it can serve both scientific and literary needs.

LAUNDRY LIST FOR PROCESS ANALYSIS

- Sequence is chronological and usually fixed; think of recipes.

- When you use this device, make sure the stages of the process are clear, by using transitions (e.g., *first, next, after two days, finally).*

- Make sure your terminology is appropriate for the reader. For example, the person who will read your essays probably does not know much about the embryonic development of frogs, so you should avoid using too-specialized terms like *Spemann organizer* or *Nieuwkoop center.*

- Verify that every step is clear; an error or omission in an intermediate step may make the rest of the process analysis very confusing. If you were describing how to braid hair, and wrote the following instructions: "First, comb or brush your hair so that it is untangled and manageable to work with. Next, take the far-right section of hair and put it over the middle section and under the far-left section."—this could be confusing to your reader because you never said to divide the hair into three sections before starting the actual braiding process.

SAMPLE QUESTION

Write a short essay in which you describe the process of how you selected the colleges to which you applied (or are going to apply to).

DRILL: REFLECT ON HOW YOU COULD USE
PROCESS ANALYSIS TO ADDRESS THE FOLLOWING TOPICS

Try making a numbered list with a few examples. Make sure you have included all the necessary steps and have used appropriate language and terminology for your reader. Remember to use transition words when you write the essay.

TOPIC 1:   How decisions are made at your school

TOPIC 2:   How to get through your high school successfully

TOPIC 3:   How to choose and keep close friends

CAUSE AND EFFECT

You just saw how process analysis is a useful rhetorical mode for explaining how to do things or how things were done; the rhetorical mode known as **cause and effect** explains *why things should be* or *should have been done*. In a sense, cause and effect explains the processes responsible for the process. You've probably received at least some rudimentary process analysis about how to use a computer at some point (first, turn on the computer; then launch your browser; log on to your IM; select someone else who is logged in....), but you probably don't know *why* all that works.

Some cause-and-effect relationships are easy to describe. For instance, read the example below from *Candide*'s Dr. Pangloss.

> "It is demonstrable," said Pangloss, "that things cannot
> be otherwise than as they are; for as all things have been
> created for some end, they must necessarily be created
> Line   for the best end. Observe, for instance, the nose is formed
> 5   for spectacles; therefore we wear spectacles. The legs
> are visibly designed for stockings; accordingly we wear
> stockings. Stones were made to be hewn and to construct
> castles; therefore My Lord has a magnificent castle, for
> the greatest baron in the province ought to be the best
> 10   lodged. Swine were intended to be eaten; therefore we
> eat pork all the year round."

In this passage, Pangloss is using a series of cause-and-effect relationships to prove his point, that "things cannot be otherwise than as they are." This rhetorical mode is everywhere, however. You see examples of this rhetorical mode all around you.

For example, if you were writing about the poor average of AP English Language and Composition test scores at your school, you could go about it in two ways. First, you could examine some *immediate* causes: Ms. What's-Her-Name retired and was replaced by a teacher who had no experience teaching and no background in English, we didn't have a good review book for the exam, or the exam is administered in Room Z during school band practice. Alternatively, you could examine some *underlying* causes for the poor exam scores: The superintendent of schools changed hiring policies (so a terrible teacher was hired); last year, funds for buying books were diverted to buying new lockers for the football team (so we had no good review book); and the room that the school band normally practices in was flooded when a pipe broke.

On this exam, the causes and effects that you choose to explore will depend on what you're asked to explain. You may have to use cause and effect in your essays, possibly in combination with one or more other rhetorical modes; you may also see a few questions in the multiple-choice section that deal with how the author uses cause and effect to make a point. When making critical decisions, writers will often consider both the immediate and the long-term effects; when analyzing an important event, writers will often examine both the immediate and the underlying causes.

LAUNDRY LIST FOR CAUSE AND EFFECT

- Do not confuse the relating of mere circumstances with a cause-and-effect relationship. For example, it is not logical to assume that socialism in Chile necessarily caused socialism in Argentina.

- Turn your causal relationships into causes and effects by using carefully chosen examples. Remember that not all causal relationships are causes and effects. However, careful use of evidence and examples can turn causal relationships into causes and effects.

- Make sure to carefully address each step in a series of causal relationships; if you don't, you risk losing your reader. Imagine the attendance secretary when she hears, "I'm sorry I'm late. We had a fire, so I had to find my cat." A better (clearer) explanation would have been: "I'm sorry I'm late. This morning at 4:00 A.M. there was an electrical fire in the garage; fortunately, there was an alarm that woke my dad, who put out the fire, but when he opened the garage door, my cat ran outside. I think it was frightened so it ran up a tree. I decided to climb up the tree and get the cat but I fell, and my mother had to take me to the emergency room."

SAMPLE QUESTION

Write an essay in which you examine the possible causes and effects of violence in the United States today.

DRILL: REFLECT ON HOW YOU COULD USE
CAUSE AND EFFECT TO ADDRESS THE FOLLOWING TOPICS

TOPIC 1: Academic dishonesty in high schools

TOPIC 2: The fear of terrorism in the United States

TOPIC 3: The changing face of ethnic America

DEFINITION

You are probably familiar with definitions; you see them every time you look up a word in the dictionary. Hopefully when you write, you try to make sure your reader understands the words that you use.

When writing your essays for the AP English Language and Composition Exam, if you happen to leave a key term unexplained or explained vaguely, even a carefully crafted essay will fall apart. This is especially true of very specialized terminology and obscure words. For example, if you are explaining a wonderful new tradition at your school and define it by synonym, you may write, "Basically, it's a Mexican *feis*." If your readers are Irish, this would be all right; if your readers were from just about anywhere else, you would need to define *feis* by putting it in a **category** (defining it in terms everyone will understand): "a *feis* is a competition for Irish dance, song, and instrumental music." Then, you could explain your project: "We want to do the same thing with traditional Mexican dance, song, and music."

For the AP exam, we have to consider *definition* in its meaning as a rhetorical mode. In this case, a paragraph—or an entire essay—is devoted to the definition of a term. Here, for example, is a paragraph that defines *feis* (pronounced "fesh").

> A *feis* is a day of competition in Irish dancing, music,
> and song. Perhaps you were wondering where all the
> Irish dancers from *Lord of the Dance* came from. All first
> Line performed at a *feis* and honed their skills through compe-
> 5 titions at various levels. A *feis* is a living legacy of Irish
> culture; it is where beginners, trying to remember their
> left from right, unknowingly dance the ancient steps of
> Ireland and pass this legacy on to the next generation.
> On the more practical side, a *feis* is to Irish performers
> 10 what a soccer game is to athletes the world over. Com-
> petitions are organized by ability (Beginner, Advanced
> Beginner, Novice, Open, Preliminary Championships,
> and Championships) and by age (Under 6, Under 7, etc).
> At a typical *feis*, there might be as many as 2,500 dancers.

The passage begins with a straightforward definition, but the definition is extended and rhetorical modes are mixed. You noted, I'm sure, the *analogy* to a soccer game; then, there is an inchoate (imperfectly formed) stab at *classification* (the divisions in the competition). You could even argue that the mention of *Lord of the Dance* serves as a kind of *example*. The rhetorical mode of *definition* can be used simply to explain a word or concept, but typically the author using it also wants to interest the reader in what's being explained.

Let's take a look at another good example of definition.

> The *Palio* is a horse race that's held twice each year
> in Siena, Italy: on July 2nd in honor of the Madonna of
> Provenzano, and on August 16th in honor of the As-
> Line sumption of the Virgin. But saying that the Palio is just
> 5 another horse race would be like calling the Superbowl
> just another football game. The Palio is not just a race.
> It is blood, sweat, and tears; it is part competition and
> part festival. According to some, it is the world's craziest
> horse race; according to others, it is Italy's most honored
> 10 tradition. One thing is clear to everyone, however: the
> Palio represents the tradition, culture, and soul of Siena.
> The actual race lasts only about a minute, but those mo-
> ments represent an entire year's worth of anticipation
> and preparation.

Again, the passage begins with a simple definition; but here, too, we have an example of another rhetorical mode—analogy (to the Superbowl).

However, the author of this passage uses an important additional tactic, known as *definition by negation.* You should be aware of this rhetorical device and use it where appropriate. In the passage above, the negation is partial—the Palio is, indeed, a race, but it is not "just a race." Most negations work in that manner; definition by negation is usually used to impress upon the reader the importance of the item under discussion or create a distinction between the item under discussion and the item with which it is being "negatively" compared. For instance, you may write, "Madonna is not a pop singer; she's a phenomenon, a true diva, a multitalented musical ambassador, and savvy business-woman." Perhaps this statement is true, but she's still a pop singer.

You may be able to use definition as a mode in your free-response essays, but most likely, you will see definition used in the passages in the multiple-choice sections. For example, you may be asked to answer a question that deals with how an author uses definition to analyze a topic.

LAUNDRY LIST FOR DEFINITION

- Keep your reason for defining something in mind as you're writing.

- Define key terms according to what you know of your audience, in other words, the readers of the essays; you don't want to bore your reader by defining terms unnecessarily, nor do you want to perplex your reader by failing to define terms that may be obscure to your audience. Keep in mind that for you, your readers are the AP English Language and Composition Exam graders.

- Explain the background (history) when it is relevant to your definition.

- Define by negation when appropriate.

- Combine definition with any number of other rhetorical modes when applicable.

SAMPLE QUESTION

Write an essay in which you use definition to analyze the role of integrity in your life.

DRILL: REFLECT ON HOW YOU COULD USE DEFINITION TO ADDRESS THE FOLLOWING TOPICS

First define each word by category; then, define each word by negation.

WORD 1: Hip-hop

WORD 2: Success

WORD 3: Love

WORD 4: Cool

DESCRIPTION

Description can help make expository or argumentative writing lively and interesting and hold the reader's interest, which is vital, of course. Think of how many essays those test graders have to read every day; as we mentioned in the techniques chapters, a large part of scoring well on the free-response section is keeping your audience interested.

Oftentimes description serves as the primary rhetorical mode for an entire essay—or even an entire book. It's typically used to communicate a scene, a specific place, or a person to the reader. Although writers tend to concentrate most on the visual aspects of descriptions, descriptions can be used to appeal to any of the reader's senses.

It is important to keep in mind that sometimes description can be objective; in these cases, the author is not describing something in a sentimental or otherwise subjective way—he or she is merely stating the facts. As an example of this, take a look at Charles Darwin's depiction of Valparaiso, the chief seaport in Chile, in *Voyage of the Beagle*.

> The town is built at the very foot of a range of hills,
> about 1,600 feet high, and rather steep. From its posi-
> tion, it consists of one long, straggling street, which
> Line runs parallel to the beach, and wherever a ravine comes
> 5 down, the houses are piled up on each side of it. The
> rounded hills, being only partially protected by very
> scanty vegetation, are worn into numberless little gul-
> lies, which expose a singularly bright red soil. From this
> cause, and from the low whitewashed houses with tile
> 10 roofs, the view reminded me of St. Cruz in Tenerife. In a
> northwesterly direction there are some fine glimpses of
> the Andes, but these mountains appear much grander
> when viewed from the neighboring hills: the great dis-
> tance at which they are situated can then more readily be
> 15 perceived.

This type of objective description tends to be drier than more subjective description. The degree of objectivity exhibited above probably doesn't thrill you—nor will it thrill the AP readers.

Fortunately, unlike most other rhetorical modes, description allows for a significant degree of subjectivity. In most descriptions, the writer attempts to communicate personal impressions of something or someone, and to do so it is necessary to draw on the powers of figurative writing; simile, metaphor, and personification are the most common.

Here is another description of a city: Nathaniel Hawthorne's impressions of Florence. The description comes not from one of Hawthorne's novels, but from one of the notebooks that he kept during his travels in Europe.

By and by, we had a distant glimpse of Florence, showing its great dome and some of its towers out of a sidelong valley, as if we were between two great waves
Line of the tumultuous sea of hills, while, far beyond, rose in
5 the distance the blue peaks of three or four of the Apennines, just on the remote horizon. There being a haziness in the atmosphere, however, Florence was little more distinct to us than the Celestial City was to Christian and Hopeful, when they spied at it from the Delectable
10 Mountains.

Florence at first struck me as having the aspect of a very new city in comparison with Rome; but, on closer acquaintance, I find that many of the buildings are antique and massive, though still the clear atmosphere,
15 the bright sunshine, the light, cheerful hues of the stucco, and—as much as anything else, perhaps—the vivacious character of the human life in the streets, take away the sense of its being an ancient city.

As we returned home over the Arno River, crossing
20 the Ponte di Santa Trinitá, we were struck by the beautiful scene of the broad, calm river, with the palaces along its shores repeated in it, on either side, and the neighboring bridges, too, just as perfect in the tide beneath as in the air above—a city of dream and shadow so close to
25 the actual one. God has a meaning, no doubt, in putting this spiritual symbol continually beside us.

Along the river, on both sides, as far as we could see, there was a row of brilliant lamps, which, in the far distance, looked like a cornice of golden light; and this
30 also shone as brightly in the river's depths. The lilies of the evening, in the quarter where the sun had gone down, were very soft and beautiful, though not so gorgeous as thousands that I have seen in America. But I believe I must fairly confess that the Italian sky, in the
35 daytime, is bluer and brighter than our own, and that the atmosphere has a quality of showing objects to better advantage. It is more than mere daylight; the magic of moonlight is somehow mixed up with it, although it is so transparent a medium of light.

This is a much more personal vision of a city. Hawthorne uses one simile to give us a better visual image of the countryside around Florence ("as if we were between two great waves of the tumultuous sea of hills"), and another to communicate the effect of the gas lamps ("like a cornice of golden light"); and he employs a metaphor ("a city of dream and shadow") to evoke his impression of the reflections in the river. In fact, virtually all of the description serves to communicate or explain *Hawthorne's* impressions of the city; here, the writer wishes to evoke and is not interested in scientific exactitude.

Keep in mind that this rhetorical device allows you a certain amount of freedom of language, but it also allows you certain liberties in organization. In Hawthorne's passage, for example, the author put down in writing his impressions in whatever order they came to him. In more objectively written descriptions, however, it often makes sense to think *spatially* when writing a visual description. You might describe a scene from left to right or front to back, for example; you might start a description of a person with the head (and end with the feet).

In the following passage, Fyodor Dostoyevsky gives us both a spatial description and a barrage of sensory impressions.

> In the first place, on entering this house, one passes
> into a very bare hall, and thence along a passage to a
> mean staircase. The reception room, however, is bright,
> *Line* clean, and spacious, and is lined with redwood and
> 5 metalwork. But the scullery you would not care to see;
> it is greasy, dirty, and odoriferous, while the stairs are
> in rags, and the walls so covered with filth that the hand
> sticks fast wherever it touches them. Also, on each land-
> ing there is a medley of boxes, chairs, and dilapidated
> 10 wardrobes; while the windows have had most of their
> panes shattered, and everywhere stand washtubs filled
> with dirt, litter, eggshells, and fish bladders. The smell is
> abominable. In short, the house is not a nice one.
>
> As to the disposition of the rooms, I have described it
> 15 to you already. True, they are convenient enough, yet
> every one of them has an atmosphere. I do not mean that
> they smell badly so much as that each of them seems to
> contain something which gives forth a rank, sickly-sweet
> odor. At first the impression is an unpleasant one, but a
> 20 couple of minutes will suffice to dissipate it, for the rea-
> son that everything here smells—people's clothes, hands,
> and everything else—and one grows accustomed to the
> rankness. Canaries, however, soon die in this house. A
> naval officer here has just bought his fifth. Birds cannot
> 25 live long in such an air. Every morning, when fish or
> beef is being cooked, and washing and scrubbing are in
> progress, the house is filled with steam. Always, too, the
> kitchen is full of linen hanging out to dry; and since my
> room adjoins that apartment, the smell from the clothes
> 30 causes me not a little annoyance. However, one can grow
> used to anything.

Note that Dostoyevsky's description first takes us through the ground floor and leads us up the staircase. Unlike the previous passages, this one appeals to our tactile ("so covered with filth that the hand sticks") and, even more prominently, olfactory senses. Choice of detail is important, and the choice of fish bladders, for example, conveys wonderfully the disgusting sights and smell. This is great writing—not only is the description effective, it's also humorous, thanks to the short comment at the end of each paragraph.

Laundry List for Description

- When possible, call on all five senses: visual, auditory, olfactory (smell), gustatory (taste), and tactile.

- Place the most striking examples at the beginnings and ends of your paragraphs (or essay) for maximum effect.

- Show, don't tell, using anecdotes and examples.

- Use concrete nouns and adjectives; nouns, not adjectives, should dominate.

- Concentrate on details that will convey the sense you're trying to get across most effectively. (Remember the fish bladders!)

- Employ figures of speech, especially similes, metaphors, and personification, when appropriate.

- When describing people, try to focus on distinctive mannerisms; if possible, you should go beyond physical appearance.

- Direct discourse (using dialogue or quotations) can be revealing and useful.

- A brief illustrative anecdote is worth a thousand words. Instead of simply using a general statement ("My friend Kai is a very generous person"), use an example ("My friend Kai is known for his generosity; the whole school knows about the time that he spent an entire weekend volunteering at a homeless shelter").

- To the extent possible, use action verbs. You could write, "The delightful aroma of chocolate chip cookies baking in the oven *crept around the corner and filled the den* with its sweetness" instead of just "The baking chocolate chip cookies *smelled* sweet."

Sample Question

Write an essay in which you describe your local shopping mall. Remember that you are not limited to physical descriptions.

Drill: Reflect on How You Could Use
Description to Address the Following Topics

First decide the general feeling you'd like to convey, and second begin to list some specifics; don't forget examples or anecdotes. When describing people, go beyond just the physical.

TOPIC 1:   A party

TOPIC 2:   Your parents

TOPIC 3:   A natural disaster (seen from personal experience or on television)

TOPIC 4:   Your favorite place to relax

TOPIC 5:   The campus of your school

NARRATION

A **narrative** is a story in which pieces of information are arranged in chronological order. You probably know that, but what you may not know is that narration can be an effective expository technique.

Decades after her experience in a Japanese internment camp, Jeanne Wakatsuki Houston decided to narrate her experiences before, during, and immediately after imprisonment. She did not want to tell the story just for the story's sake; she wanted to relay her experience to the public to exorcize personal demons and to raise public awareness about this period in history. Here is a passage from this *personal narrative*. The passage describes the period after the Wakatsuki family had lost their house in Ocean Park, California, when they were forced into detention.

> My own family, after three years of mess hall liv-
> ing, collapsed as an integrated unit. Whatever dignity
> or feeling of filial strength we may have known before
> Line   December 1941 was lost, and we did not recover it until
> 5   many years after the war, not until after Papa died and
> we began to come together, trying to fill the vacuum his
> passing left in all our lives.
>
> The closing of the camps, in the fall of 1945, only ag-
> gravated what had begun inside. Papa had no money
> 10   then and could not get work. Half of our family had
> already moved to the East Coast, where jobs had opened
> up for them. The rest of us were relocated into a former
> defense workers' housing project in Long Beach. In that
> small apartment there never was enough room for all of
> 15   us to sit down for a meal. We ate in shifts, and I yearned
> all the more for our huge round table in Ocean Park.
>
> Soon after we were released I wrote a paper for a
> seventh-grade journalism class, describing how we
> used to hunt grunion before the war. The whole family
> 20   would go down to Ocean Park Beach after dark, when
> the grunion were running, and build a big fire on the
> sand. I would watch Papa and my older brothers splash
> through the moonlit surf to scoop out the fish, then we'd
> rush back to the house where Mama would fry them up
> 25   and set the sizzling pan on the table, with soy sauce and
> horseradish, for a midnight meal. I ended the paper with
> this sentence: "The reason I want to remember this is
> because I know we'll never be able to do it again."

You may be asked to use personal narrative when writing your essays on the AP English Language and Composition test; and you will certainly be asked to *analyze* narratives that employ this rhetorical mode.

Additionally, sometimes you'll see questions on the essay section of the AP exam that will ask you to relate someone else's experience to illustrate a point. In essence, you'll be asked to write a narrative in the third person, but choose wisely. For example, if you're asked to "relate an experience where someone you know (directly or indirectly) overcame incredible obstacles to reach a goal," you wouldn't want to narrate the story of your cat, who managed to catch an elusive mouse.

In the following passage, Booker T. Washington uses narrative to explain how his view on education developed. Watch for changes between the first- and third-person style of narration.

When a mere boy, I saw a young colored man, who
had spent several years in school, sitting in a common
cabin in the South, studying a French grammar. I noted
Line the poverty, the untidiness, the want of system, and
5 thrift that existed about the cabin, notwithstanding
his knowledge of French and other academic subjects.
Another time, when riding on the outer edges of a
town in the South, I heard the sound of a piano coming from a cabin of the same kind. Contriving some
10 excuse, I entered and began a conversation with the
young colored woman who was playing, and who had
recently returned from a boarding-school, where she had
been studying instrumental music among other things.
Despite the fact that her parents were living in a rented
15 cabin, eating poorly cooked food, surrounded with
poverty, and having almost none of the conveniences of
life, she had persuaded them to rent a piano for four or
five dollars per month. Many such instances as these, in
connection with my own struggles, impressed upon me
20 the importance of making a study of our needs as a race,
and applying the remedy accordingly.

Some one may be tempted to ask, Has not the negro
boy or girl as good a right to study a French grammar
and instrumental music as the white youth? I answer,
25 Yes, but in the present condition of the negro race in
this country there is need of something more. Perhaps I
may be forgiven for the seeming egotism if I mention the
expansion of my own life partly as an example of what
I mean. My earliest recollection is of a small one-room
30 log hut on a large slave plantation in Virginia. After the
close of the war, while working in the coal-mines of West
Virginia for the support of my mother, I heard in some
accidental way of the Hampton Institute.

When I learned that it was an institution where a
35 black boy could study, could have a chance to work for
his board, and at the same time be taught how to work
and to realize the dignity of labor, I resolved to go there.
Bidding my mother good-by, I started out one morning
to find my way to Hampton, though I was almost pen-
40 niless and had no definite idea where Hampton was. By
walking, begging rides, and paying for a portion of the
journey on the steam-cars, I finally succeeded in reaching the city of Richmond, Virginia. I was without money
or friends. I slept under a sidewalk, and by working on
45 a vessel next day I earned money to continue my way to
the institute, where I arrived with a surplus of fifty cents.
At Hampton I found the opportunity—in the way of
buildings, teachers, and industries provided by the generous—to get training in the class-room and by practical
50 touch with industrial life, to learn thrift, economy, and

push. I was surrounded by an atmosphere of business, Christian influence, and a spirit of self-help that seemed to have awakened every faculty in me, and caused me for the first time to realize what it meant to be a man
55 instead of a piece of property.

While there I resolved that when I had finished the course of training I would go into the far South, into the Black Belt of the South, and give my life to providing the same kind of opportunity for self-reliance and self-
60 awakening that I had found provided for me at Hampton.

Notice that in the first paragraph, the narration slips briefly into the third person—Washington is telling the story of the girl, not his own. Likewise, Washington presents the story of the boy studying French from his point of view. In these two instances, Washington switches from first to third person with ease, so that the transition is optimally effective and unnoticeable. The second paragraph effortlessly transitions to a personal anecdote, which is continued in the third paragraph. The final paragraph justifies the narrative: Washington's life story leads to his commitment to establish his own institute—called the Tuskegee Normal and Industrial Institute—deep in the South.

LAUNDRY LIST FOR NARRATION

- When possible, structure the events in chronological order.

- Make your story complete: make sure you have a beginning, middle, and end.

- Provide a realistic setting (typically at the beginning). Notice how Booker T. Washington provides a setting in this passage with just a few details: "a young colored man," "a common cabin in the South," "the poverty, the untidiness, the want of system, and thrift that existed about the cabin."

- Whenever possible, use action verbs; for example, write "the fighters *tumbled* to the ground," rather than "there *were* fallen soldiers on the ground."

- Provide concrete and specific details.

- Show, don't tell. This is another way of saying that you should use anecdotes and examples whenever possible.

- Establish a clear point of view; if it's clear who is narrating and why, then it will be easier to choose relevant details.

- Include appropriate amounts of direct discourse (dialogue or quotations).

SAMPLE QUESTION

"A college education is not necessary for success." Relate an experience of someone you know (directly or indirectly) that defends, challenges, or qualifies this statement.

DRILL: REFLECT ON HOW YOU COULD USE NARRATION TO ADDRESS THE FOLLOWING TOPICS

Think of a personal experience (or an experience of someone you know) that pertains to the topic. Determine how you would best describe this experience. Come up with a few anecdotes or examples.

TOPIC 1: Danger when eating becomes an obsession

TOPIC 2: Hardship is a necessary part of our education

INDUCTION AND DEDUCTION

You will probably find that the rhetorical modes of induction and deduction are most useful when you're writing the argumentative essay, although they will be helpful on the rhetorical analysis essay too.

Induction is a process in which specific examples are used to reach a general conclusion. If you took the AP European History Exam and did not like the experience and followed by taking the AP Calculus Exam and did not like the experience, you might arrive at the following general conclusion: AP exams are always an unpleasant experience. If, when you were young, you found that you didn't like broccoli, asparagus, or cabbage, your parents might have concluded that you didn't like vegetables. In both cases, the conclusion would be of questionable value because there is not enough evidence to justify the generalization.

Assume that you want to argue that your English teacher is in a bad mood every time the Boston Red Sox lose a game to the New York Yankees. You could substantiate that generalization by recalling certain tantrums that he threw and comparing those days with the dates of Red Sox losses. This would substantiate your claim but not prove it, especially if you didn't even know if your teacher saw the games. After all, what if something else happened to coincide with the games and was the real cause of his bad temper, such as traffic jams on the way home from school?

We tend to believe in generalizations arrived at through induction, whether they can actually be proved. The Food and Drug Administration, for example, has to follow the inductive reasoning of scientists; just because a certain drug produced the desired results—and didn't produce an undesirable result, such as death—20,000 experimental cases does not prove that the same results will occur when 20,000,000 people take the drug.

Deduction involves the use of a generalization to draw a conclusion about a specific case. For example, if you read in the morning paper that all schools in your county would be closed that day because of inclement weather, you could conclude that you won't have to go to school. You just used deductive reasoning.

LAUNDRY LIST FOR INDUCTION AND DEDUCTION

- Induction proceeds from the specific to a generalization. For example, your class-mate Ricky plays on the school's football and basketball teams, and he has ice hockey posters all over his bedroom at home. You could conclude that Ricky likes all sports in general.

- Make sure you have sufficient evidence to support your claim.

- Deduction is the process of applying a generalization to a specific case. For example, your cousin Jennifer told you that she hates dancing and loud music. From this, you could safely say that she probably wouldn't want to come with you to the hot new nightclub opening this weekend.

- Make sure your generalization has sufficient credibility before applying it to specific cases. For example, it would be an unfair generalization to assume that all baseball players use or have used anabolic steroids.

SAMPLE QUESTION

Write a short essay in which you analyze the following statement: *Contemporary films are a reflection of today's values.*

DRILL: REFLECT ON HOW YOU COULD USE
INDUCTION TO SUBSTANTIATE THE FOLLOWING THESES

THESIS 1: Academic honesty is alive and well.

THESIS 2: High schools don't really care about their mission to educate.

THESIS 3: Computer games have beneficial effects.

THESIS 4: Children generally demonstrate more wisdom than their parents.

In this chapter we looked at a few more rhetorical modes that will be extremely useful to you on test day. Remember that these can be used in combination with each other *and*, further complicating matters, in combination with the modes in the previous chapter. Hopefully, these modes have given you some ideas about how you can structure your essays into coherent works that the test readers will understand and maybe even enjoy.

Here we are at the end of the review section of the book. You are now ready to take the practice tests; you may be dreading these now, but we know that once you begin, you'll see that you know a lot more than you think you do! If you've worked through the book up to this point and complete these practice exams, you'll certainly be ready for test day.

Good luck!

KEY TERMS

complex rhetorical modes

process analysis

cause and effect

definition

category

description

narration

narrative

induction

deduction

The Princeton Review AP English Language and Composition Practice Tests and Explanations

12

Practice Test 1

AP® English Language and Composition Exam

DO NOT OPEN THIS BOOKLET UNTIL YOU ARE TOLD TO DO SO.

At a Glance

Total Time
1 hour
Number of Questions
54
Percent of Total Grade
45%
Writing Instrument
Pencil required

Instructions

Section I of this examination contains 54 multiple-choice questions. Fill in only the ovals for numbers 1 through 54 on your answer sheet.

Indicate all of your answers to the multiple-choice questions on the answer sheet. No credit will be given for anything written in this exam booklet, but you may use the booklet for notes or scratch work. After you have decided which of the suggested answers is best, completely fill in the corresponding oval on the answer sheet. Give only one answer to each question. If you change an answer, be sure that the previous mark is erased completely. Here is a sample question and answer.

Sample Question   Sample Answer

Chicago is a   Ⓐ ● Ⓒ Ⓓ Ⓔ
(A) state
(B) city
(C) country
(D) continent
(E) village

Use your time effectively, working as quickly as you can without losing accuracy. Do not spend too much time on any one question. Go on to other questions and come back to the ones you have not answered if you have time. It is not expected that everyone will know the answers to all the multiple-choice questions.

About Guessing

Many candidates wonder whether or not to guess the answers to questions about which they are not certain. Multiple choice scores are based on the number of questions answered correctly. Points are not deducted for incorrect answers, and no points are awarded for unanswered questions. Because points are not deducted for incorrect answers, you are encouraged to answer all multiple-choice questions. On any questions you do not know the answer to, you should eliminate as many choices as you can, and then select the best answer among the remaining choices.

This page intentionally left blank.

ENGLISH LANGUAGE AND COMPOSITION
SECTION I
Time—1 hour

Directions: This part consists of selections from prose works and questions on their content, form, and style. After reading each passage, choose the best answer to each question and completely fill in the corresponding oval on the answer sheet.

Note: Pay particular attention to the requirement of questions that contain the words NOT, LEAST, or EXCEPT.

Questions 1–10. Read the following passage carefully before you choose your answers.

(The following passage is from Jonathan Swift's 1729 essay "A Modest Proposal.")

There only remains one hundred and twenty thousand children of poor parents annually born. The question therefore is, how this number shall be reared
Line and provided for, which, as I have already said, under
5 the present situation of affairs, is utterly impossible by all the methods hitherto proposed. For we can neither employ them in handicraft or agriculture; we neither build houses (I mean in the country) nor cultivate land: they can very seldom pick up a livelihood by stealing,
10 till they arrive at six years old, except where they are of towardly parts, although I confess they learn the rudiments much earlier, during which time, they can however be properly looked upon only as probationers, as I have been informed by a principal gentleman in
15 the county of Cavan, who protested to me that he never knew above one or two instances under the age of six, even in a part of the kingdom so renowned for the quickest proficiency in that art.
I am assured by our merchants, that a boy or a
20 girl before twelve years old is no salable commodity; and even when they come to this age they will not yield above three pounds, or three pounds and half-a-crown at most on the exchange; which cannot turn to account either to the parents or kingdom, the charge of
25 nutriment and rags having been at least four times that value.
I shall now therefore humbly propose my own thoughts, which I hope will not be liable to the least objection.
30 I have been assured by a very knowing American of my acquaintance in London, that a young healthy child well nursed is at a year old a most delicious, nourishing, and wholesome food, whether stewed, roasted, baked, or boiled; and I make no doubt that it
35 will equally serve in a fricassee or a ragout.
I do therefore humbly offer it to public consideration that of the hundred and twenty thousand children already computed, twenty thousand may be

reserved for breed, whereof only one-fourth part to be
40 males; which is more than we allow to sheep, black cattle or swine; and my reason is, that these children are seldom the fruits of marriage, a circumstance not much regarded by our savages, therefore one male will be sufficient to serve four females. That the remaining
45 hundred thousand may, at a year old, be offered in the sale to the persons of quality and fortune through the kingdom; always advising the mother to let them suck plentifully in the last month, so as to render them plump and fat for a good table. A child will make two
50 dishes at an entertainment for friends; and when the family dines alone, the fore or hind quarter will make a reasonable dish, and seasoned with a little pepper or salt will be very good boiled on the fourth day, especially in winter.
55 I have reckoned upon a medium that a child just born will weigh 12 pounds, and in a solar year, if tolerably nursed, increaseth to 28 pounds.
I grant this food will be somewhat dear, and therefore very proper for landlords, who, as they have
60 already devoured most of the parents, seem to have the best title to the children.

1. This text can best be described as

    (A) scientific
    (B) satirical
    (C) forthright
    (D) humanitarian
    (E) sadistic

2. In the first, second, and fourth paragraphs the author relies on dubious

    (A) similes
    (B) *ad hominem* arguments
    (C) extended metaphors
    (D) arguments from authority
    (E) appeals to ignorance

GO ON TO THE NEXT PAGE.

3. "Probationers" (line 13) are

   (A) children learning how to steal
   (B) children on probation
   (C) adults on probation
   (D) apprentices working at a trade
   (E) young artists

4. The phrase "the charge of nutriment and rags having been at least four times that value" (lines 24-26) is humorous because

   (A) food was relatively cheap at that time
   (B) "four times" is a hyperbole
   (C) rags could be found free
   (D) we don't know who is being charged
   (E) "rags" is unexpected diction

5. The word "fricassee" (line 35) is best interpreted to mean

   (A) animal
   (B) child
   (C) dish
   (D) place
   (E) master

6. Which of the following rhetorical devices does the author employ in lines 36-44?

   (A) process analysis
   (B) example
   (C) cause and effect
   (D) deductive reasoning
   (E) analogy

7. The phrase "always advising the mother to let them suck plentifully in the last month" (lines 47-48) extends the comparison between the children and

   (A) properly nourished mammals
   (B) poor and ruthless parents
   (C) savages
   (D) animals raised for slaughter
   (E) the poor treatment of animals

8. In line 58, "dear" means

   (A) expensive
   (B) sweet
   (C) cherished
   (D) unforgettable
   (E) unhealthy

9. In context, "devoured" (line 60) is an effective word choice because

   (A) it fits both figuratively and literally
   (B) it is appropriate only literally
   (C) it is indicative of the landlords' plight
   (D) it works as a sentimental appeal
   (E) it reveals the author's point of view

10. According to the author, the proposal

    (A) makes good economic sense and helps the poor
    (B) provides food for the needy and the rich, alike
    (C) makes good economic sense but does not benefit the poor or rich
    (D) benefits the rich in several ways
    (E) benefits everyone in many ways

GO ON TO THE NEXT PAGE.

Questions 11-14. Read the following passage carefully before you choose your answers.

(The following passage is excerpted from a contemporary article in a scholarly journal.)

The most obvious joke in the title of Swift's *Travels into Several Remote Nations of the World* is that what purports to be a chronicle of several excursions to
Line remote nations turns out to be a satiric anatomy of
5 specifically English attitudes and values. But there is a second joke. Many of the supposedly unfamiliar and exotic sights Gulliver sees in his sixteen years and seven months of wandering in remote nations, and even the radically altered perspectives from which he
10 sees them (as diminutive landscapes, giant people, intelligent animals, etc.), could have been seen or experienced in a few days by anyone at the tourists sights, public entertainments, shows, spectacles, and exhibitions in the streets and at the fairs of London.

15 It is not surprising that *Gulliver's Travels* should be filled with the shows and diversions of London. All the Scriblerians were fascinated with popular entertainments; collectively and individually, they satirized them in many of their works. Swift shared
20 this fascination with his fellow Scriblerians, and he transforms the sights and shows of London into an imaginative center of *Gulliver's Travels*.

1

Gulliver himself senses that the wonders he sees in remote nations resemble popular entertainments
25 back home in England when he notes that the capital city of Lilliput "looked like the painted Scene of a City in a Theatre."[1] And other popular entertainments would allow Londoners to see many of the same sights Gulliver saw in Lilliput. A Londoner could experience
30 what a miniature city looked like to the giant Gulliver by going to see the papier-mâché and clay architectural and topographical models displayed at fairs and in inns, some of which were extraordinarily elaborate and detailed, such as the model of Amsterdam exhibited
35 in 1710, which was twenty feet wide and twenty to thirty feet long, "with all the Churches, Chappels, Stadt house, Hospitals, noble Buildings, Streets, Trees, Walks, Avenues, with the Sea, Shipping, Sluices, Rivers, Canals &c., most exactly built to admiration."[2]
40 Miniature people, as well as miniature landscapes, could be seen in one of the most popular diversions in London, the peepshows, which were enclosed boxes containing scenes made out of painted board, paper

flats, and glass panels and given the illusion of depth
45 by mirrors and magnifying glasses. All of this was seen through a hole bored in one side. Among the most popular scenes were interiors, particularly palace interiors of European royalty, and so there is a direct analogy between peering in the hole of a peepshow
50 and Gulliver's looking into the palace in Lilliput: "I applied my Face to the Windows of the middle Stories, and discovered the most splendid Apartments that can be imagined. There I saw the Empress, and the young Princes in their several Lodgings. Her Imperial
55 Majesty was pleased to smile very graciously upon me, and gave me out the window her Hand to kiss." The queen's movements could have been seen in the peepshows, too, for clockwork animating the figures was introduced early in the century. And much the
60 same illusion of a living, miniature world could be found in another popular diversion, the "moving picture," a device in which cutout figures were placed within a frame and activated by jacks and wheels. This curiosity fascinated contemporary Londoners: "The
65 landscape looks as an ordinary picture till the clock-work behind the curtain be set at work, and then the ships move and sail distinctly upon the sea till out of sight; a coach comes out of town, the motion of the horses and wheels are very distinct, and a gentleman in
70 the coach that salutes the company; a hunter also and his dogs keep their course till out of sight." Swift saw this same moving picture, or one very much like it, and was impressed.

11. The purpose of the passage is most likely to

(A) describe the cultural landscape in *Gulliver's Travels*

(B) draw a comparison between the fictional world Gulliver experienced and the similar imaginative elements of eighteenth-century London

(C) point out the superfluous nature of entertainment in Swift's London

(D) provide evidence that Swift's satire is derived from the natural curiosity of European royalty

(E) discredit the notion that *Gulliver's Travels* is a wholly original work

---

1 *Gulliver's Travels*, in *The Prose Works of Jonathan Swift*, ed. Herbert Davis, 14 vols. (Oxford: B. Blackwell, 1939–68), XI:13

2 Quoted in John Ashton, *Social Life in the Reign of Queen Anne* (New York: Chatto and Windus, 1883), 219–20

GO ON TO THE NEXT PAGE.

12. The footnote 1 in line 27 indicates that

   (A) the article first appeared as an addendum to *Gulliver's Travels*
   (B) *Gulliver's Travels* was first published in 1939
   (C) the quotation "looked like the…Theater" was excerpted from *Gulliver's Travels*, part of a 14 volume set of Swift's works
   (D) the quotation "looked like the…Theater" was originally written by Herbert Davis
   (E) *Gulliver's Travels* was reprinted in its entirety in 1939, and credited to Herbert Davis instead of Swift

13. The footnote 2 in line 39 indicates

   (A) the quotation was taken from a professional journal
   (B) the quotation refers to a 1710 exhibit in Amsterdam
   (C) the quotation originally appeared in *Gulliver's Travels* in 1883
   (D) the quotation, describing a miniature exhibition of Amsterdam, first appeared in a book by John Ashton
   (E) the quotation was originally published in a newspaper

14. The detail in lines 50-56 suggest the scene is viewed by which of the following?

   (A) an impartial anthropologist
   (B) an intrigued visitor
   (C) a critical literary scholar
   (D) an argumentative architect
   (E) a struggling writer

GO ON TO THE NEXT PAGE.

Questions 15-22. Read the following passage carefully before you choose your answers.

(The following passage is from a recent work by an art historian.)

It can be demonstrated quite satisfactorily that although Romanticism does not erupt into painting until the very end of the eighteenth century it is
Line comparatively untrammeled in literature long before
5 this date. One might remember in this connection not necessarily Jean-Jacques Rousseau, often invoked almost automatically as the patron saint of the movement, but a novelist like the Abbé Prévost, who, in the 1730s and 1740s, writes novels with a
10 full repertory of Gothic effects, such as crêpe-hung mortuary chambers and doomed travelers who insist on telling their life stories to their hapless neighbours in stage-coaches. Even more relevant than the novelists are a number of dramatists who accomplish a
15 revolution in theatrical behaviour which is of singular importance for the morphology of Romanticism. Nivelle de la Chausée, Diderot, and their numerous and more obscure followers create a type of dramatic genre which calls for the actors to go out of their way
20 to give gratuitous demonstrations of the intensity with which they feel. For a long time these demonstrations were confined to tragic-comedies, or *comédies larmoyantes*, in which the gesticulating characters, often morbid, always extravagant, were united at curtain fall,
25 but when they were transposed to a form of tragedy, dealing with contemporary problems, as they were in the works of the pre-Revolutionary dramatist Louis-Sébastien Mercier, one is already very close to the more rhetorical aspect of Romantic paintings.

15. It can be inferred from this passage that

(A) Rousseau's novels predate those of Abbé Prévost
(B) most critics concur that French Romanticism began with Abbé Prévost's works
(C) Nivelle de la Chausée is most famous for his novels
(D) the eighteenth-century novel is not relevant to the discussion of French Romanticism
(E) Romantic paintings often depict emotional contemporary issues

16. It can be inferred from this passage that Romantic works often include

(A) scenes in gloomy interiors
(B) battles with Goths
(C) scenes from the Wild West
(D) discussions with neighbors
(E) vividly decorated chambers

17. The word "morphology" (line 16) most closely means

(A) structure
(B) sickness
(C) psychology
(D) death
(E) revolution

18. The "gratuitous demonstrations" (line 20) are

(A) free of charge
(B) calm portrayals
(C) not directly tied to the plot
(D) tips for the actors
(E) gratifying plays

19. The "*comédies larmoyantes*" (lines 22-23) are characterized by

(A) the overwrought emotionalism of the characters
(B) the subdued control of the action
(C) complicated rhetoric
(D) the death of the main characters at the end of the play
(E) extravagant sets

20. "Revolutionary" (line 27) is capitalized because it

(A) refers to a specific revolution
(B) designates a literary movement
(C) is a key word in the passage
(D) is part of the author's title
(E) refers to a specific dramatist

21. The last sentence (lines 21-29) in the passage is

(A) a periodic sentence
(B) a run-on sentence
(C) a metaphorical conclusion
(D) not to be taken literally
(E) an attack on the dramatist Mercier

22. Most likely, the passage is part of

(A) a historical study of drama
(B) a textbook on history
(C) a study of Romanticism
(D) an article in a travel magazine
(E) a political history of France

GO ON TO THE NEXT PAGE.

Questions 23-33. Read the following passage carefully before you choose your answers.

(The following passage is from A Vindication of the Rights of Women *by Mary Wollstonecraft in 1792.)*

My own sex, I hope, will excuse me, if I treat
them like rational creatures, instead of flattering their
fascinating graces, and viewing them as if they were in
Line a state of perpetual childhood, unable to stand alone.
5 I earnestly wish to point out in what true dignity
and human happiness consists—I wish to persuade
women to endeavour to acquire strength, both of
mind and body, and to convince them that the soft
phrases, susceptibility of heart, delicacy of sentiment,
10 and refinement of taste, are almost synonymous with
epithets of weakness, and that those beings who are
only the objects of pity and that kind of love, which
has been termed its sister, will soon become objects of
contempt.
15 Dismissing then those pretty feminine phrases,
which the men condescendingly use to soften our
slavish dependence, and despising that weak elegancy
of mind, exquisite sensibility, and sweet docility of
manners, supposed to be the sexual characteristics
20 of the weaker vessel, I wish to show that elegance
is inferior to virtue, that the first object of laudable
ambition is to obtain a character as a human being,
regardless of the distinction of sex; and that secondary
views should be brought to this simple touchstone.
25 This is a rough sketch of my plan; and should I
express my conviction with the energetic emotions
that I feel whenever I think of the subject, the dictates
of experience and reflection will be felt by some of
my readers. Animated by this important object, I
30 shall disdain to cull my phrases or polish my style;—I
aim at being useful, and sincerity will render me
unaffected; for, wishing rather to persuade by the
force of my arguments, than dazzle by the elegance of
my language, I shall not waste my time in rounding
35 periods, nor in fabricating the turgid bombast of
artificial feelings, which, coming from the head, never
reach the heart—I shall be employed about things,
not words!—and, anxious to render my sex more
respectable to members of society, I shall try to avoid
40 that flowery diction which has slided from essays
into novels, and from novels into familiar letters and
conversation.
These pretty nothings—these caricatures of the real
beauty of sensibility, dropping glibly from the tongue,
45 vitiate the taste, and create a kind of sickly delicacy that
turns away from simple unadorned truth; and a deluge
of false sentiments and overstretched feelings, stifling
the natural emotions of the heart, render the domestic

pleasures insipid, that ought to sweeten the exercise
50 of those severe duties, which educate a rational and
immortal being for a nobler field of action.
The education of women has, of late, been more
attended to than formerly; yet they are still reckoned
a frivolous sex, and ridiculed or pitied by the writers
55 who endeavour by satire or instruction to improve
them. It is acknowledged that they spend many of the
first years of their lives in acquiring a smattering of
accomplishments: meanwhile strength of body and
mind are sacrificed to libertine notions of beauty, to
60 the desire of establishing themselves—the only way
women can rise in the world—by marriage. And this
desire making mere animals of them, when they marry
they act as such children may be expected to act—they
dress; they paint, and nickname God's creatures—
65 Surely these weak beings are only fit for a seraglio!—
Can they govern a family, or take care of the poor babes
whom they bring into the world?

23. In the initial paragraph, the author employs both

   (A) apology and classification
   (B) irony and exposition
   (C) analogy and extended metaphor
   (D) flattery and epithets
   (E) induction and persuasion

24. In the initial paragraph, the author decries

   (A) traditional feminine attributes
   (B) traditional male attributes
   (C) modern sexuality
   (D) the importance of love
   (E) the importance of sentiments

25. In the initial paragraph, the author suggests that

   (A) men prefer strong women
   (B) a man will never truly love a strong woman
   (C) men never respect strong women
   (D) women need emotional and physical strength
   (E) women need intellectual and physical strength

26. The author ties the second paragraph to the first by
   using the words

   (A) "vessel" and "touchstone"
   (B) "soften" and "inferior"
   (C) "laudable" and "sex"
   (D) "slavish" and "virtue"
   (E) "soften" and "weak"

GO ON TO THE NEXT PAGE.

27. The word "vessel" (line 20) is a metaphor for

    (A) sex
    (B) woman
    (C) man
    (D) phrase
    (E) character

28. The author suggests that a woman's worth may be best judged by

    (A) comparing her with a praiseworthy man
    (B) examining the elegance of her writing
    (C) evaluating the strength of her character
    (D) evaluating her physical beauty
    (E) examining her manners

29. The author proposes to write in a manner that is both

    (A) cogent and emotional
    (B) polished and intellectual
    (C) ornate and rhetorical
    (D) elegant and cerebral
    (E) convincing and flowery

30. The words "pretty nothings" (line 43) are a reprise of

    (A) "letters and conversation" (lines 41-42)
    (B) "essays" and "novels" (lines 40-41)
    (C) "flowery diction" (line 40)
    (D) "rounding periods" (lines 34-35)
    (E) "members of society" (line 39)

31. With the phrase "dropping glibly from the tongue" (line 44) the author begins

    (A) a caricature of women
    (B) a critique of turgid bombast
    (C) a panegyric of sugary writing
    (D) an analysis of sentimental writing
    (E) an extended metaphor

32. One can infer from the passage that to become strong human beings, rather than mere children, young women need

    (A) an education different from that of young men
    (B) more understanding husbands
    (C) obliging husbands
    (D) a good marriage
    (E) the same education as that of young men

33. The tone of the final paragraph is

    (A) sardonic
    (B) condescending
    (C) ironic
    (D) sarcastic
    (E) haughty

GO ON TO THE NEXT PAGE.

Questions 34-41. Read the following passage carefully before you choose your answers.

(*The following passage is from Neil Postman's 1995 book,* The End of Education.)

But it is important to keep in mind that the engineering of learning is very often puffed up, assigned an importance it does not deserve. As an old
Line saying goes, *There are one and twenty ways to sing tribal*
5 *lays, and all of them are correct.* So it is with learning. There is no one who can say that this or that is the best way to know things, to feel things, to see things, to remember things, to apply things, to connect things and that no other will do as well. In fact, to make
10 such a claim is to trivialize learning, to reduce it to a mechanical skill.

Of course, there are many learnings that are little else but a mechanical skill, and in such cases, there well may be a best way. But to become a different
15 person because of something you have learned—to appropriate an insight, a concept, a vision, so that your world is altered—that is a different matter. For that to happen, you need a reason. And this is the metaphysical problem I speak of.
20 A reason, as I use the word here, is different from a motivation. Within the context of schooling, motivation refers to a temporary psychic event in which curiosity is aroused and attention is focused. I do not mean to disparage it. But it must not be confused with a reason
25 for being in a classroom, for listening to a teacher, for taking an examination, for doing homework, for putting up with school even if you are not motivated.

This kind of reason is somewhat abstract, not always present in one's consciousness, not at all easy to
30 describe. And yet for all that, without it schooling does not work. For school to make sense, the young, their parents, and their teachers must have a god to serve, or, even better, several gods. If they have none, school is pointless. Nietzsche's famous aphorism is relevant
35 here: "He who has a *why* to live can bear with almost any *how*." This applies as much to learning as to living.

To put it simply, there is no surer way to bring an end to schooling than for it to have no end.

34. The "engineering of learning" (line 2) most nearly means

(A) development of schools
(B) building of schools
(C) educational methodology
(D) building up of knowledge
(E) study of engineering

35. The "old saying" (lines 3-4) serves as

(A) an analogy to the sentences that follow
(B) a contrast to the sentences that follow
(C) an illustration of the first sentence
(D) a historical interlude
(E) a tribute to tribal lays

36. The series of infinitives in the initial paragraph emphasizes that the learning process is

(A) long and tedious
(B) multifaceted and impersonal
(C) active and varied
(D) difficult and trivial
(E) mechanical and complicated

37. According to the author, motivation is

(A) not important
(B) synonymous with reason
(C) abstract and fleeting
(D) momentary and concrete
(E) psychological and enduring

38. Both the first and third paragraphs contain

(A) aphorisms
(B) ironical statements
(C) syllogistic reasoning
(D) *ad hominem* arguments
(E) notable parallelism

39. In line 32, "god" most nearly means

(A) religion
(B) deity
(C) reason
(D) person
(E) Nietzsche

40. The author employs the argument from authority as

(A) a contrast to his point of view
(B) a relevant concrete example
(C) an apt analogy
(D) an example of cause and effect
(E) an illustration of the cruelty in schools

41. The paradox in the final sentence rests on

(A) different meanings of "end"
(B) a crass simplification
(C) the comparison between schooling and learning
(D) the eternal process of learning
(E) a new way of bringing schooling to an end

GO ON TO THE NEXT PAGE.

Questions 42-47. Read the following passage carefully before you choose your answers.

(The following passage is from Plessy v. Ferguson, *1896.)*

It is one thing for railroad carriers to furnish, or to be required by law to furnish, equal accommodations for all whom they are under a legal duty to carry.
Line It is quite another thing for government to forbid
5 citizens of the white and black races from traveling in the same public conveyance, and to punish officers of railroad companies for permitting persons of the two races to occupy the same passenger coach. If a state can prescribe, as a rule of civil conduct, that
10 whites and blacks shall not travel as passengers in the same railroad coach, why may it not so regulate the use of the streets of its cities and towns as to compel white citizens to keep on one side of a street, and black citizens to keep on the other? Why may it not,
15 upon like grounds, punish whites and blacks who ride together in street cars or in open vehicles on a public road or street? Why may it not require sheriffs to assign whites to one side of a court room, and blacks to the other? And why may it not also prohibit
20 the commingling of the two races in the galleries of legislative halls or in public assemblages convened for the consideration of the political questions of the day? Further, if this statute of Louisiana is consistent with the personal liberty of citizens, why may not the state
25 require the separation in railroad coaches of native and naturalized citizens of the United States, or of Protestants and Roman Catholics?

The white race deems itself to be the dominant race in this country. And so it is, in prestige, in
30 achievements, in education, in wealth, and in power. So, I doubt not, it will continue to be for all time, if it remains true to its great heritage, and holds fast to the principles of constitutional liberty. But in view of the constitution, in the eye of the law, there is in this
35 country no superior, dominant, ruling class of citizens. There is no caste here. Our constitution is color-blind, and neither knows nor tolerates classes among citizens. In respect of civil rights, all citizens are equal before the law. The humblest is the peer of the most powerful.
40 The law regards man as man, and takes no account of his surroundings or of his color when his civil rights as guarantied by the supreme law of the land are involved. It is therefore to be regretted that this high tribunal, the final expositor of the fundamental
45 law of the land, has reached the conclusion that it is competent for a state to regulate the enjoyment by citizens of their civil rights solely upon the basis of race.

In my opinion, the judgment this day rendered will,
50 in time, prove to be quite as pernicious as the decision made by this tribunal in the Dred Scott Case.
It was adjudged in that case that the descendants of Africans who were imported into this country, and sold as slaves, were not included nor intended to be
55 included under the word "citizens" in the constitution, and could not claim any of the rights and privileges which that instrument provided for and secured to citizens of the United States; that, at the time of the adoption of the constitution, they were "considered
60 as a subordinate and inferior class of beings, who had been subjugated by the dominant race, and, whether emancipated or not, yet remained subject to their authority, and had no rights or privileges but such as those who held the power and the government might
65 choose to grant them." The recent amendments of the constitution, it was supposed, had eradicated these principles from our institutions.
I am of opinion that the state of Louisiana is inconsistent with the personal liberty of citizens, white
70 and black, in that state, and hostile to both the spirit and letter of the constitution of the United States. If laws of like character should be enacted in the several states of the Union, the effect would be in the highest degree mischievous. Slavery, as an institution
75 tolerated by law, would, it is true, have disappeared from our country; but there would remain a power in the states, by sinister legislation, to interfere with the full enjoyment of the blessings of freedom, to regulate civil rights, common to all citizens, upon the basis of
80 race, and to place in a condition of legal inferiority a large body of American citizens, now constituting a part of the political community, called the "People of the United States," for whom, and by whom through representatives, our government is administered.
85 Such a system is inconsistent with the guaranty given by the constitution to each state of a republican form of government, and may be stricken down by congressional action, or by the courts in the discharge of their solemn duty to maintain the supreme law of
90 the land, anything in the constitution or laws of any state to the contrary notwithstanding.
For the reason stated, I am constrained to withhold my assent from the opinion and judgment of the majority.

42. The speaker in this passage is

(A) delivering a political speech
(B) rendering a legal judgment
(C) reminiscing about the past
(D) a state governor
(E) involved with the railroad company

GO ON TO THE NEXT PAGE.

43. In the first paragraph, the series of rhetorical questions serves the speaker's strategy of reasoning by

    (A) appeals to authority
    (B) analogy
    (C) description
    (D) induction
    (E) deduction

44. Based on the passage, the speaker holds that

    (A) racial equality will become a reality in America
    (B) civil equality is guaranteed by the Constitution
    (C) racial equality is guaranteed by the Constitution
    (D) both civil and racial equality are guaranteed by the Constitution
    (E) neither civil nor racial equality is guaranteed by the Constitution

45. In line 50, "pernicious" most nearly means

    (A) just
    (B) unjust
    (C) useful
    (D) propitious
    (E) harmful

46. In the speaker's opinion, the Louisiana law is subject to censure by

    (A) either the United States Congress or the United States Supreme Court
    (B) Louisiana legislation only
    (C) United States legislation only
    (D) the people of Louisiana only
    (E) neither the United States Congress nor the United States Supreme Court

47. The style of the entire passage can be best described as

    (A) ornate and whimsical
    (B) dry and objective
    (C) abstract and legalistic
    (D) terse and opinionated
    (E) probing and subtle

GO ON TO THE NEXT PAGE.

Questions 48-54. Read the following passage carefully before you choose your answers.

(The following passage is excerpted from the British Prime Minister's 1846 speech about the repeal of the Corn Laws.)

Sir, believe me, to conduct the Government of this country is a most arduous duty; I may say it without irreverence, that these ancient institutions, like our
Line physical frames, are "fearfully and wonderfully
5 made." It is no easy task to ensure the united action of an ancient monarchy, a proud aristocracy, and a reformed constituency. I have done everything I could do, and have thought it consistent with true Conservative policy to reconcile these three branches
10 of the State. I have thought it consistent with true Conservative policy to promote so much of happiness and contentment among the people that the voice of disaffection should be no longer heard, and that thoughts of the dissolution of our institutions should
15 be forgotten in the midst of physical enjoyment. These were my attempts, and I thought them not inconsistent with true and enlarged Conservative policy. These were my objects in accepting office—it is a burden too great for my physical, and far beyond
20 my intellectual structure; and to be relieved from it with perfect honour would be the greatest favour that could be conferred on me. But as a feeling of honour and strong sense of duty require me to undertake those responsible functions, I declare, Sir, that I am ready to
25 incur these risks, to bear these burdens, and to front all these honourable dangers. But, Sir, I will not take the step with mutilated power and shackled authority. I will not stand at the helm during, such tempestuous nights as I have seen, if the vessel be not allowed fairly
30 to pursue the course which I think she ought to take. I will not, Sir, undertake to direct the course of the vessel by the observations which have been taken in 1842. I will reserve to myself the marking out of that course; and I must, for the public interest, claim for myself the
35 unfettered power of judging of those measures which I conceive will be better for the country to propose.
Sir, I do not wish to be the Minister of England; but while I have the high honour of holding that Office, I am determined to hold it by no servile tenure. I
40 will only hold that office upon the condition of being unshackled by any other obligations than those of consulting the public interests, and of providing for the public safety.

48. The opening sentence of the passage contains

(A) an expression of fear
(B) an appeal to authority
(C) a humorous simile
(D) an irreverent attack
(E) equivocation

49. The speaker is addressing

(A) a friend
(B) a group of his peers
(C) a king
(D) a crowd of voters
(E) his political adversaries

50. The most significant transition takes place in

(A) line 10 ("I have thought it consistent…")
(B) line 18 ("These were my objects…")
(C) line 22 ("But as a feeling of honour…")
(D) line 26 ("But, Sir, I will not…")
(E) lines 30-31 ("I will not, Sir, undertake…")

51. All of the following are part of the same extended metaphor EXCEPT

(A) "helm" (line 28)
(B) "vessel" (line 29)
(C) "fairly" (line 29)
(D) "course" (line 30)
(E) "unshackled" (line 41)

52. Which term in the first paragraph serves to prepare the dominant point of the final paragraph?

(A) "disaffection" (line 13)
(B) "enjoyment" (line 15)
(C) "dangers" (line 26)
(D) "tempestuous" (line 28)
(E) "unfettered" (line 35)

53. Based on the passage, the speaker's motivation to serve as Prime Minister is dictated mostly by

(A) greed
(B) political ambition
(C) sense of honor
(D) political power
(E) youthful exuberance

54. The tone of the entire passage

(A) remains consistently cynical
(B) shifts according to the speaker's mood
(C) shifts from light to serious
(D) becomes more frivolous in the final paragraph
(E) remains consistently lighthearted

END OF SECTION I

AP® English Language and Composition Exam

SECTION II: Free-Response Questions

DO NOT OPEN THIS BOOKLET UNTIL YOU ARE TOLD TO DO SO.

At a Glance

Total Time
2 hours, plus a 15-minute reading period
Number of Questions
3
Percent of Total Grade
55%
Writing Instrument
Pen required

Instructions

Section II of this examination requires answers in essay form. To help you use your time well, the coordinator will announce the time at which each question should be completed. If you finish any question before time is announced, you may go on to the following question. If you finish the examination in less than the time allotted, you may go back and work on any essay question you want.

Each essay will be judged on its clarity and effectiveness in dealing with the requirements of the topic assigned and on the quality of the writing. After completing each question, you should check your essay for accuracy of punctuation, spelling, and diction; you are advised, however, not to attempt many longer corrections. Remember that quality is far more important than quantity.

Write your essays with a pen, preferably in black or dark blue ink. Be sure to write CLEARLY and LEGIBLY. Cross out any errors you make.

The questions for Section II are printed in the green insert. You are encouraged to use the green insert to make notes and to plan your essays, but be sure to write your answers in the pink booklet. Number each answer as the question is numbered in the examination. Do not skip lines. Begin each answer on a new page in the pink booklet.

ENGLISH LANGUAGE AND COMPOSITION
SECTION II
Time—2 hours

Question 1

(Suggested writing time—40 minutes. This question counts for one-third of the total essay section score.)

In democratic nations today, the ability to vote is presumed. Many consider this right a "natural right," while others consider it a privilege or even a civic duty.

Carefully read the following six sources, including the introductory information for each source. Then synthesize information from at least three of the sources and incorporate it into a coherent, well-written essay that develops a position on the most important consideration in granting suffrage to women in America.

Make sure that your argument is central; use the sources to illustrate and support your reasoning. Avoid merely summarizing the sources. Indicate clearly which sources you are drawing from, whether through direct quotation, paraphrase, or summary. You may cite the sources as Source A, Source B, etc., or by using the descriptions in parentheses.

Source A	(Anthony lecture)
Source B	(*Daily Graphic*)
Source C	(Hunt)
Source D	(66th Congress)
Source E	(*Minor v. Happersett*)
Source F	(*Woman's Sphere*)

GO ON TO THE NEXT PAGE.

Source A

Anthony, Susan B. "Is It a Crime for a Citizen of the United States to Vote?" 3 April 1873.

The following passage is the opening of a speech given by Susan B. Anthony, who in 1872 was arrested and charged with voting illegally.

Friends and Fellow-citizens: I stand before you to-night, under indictment for the alleged crime of having voted at the last Presidential election, without having a lawful right to vote. It shall be my work this evening to prove to you that in thus voting, I not only committed no crime, but, instead, simply exercised my citizen's right, guaranteed to me and all United States citizens by the National Constitution, beyond the power of any State to deny.

Our democratic-republican government is based on the idea of the natural right of every individual member thereof to a voice and a vote in making and executing the laws. We assert the province of government to be to secure the people in the enjoyment of their unalienable rights. We throw to the winds the old dogma that governments can give rights. Before governments were organized, no one denies that each individual possessed the right to protect his own life, liberty and property. And when 100 or 1,000,000 people enter into a free government, they do not barter away their natural rights; they simply pledge themselves to protect each other in the enjoyment of them, through prescribed judicial and legislative tribunals. They agree to abandon the methods of brute force in the adjustment of their differences, and adopt those of civilization.

Nor can you find a word in any of the grand documents left us by the fathers that assumes for government the power to create or to confer rights. The Declaration of Independence, the United States Constitution, the constitutions of the several states and the organic laws of the territories, all alike propose to protect the people in the exercise of their God-given rights. Not one of them pretends to bestow rights.

"All men are created equal, and endowed by their Creator with certain unalienable rights. Among these are life, liberty and the pursuit of happiness. That to secure these, governments are instituted among men, deriving their just powers from the consent of the governed."

Here is no shadow of government authority over rights, nor exclusion of any from their full and equal enjoyment. Here is pronounced the right of all men, and "consequently," as the Quaker preacher said, "of all women," to a voice in the government. And here, in this very first paragraph of the declaration, is the assertion of the natural right of all to the ballot; for, how can "the consent of the governed" be given, if the right to vote be denied. Again:

"That whenever any form of government becomes destructive of these ends, it is the right of the people to alter or abolish it, and to institute a new government, laying its foundations on such principles, and organizing its powers in such forms as to them shall seem most likely to effect their safety and happiness."

Surely, the right of the whole people to vote is here clearly implied. For however destructive in their happiness this government might become, a disfranchised class could neither alter nor abolish it, nor institute a new one, except by the old brute force method of insurrection and rebellion. One-half of the people of this nation to-day are utterly powerless to blot from the statute books an unjust law, or to write there a new and a just one.

GO ON TO THE NEXT PAGE.

Source B

Wust, Thomas. Untitled political cartoon. The Daily
Graphic. 1873.

The following is a political cartoon.

GO ON TO THE NEXT PAGE.

Source C

United States v. Susan B. Anthony (1873).

The following passage is excerpted from Judge Ward Hunt's instructions to the jury.

The right of voting, or the privilege of voting, is a right or privilege arising under the Constitution of the State, and not of the United States. The qualifications are different in the different States. Citizenship, age, sex, residence, are variously required in the different States, or may be so. If the right belongs to any particular person, it is because such person is entitled to it by the laws of the State where he offers to exercise it, and not because of citizenship of the United States. If the State of New York should provide that no person should vote until he had reached the age of 31 years, or after he had reached the age of 50, or that no person having gray hair, or who had not the use of all his limbs, should be entitled to vote, I do not see how it could be held to be a violation of any right derived or held under the Constitution of the United States. We might say that such regulations were unjust, tyrannical, unfit for the regulation of an intelligent State; but if rights of a citizen are thereby violated, they are of that fundamental class derived from his position as a citizen of the State, and not those limited rights belonging to him as a citizen of the United States. (…)

If she believed she had a right to vote, and voted in reliance upon that belief, does that relieve her from the penalty? It is argued that the knowledge referred to in the act relates to her knowledge of the illegality of the act, and not to the act of voting; for it is said that she must know that she voted. Two principles apply here: First, ignorance of the law excuses no one; second, every person is presumed to understand and to intend the necessary effects of his own acts. Miss Anthony knew that she was a woman, and that the constitution of this State prohibits her from voting. She intended to violate that provision—intended to test it, perhaps, but certainly intended to violate it. The necessary effect of her act was to violate it, and this side is presumed to have intended. There was no ignorance of any fact, but all the facts being known, she undertook to settle a principle in her own person. She takes the risk, and she cannot escape the consequences. It is said, and authorities are cited to sustain the position, that there can be no crime unless there is a culpable intent; to render one criminally responsible a vicious will must be present. A commits a trespass on the land of B, and B, thinking and believing that he has a right to shoot an intruder on his premises, kills A on the spot. Does B's misapprehension of his rights justify his act? Would a Judge be justified in charging the jury that if satisfied that B supposed he had a right to shoot A he was justified, and they should find a verdict of not guilty? No Judge would make such a charge. To constitute a crime, it is true that there must be a criminal intent, but it is equally true that knowledge of the facts of the case is always held to supply this intent. An intentional killing bears with it evidence of malice in law. Whoever, without justifiable cause, intentionally kills his neighbor is guilty of a crime. The principle is the same in the case before us, and in all criminal cases. (…)

Upon this evidence I suppose there is no question for the jury and that the jury should be directed to find a verdict of guilty.

GO ON TO THE NEXT PAGE.

Source D

Joint resolution of the 66th Congress, May 19, 1919.

Sixty-sixth Congress of the United States of America;

At the First Session,

Begun and held at the City of Washington on Monday, the nineteenth day of May, one thousand nine hundred and nineteen.

JOINT RESOLUTION

Proposing an amendment to the Constitution extending the right of suffrage to women.

Resolved by the Senate and House of Representatives of the United States of America in Congress assembled (two-thirds of each House concurring therein), That the following article is proposed as an amendment to the Constitution, which shall be valid to all intents and purposes as part of the Constitution when ratified by the legislatures of three-fourths of the several States.

"ARTICLE ————.

"The right of citizens of the United States to vote shall not be denied or abridged by the United States or by any State on account of sex.

"Congress shall have power to enforce this article by appropriate legislation."

F. H. Gillett.

Speaker of the House of Representatives.

Thos. R. Marshall.

Vice President of the United States and
President of the Senate.

GO ON TO THE NEXT PAGE.

Source E

<u>Minor v. Happersett</u>, 88 U.S. 162 (1874)

The following passage is excerpted from the Opinion of the Court.

In October, 1874, the Supreme Court voted unanimously that the Constitution of the United States does not confer on women the right to vote in federal elections.

When the Federal Constitution was adopted, all the States, with the exception of Rhode Island and Connecticut, had constitutions of their own. These two continued to act under their charters from the Crown. Upon an examination of those constitutions we find that in no State were all citizens permitted to vote. Each State determined for itself who should have that power. Thus, in New Hampshire, "every male inhabitant of each town and parish with town privileges, and places unincorporated in the State, of twenty-one years of age and upwards, excepting paupers and persons excused from paying taxes at their own request," were its voters; in Massachusetts "every male inhabitant of twenty-one years of age and upwards, having a freehold estate within the commonwealth of the annual income of three pounds, or any estate of the value of sixty pounds"; in Rhode Island "such as are admitted free of the company and society" of the colony; in Connecticut such persons as had "maturity in years, quiet and peaceable behavior, a civil conversation, and forty shillings freehold or forty pounds personal estate," if so certified by the selectmen. (…)

Certainly, if the courts can consider any question settled, this is one. For nearly ninety years the people have acted upon the idea that the Constitution, when it conferred citizenship, did not necessarily confer the right of suffrage. If uniform practice long continued can settle the construction of so important an instrument as the Constitution of the United States confessedly is, most certainly it has been done here. Our province is to decide what the law is, not to declare what it should be.

We have given this case the careful consideration its importance demands. If the law is wrong, it ought to be changed; but the power for that is not with us. The arguments addressed to us bearing upon such a view of the subject may perhaps be sufficient to induce those having the power, to make the alteration, but they ought not to be permitted to influence our judgment in determining the present rights of the parties now litigating before us. No argument as to woman's need of suffrage can be considered. We can only act upon her rights as they exist. It is not for us to look at the hardship of withholding. Our duty is at an end if we find it is within the power of a State to withhold.

Being unanimously of the opinion that the Constitution of the United States does not confer the right of suffrage upon any one, and that the constitutions and laws of the several States which commit that important trust to men alone are not necessarily void, we affirm the judgment.

GO ON TO THE NEXT PAGE.

Source F

Nineteenth-century political cartoon.

Woman Devotes Her Time to Gossip and Clothes Because She Has Nothing Else to Talk About. Give Her
Broader Interests and She Will Cease to Be Vain and Frivolous.

GO ON TO THE NEXT PAGE.

Question 2

(Suggested time—40 minutes. This question counts for one-third of the total essay section score.)

The passages that follow were published shortly after the appearance of Mary Shelley's *Frankenstein* (1818). At that time, very few people knew the identity of the author. The first passage has been extracted from an anonymous piece from *The Quarterly Review*. The second passage is part of (Sir) Walter Scott's review of *Frankenstein* in *Blackwood's Edinburgh Magazine*.

Read the passages carefully. Then write an essay in which you compare and contrast the manner in which each critic uses language to convey a point of view.

Passage 1

On board this ship poor Frankenstein, after
telling his story to Mr. Walton, who has been so kind
to write it down for our use, dies of cold, fatigue,
Line and horror; and soon after, the monster, who had
5 borrowed (we presume from the flourishing colony
of East Greenland) a kind of raft, comes alongside
the ship, and notwithstanding his huge bulk, jumps
in at Mr. Walton's cabin window, and is surprised by
that gentleman pronouncing a funeral oration over
10 the departed Frankenstein; after which, declaring that
he will go back to the Pole, and there burn himself
on a funeral pyre (of ice, we conjecture) of his own
collecting, he jumps again out the window into his raft,
and is out of sight in a moment.
15 Our readers will guess from this summary,
what a tissue of horrible and disgusting absurdity
this work presents. It is piously dedicated to Mr.
Godwin, and is written in the spirit of his school.
The dreams of insanity are embodied in the strong
20 and striking language of the insane, and the author,
notwithstanding the rationality of his preface, often
leaves us in doubt whether he is not as mad as his
hero. Mr. Godwin is the patriarch of a literary family,
whose chief skill is in delineating the wanderings of
25 the intellect, and which strangely delights in the most
affecting and humiliating of human miseries. His
disciples are a kind of out pensioners of Bedlam, and
like "Mad Bess" or "Mad Tom," are occasionally visited
with paroxysms of genius and fits of expression, which
30 makes sober-minded people wonder and shudder.
But when we have thus admitted that *Frankenstein*
has passages which appall the mind and make the flesh
creep, we have given it all the praise (if praise it can
be called) which we dare to bestow. Our taste and our
35 judgment alike revolt at this kind of writing, and the

greater the ability with which it may be executed
the worse it is—it inculcates no lesson of conduct,
manners, or morality; it cannot mend, and will not
even amuse its readers, unless their taste have been
40 deplorably vitiated—it fatigues the feelings without
interesting the understanding; it gratuitously
harasses the sensations. The author has powers,
both of conception and language, which employed
in a happier direction might, perhaps (we speak
45 dubiously), give him a name among these whose
writings amuse or amend their fellow-creatures; but
we take the liberty of assuring him, and hope that
he may be in a temper to listen to us, that the style
which he has adopted in the present publication
50 merely tends to defeat his own purpose, if he really
had any other object in view than that of leaving the
wearied reader, after a struggle between laughter
and loathing, in doubt whether the head or the heart
of the author be the most diseased.

GO ON TO THE NEXT PAGE.

Passage 2

Exhausted by his sufferings, but still breathing vengeance against the being which was at once his creature and his persecutor, this unhappy victim to
Line physiological discovery expires just as the clearing
5   away of the ice permits Captain Walton's vessel to hoist sail for the return to Britain. At midnight, the daemon, who had been his destroyer, is discovered in the cabin, lamenting over the corpse of the person who gave him being. To Walton he attempts to justify his resentment
10 towards the human race, while, at the same time, he acknowledges himself a wretch who had murdered the lovely and the helpless, and pursued to irremediably ruin his creator, the select specimen of all that was worthy of love and admiration.
15   "Fear not," he continues, addressing the astonished Walton, "that I shall be the instrument of future mischief. My work is nearly complete. Neither yours nor any man's death is needed to consummate the series of my being, and accomplish that which must
20 be done; but it requires my own. Do not think that I shall be slow to perform this sacrifice. I shall quit your vessel on the ice-raft which brought me hither, and shall seek the most northern extremity of the globe; I shall collect my funeral pile and consume to ashes this
25 miserable frame, that its remains may afford no light to any curious and unhallowed wretch, who would create such another as I have been...."
        "He sprung from the cabin-window, as he said this, upon the ice-raft which lay close to the vessel. He was
30 soon borne away by the waves, and lost in darkness and distance."
        Whether this singular being executed his purpose or not must necessarily remain an uncertainty, unless the voyage of discovery to the north pole should throw any
35 light on the subject.
        So concludes this extraordinary tale, in which the author seems to us to disclose uncommon powers of poetic imagination. The feeling with which we perused the unexpected and fearful, yet, allowing the
40 possibility of the event, very natural conclusion of Frankenstein's experiment, shook a little even our firm nerves; although such and so numerous have been the expedients for exciting terror employed by the romantic writers of the age, that the reader may adopt
45 Macbeth's words with a slight alteration:
        "We have supp'd full with horrors
        Direness, familiar to our 'callous' thoughts,
        Cannot once startle us."
        It is no slight merit in our eyes that the tale, though
50 wild in incident, is written in plain and forcible English, without exhibiting that mixture of hyperbolical Germanisms with which tales of wonder are usually told, as if it were necessary that the language should

be as extravagant as the fiction. The ideas of the author
55 are always clearly as well as forcibly expressed; and his descriptions of landscape have in them the choice requisites of truth, freshness, precision, and beauty.

GO ON TO THE NEXT PAGE.

Question 3

(Suggested time—40 minutes. This question counts for one-third of the total essay section score.)

Read carefully the passage below. Then write an essay in which you support, refute, or qualify the claim that a "neutral" stand on race perpetuates racial imbalance.

> *I am saying that sometimes colorblindness is racism. I know that sounds counterintuitive, but let me go on.*
>
> *Think of society as comprised of lots of different groups of people, identified by their race, gender, etc. Neutrality in our society is supposed to be the great equalizer because we believe that, if we don't favor any one group, things will work themselves out and become more equal. But the thing is this: neutrality has this effect only if there is no previous social or historical context. But that's not how the real world is. There is, in fact, a social and historical context for every situation. So if I were being "neutral" and viewing everyone as being the same, ignoring personal contexts, I wouldn't be promoting equality because I would be ignoring the differences that exist and allowing the inequalities to continue to exist, given that I wouldn't do anything to help change them. Identifying problems and actively promoting solutions are necessary to effect useful change; being neutral is consenting to the status quo.*

STOP

END OF EXAM

13

Practice Test 1: Answers and Explanations

EXPLANATIONS TO THE MULTIPLE-CHOICE SECTION

1. **B** This first passage, taken from Jonathan Swift's "A Modest Proposal" is a relatively easy one. If you take the author's proposal seriously, then four of the answers [(A), (C), (D), and (E)] are plausible; of course, the key is to understand that the author is not making a serious proposal, but, rather, he is satirizing other so-called scientific studies that, under the guise of humanitarianism, tend to offer cruel (if not sadistic) "solutions" to poverty. Therefore, (B) is the only acceptable answer.

2. **D** Even if you are not familiar with the term "arguments from authority," you can easily guess the meaning. The authorities cited are "a principal gentleman in the county of Cavan" (paragraph 1), "our merchants" (paragraph 2), and "a very knowing American of my acquaintance in London" (paragraph 4). These are, of course, dubious authorities, indeed, which is one of the sources of humor in the passage.

   The easiest and fastest way to use POE in this case is to examine the shortest of the paragraphs, the fourth. Clearly, there are no similes (A) or extended metaphors (C) in the fourth paragraph, so there is no need to check the first or second paragraphs for these rhetorical devices. The other two answers are more esoteric, but logic leads you to eliminate them, even if you do not fully understand them as rhetorical terms. There is nothing approximating an appeal in paragraph four, so you can eliminate that answer easily; there is also no attempt to argue a point (B).

3. **A** Answers (B) and (C) are shallowly associated with the word "probationers," which appears in the question (and text), and are easily dismissed. Answer (E) tempts you to make a hasty association between the last word in the paragraph ("art") and a practitioner of art. This narrows the choices to (A) and (D); however, it is clear that the children's "livelihood" is not a formal trade, but mere thievery—the only "trade" left open to indigent children during the incipient stages of the Industrial Revolution. So "probationers" refers to "children learning how to steal," or choice A.

4. **E** The humor comes from the clever juxtaposition of the phrase "nutriment and rags." The first term is even more formal than what we may expect (food), and this creates an expectation for the second term: clothing. Instead, the author hits the reader with an unexpected substitute for clothes: rags. The other answers appear to be more or less plausible, but none has anything to do with humor. Hyperbole (B) was thrown in gratuitously; often, students will be tricked into selecting an answer simply because it contains a rhetorical term and appears to be the most sophisticated choice.

5. **C** You may or may not be familiar with this word, but when you read it in context, the answer to this question becomes apparent—the entire paragraph is about food, and certainly you understand the other terms (*stewed, roasted, baked, boiled*). Reading the term in context allows you to eliminate the other choices: "animal," "child," "place," and "master."

6. **A** The best approach to this question is to use POE. You can eliminate answers (B) and (C) right away. If you remember that "deductive reasoning" means starting with a generality and working logically to a specific conclusion, you can see that answer (D) is way off base too. Answer (E) may be tempting because of the existence of the phrase "which is more than we allow to sheep, black cattle, or swine" in the paragraph, but this paragraph is not dominated by analogy. Although this comparison is extended, it is not really a pattern.

"Process analysis" (A) is the best answer; in this paragraph, the author analyzes a problem and proposes a process that will bring about a solution. The proposal describes the process for breeding, fattening, and preparing this very unusual source of protein.

7. **D** This question is related to the previous one. The proposal is to fatten the children for slaughter, just as if they were livestock (sheep, cattle, or pigs).

8. **A** By using POE, you should be able to narrow your choices down to (A) and (C) very quickly. The author is saying that the new meat will be expensive, and only the rich landlords will be able to afford it.

9. **A** By this point, you must have digested (forgive the pun) the satire, so you understand that the landlords have "devoured" the parents by charging unreasonably high rents and that, according to the author, they may as well literally devour (eat) their poor tenants' children. It is understandable that answer (E) may tempt you, but the diction in this sentence is hardly a revelation. We have understood the point of view all along; behind the comical satire is the rage of a man disgusted by the exploitation of the poor by the rich.

10. **D** This farcical proposal does make good economic sense, but it does not help the poor; clearly, this eliminates answers (A), (B), and (E). The "only" in answer (C) allows us to discard that choice too. The proposal benefits the rich by providing a plentiful source of a food that, among other things, will be both chic and appropriate for a wide variety of dishes. Also, by slaughtering the children when they are infants, society will not have to worry about providing for older children, who are too young to work but old enough to need clothing and food. Ostensibly, this responsibility falls on those who have money, the rich; if this cost is eliminated, then again the rich benefit.

11. **B** To answer this question, you need to think in terms of main idea. This is a fairly straightforward question that asks you to consider the type of material you are reading and what the author is saying within that context. In this piece of literary criticism, the author is making a connection between what Gulliver experienced and what an eighteenth-century Londoner might have seen exhibited in fairs and inns.

12. **C** Footnote questions were added to the test in response to concerns raised by colleges and universities. In these days of easy access to information via the internet, colleges are becoming increasingly concerned that students do not take seriously the intellectual property of authors and end up plagiarizing, wittingly or not. Footnotes give information about authorship and publication place and date and can also provide hints as to the purpose of a piece of writing or its context. This particular footnote simply indicates that the quote about Lilliput does, indeed, come from *Gulliver's Travels*, part of a 14-volume set of works by Swift.

13. **D** This quote from *Social Life in the Reign of Queen Anne* helps to set an elaborate scene, and the footnote helps to lend credibility to Todd's purpose in describing the imaginative miniature worlds of Swift's day.

14. **C** By paying attention to the title, the author, the subject matter, and the footnotes you should be able to use POE to weed out (B) and (C), and while the subject matter of this essay might be of interest to an anthropologist (A), the content and format is consistent with literary criticism.

15. **E** In approaching this question, you'll definitely want to use POE. You can infer several things from the first part of the passage.

    1. The passage is about French Romanticism.

    2. Typically, critics agree that French Romanticism begins in the late eighteenth century.

    3. Typically, critics agree that Jean-Jacques Rousseau is the first great French Romantic.

    4. This author emphasizes that French Romanticism is important much earlier in the eighteenth century.

    5. This author believes that the novels of Abbé Prévost, who wrote Romantic works in the first half of the century, provide good examples of this earlier phenomenon.

    Thus, answer (A) is clearly false; the reverse is true. The same can be said for (B)—few critics believe this; most critics believe that "the patron saint" is Rousseau. It is easy to eliminate (D). If the novel is not relevant, then why does the critic spend half of the passage discussing it? It is true that the author proposes drama as an even more relevant genre, but that doesn't imply that the consideration of the novel was inappropriate.

    The author discusses Nivelle de la Chaussée along with the group of playwrights; thus, it is reasonable to assume that plays, not novels, are that author's claim to fame. Therefore, you're left with (E); and from how the author has described the books and paintings "often depict emotional contemporary issues."

16. **A** You should be able to eliminate choices (B) and (C) right away. Choice (C) is just ridiculous, and as for (B), the Gothic effects have to do with Gothic art (architecture) and the so-called Gothic Revival. Choice (D) doesn't seem to have much to do with the passage, so get rid of it.

    You may get caught up with answer (E); the problem with this answer is the word "vividly." However, between (A) and (E), you should be able to determine that (A) is the better choice, upon reviewing the passage. If you are unfamiliar with Gothic romances, the phrase "such as crêpe-hung mortuary chambers" is the key to arriving at the correct answer.

17. **A** Hopefully, POE can help you narrow your choices to (A) and (C). If you are unsure, plug each proposed answer into the sentence and see if the resulting sentence makes sense in the context of what you have read. "Morphology" refers to the form or structure of something. How does (A) sound? "…the revolution in theatrical behavior which is of singular importance for the <u>structure</u> (or form) of Romanticism." That isn't bad; it's the best of the answer choices!

18. **C** The only overt attempts to trick you are in (D) and (E). When you go to a restaurant, the "gratuity" is the tip; "gratuitous" and "gratifying" contain the same initial letters. Even if you do not know the correct answer, you should never fall for this kind of trick; seldom or never will the question and the correct answer have a relationship such as this one.

    Words like *intensity* and *gesticulating* should lead you to the correct answer. In this case, the author is saying that the actors "go out of their way to give gratuitous demonstrations of the intensity with which they feel," which implies that their demonstrations are not directly tied to the plot; this shows that (C) is correct. Note that (B) is the exact opposite of the correct answer.

19. **A** This question is related to the previous ones in many respects. Furthermore, answers (C), (D), and (E) are not substantiated in any way by the text, and (B) is the opposite of what is true. A large clue in the passage that should have guided you toward the correct answer is the phrase "the gesticulating characters, often morbid, always extravagant." This implies that the characters were, as (A) states, emotionally overwrought.

20. **A** The word "Revolutionary" is capitalized because it refers to a specific revolution: the French Revolution (of 1789).

21. **A** Remember that a periodic sentence is a long, complex, grammatically correct sentence. This is definitely a long sentence, but it flows well and is grammatically correct.

22. **C** Using POE, you can eliminate all the incorrect answers with ease. Clearly, the passage goes beyond a discussion of theater (A), has nothing to do with political history (E), and is far too scholarly to interest tourists (D). Although, conceivably, it could come from a history text (B), the entire passage only deals with Romanticism, and seems to get into a little too much depth, and controversially, to be appropriate for a history text.

23. **B** Again, POE is the best way to approach this question. Answers (A), (C), (D), and (E) are at least half wrong (therefore completely wrong). Take a look at (B). The author is being ironic when she says in the first line, "My own sex, I hope, will excuse me, if I treat them like rational creatures...." The second part of choice (B), "exposition," is defined as "a setting forth of meaning or intent," and that is exactly what the author is doing in this first paragraph. Answer choice (B) is correct. For the record, note that, in this context, the author's "apology" has nothing to do with being sorry; it most nearly means "defense of an idea."

24. **A** The author addresses women directly and pretends to excuse herself for addressing them as strong, confident people, instead of the weak, overly sentimental creatures that society wants (and expects) them to be.

25. **E** Your choice should boil down to (D) and (E). When the author says, "I wish to persuade women to endeavour to acquire strength, both of mind and body," she means intellectual and physical strength. Had she wanted to stress emotional strength, she would have replaced mind with heart.

26. **E** *Softer* and *weak* are important adjectives of both paragraphs; the author uses them in the second paragraph to tie this paragraph in with the first one.

27. **A** No doubt you can narrow your choices to (A) and (B). The best way to approach this type of question is to substitute in the answer choices for the original word and see which one makes the most sense. Try (A): "...supposed to be the sexual characteristics of the weaker <u>sex</u>....". This seems great, but try (B) too, just in case: "...supposed to be the sexual characteristics of the weaker <u>woman</u>..." Not as good. Naturally, in this case, the weaker sex is woman, but you are asked to find the meaning for "vessel" only. Choice (A) is the best answer.

28. **C** Again, there are only two reasonable answers: (A) and (C). The author states that "the first object of laudable ambition is to obtain a character as a human being, regardless of the distinction of sex." Thus, one must eliminate answer (A) because she is not suggesting that a comparison be made between a man and woman.

29. **A** The author wishes to convince the reader by the force of her cogent arguments and the sincerity of her emotions, so the answer is (A). If you don't have "cogent" on your vocabulary list, put it on now. It means "appealing to the intellect or powers of reasoning; convincing." You can eliminate the other choices: The author states unequivocally that she does not wish to polish her style, to employ the bombast and periodic sentences of a rhetorical style, to write elegantly, or to use flowery diction.

30. **C** The author points out—and rightfully so—that the flowery diction expected of women relegated them to a world outside of that of men. The difference in the social level of men and women was reflected in the way they used language; only men could use the crude words that attempt to express the crude realities of life. Women were not supposed to know those same crude realities, and, therefore, could not use the crude words that fit with those realities.

31. **E** The sugary diction becomes associated with the taste of a cloyingly sweet delicacy; this is an extended metaphor so POE allows you to eliminate (A), (B), and (D). This is not a caricature of women, nor is it a critique of bombast (remember, pompous speech or writing). If you do not know the meaning of "panegyric," then add it to your list of vocabulary. Panegyric means "statement of high praise." It should be clear that the author does not sing the praises of sugary writing.

32. **E** Since, in this passage, the author suggests that women have the capacity to be independent equals of men, she is most likely to agree that if women are educated in the same manner as men, then they would be more likely to be equals with men in the eyes of the world.

33. **A** Use POE, especially if you don't know what answer choice (A) means. (Sardonic means "harsh, bitter, or caustic.") Although sarcasm is stronger than irony, both answer choices (C) and (D) involve saying one thing and meaning the opposite, so both are incorrect: The author means what she says. It is difficult to imagine a feminist author addressing other women in a condescending or haughty fashion. Only answer (A) remains.

34. **C** What is the entire passage about? It is about learning, and most importantly, the reason for learning. This is simply a big-picture question in disguise. In this passage, the writer claims that teaching methodologies are overrated because there are many ways to teach and learn; what is important is a reason for learning.

35. **A** The phrase "So it is with learning," which follows the example of the ways to learn tribal lays, is a big clue that should tell you that an analogy is being used here. Besides, none of the other answers is plausible; POE can lead you with certainty to the correct answer.

36. **C** Don't be thrown off by the use of the term "infinitives" in this question. Infinitives are simply verb forms that function as substantives, while retaining some verb characteristics. Some examples of infinitives are "We want him to win the lottery," or "To go willingly will prove that you are innocent." So this question specifically refers to the line "There is no one who can say that this or that is the best way to know things, to feel things, to see things, to remember things, to apply things, to connect things and that no other will do as well." From the context—and from your own experience, one hopes—learning is a positive experience, so any answer choice that uses a negative adjective should be eliminated. Learning is (not supposed to be) "tedious" (A), "impersonal" (B), "trivial" (D), or even "mechanical" (E); using POE leaves us with only (C). In fact, learning is an active and a varied process.

37. **D** If you understand the passage, you should be able to quickly narrow your choices to (C) and (D); motivation, in the author's words, is fleeting (or momentary). Although the author does not say outright that a motivation is concrete, he does set up a clear rhetorical contrast between motivation and reason. Given that he describes reason as abstract, it figures that motivation should be roughly the opposite—or at least not the same. The only textual clue that tells us motivation is concrete is the word *event*.

38. **E** We have already drawn attention to the string of infinitives in the first paragraph; in the third paragraph, you may have already noticed the parallel series of prepositional phrases (in which the preposition "to" is repeated). Choice (E), or "notable parallelism," is correct.

Let's go through the other choices. An "aphorism" is a pithy saying or proverb. "Syllogistic reasoning" proceeds along the lines of a syllogism: a major premise, a minor premise, and a conclusion. Here is an example of syllogistic reasoning: All Princeton Review books are useful; this is a Princeton Review book; therefore, this book is useful. *Ad hominem* arguments consist of attacks against a person's character. If you were to say, "This book must be awful because you wrote it," you would be adducing an *ad hominem* argument to prove your point.

39. **C** Answers (A) and (B) are snares for the careless reader who fails to consider the context in which the word is used; "god" in this case has nothing to do with religion. The entire second half of the text is the reason for education. One big clue that the author isn't using the word "god" literally, is the phrase "…must have a god to serve, or, even better, several gods." If this were a literal use of "god," then the term would not have been pluralized later.

40. **C** In this case, the authority is Nietzsche, and the author gives us a clear rhetorical statement of his use of analogy in the sentence that follows the quote: "This applies as much to learning as to living."

41. **A** Perhaps this is a good time to review two terms that are closely related: *oxymoron* and *paradox*. An oxymoron is an apparent contradiction of terms; a paradox is an apparent contradiction of ideas. The important word here is *apparent*.

In this case, the last sentence is built on an apparent contradiction of terms: Schooling will be brought to an end if it has no end. Nonsense? No. We are supposed to understand that, in context, the second "end" is synonymous with reason (or goal or objective).

42. **B** If you missed the implications of the final statement, then you could eliminate (C) and (E) and guess. Choices (A) and (D) are similar in meaning, and both imply that the speaker is a politician—of which we have no proof. Choice (B) is your best bet. Of course, if you noticed the allusions to law in the body of the text and the judgment of the final statement, then you may have realized that the passage is the dissenting opinion of a judge in a federal case—and you would have been correct to assume that this was a case that went before the Supreme Court.

43. **B** Perhaps the biggest clue that tells us analogy is being employed is the phrase "upon like grounds." Naturally, almost everyone would agree that it would be unthinkable, for example, to segregate passengers by religion (Catholic and Protestant). If we agree that this (and the other examples) are analogous to the case before the court (segregation of passengers by race), then we are forced to agree with this judge.

44. B Were you tempted to choose (C)? Did you choose (C)? If so, you fell into a trap. Today, it would be normal to expect this judge to propose both civil and racial equality, but the judge bases his arguments solely on the issue of civil rights. In fact, the judge says that the white race is the dominant one "in prestige, in achievements, in education, in wealth, and in power. So, I doubt not, it will continue to be for all time, if it remains true to its great heritage, and holds fast to the principles of constitutional liberty." Based on the passage, the speaker appears not to believe that racial equality will ever be a reality, although civil equality exists.

45. E If you do not know the meaning of the word, begin with POE. Immediately, you will see that (A) and (C) can be eliminated; they mean things that are opposite to the speaker's tone and meaning. If you know that "propitious" is roughly equivalent to (C), "useful," you can eliminate that choice as well. As for choice (B), although "unjust," like "harmful," fits the context, the latter choice is the better synonym for the original term ("pernicious"). Of course, as long as you can narrow the choices down to two or three, you should take a guess even if you are not sure. The definition of pernicious is: "causing great harm."

46. A In this passage, the phrases "may be stricken down by congressional action, or by the courts" and "duty to maintain the supreme law of the land" provide the answer; the Louisiana law is subject to censure by either the United States Congress or the United States Supreme Court.

47. D POE is the way to go on this one. Remember to look for one inappropriate word in each answer. Neither adjective in answer (A) is really appropriate, so you can eliminate (A). Try (B). Although one may argue that the style is "dry," it is not "objective"—the speaker is arguing only one side of an issue; so (B) is out. How about (C)? Of course, the passage could be thought of as "legalistic," but it is not at all "abstract"—so get rid of (C). As for (E), the passage is "probing," but it is certainly not "subtle." The speaker comes right out and says what he believes, calling this decision as pernicious as the Supreme Court's judgment of the Dred Scott Case. (In the Dred Scott case, the Supreme Court upheld a lower court ruling that the state of Louisiana could fine the railroad company for letting African Americans ride in the same carriages as whites, a situation that was prohibited by Louisiana state law.)

48. C The simile in this first sentence compares the great and ancient parliamentary institutions with the august, but somewhat ancient bodies of the members of Parliament. The speaker is warming up his audience with a bit of humor before launching into what amounts to a very serious ultimatum: that the speaker will continue to serve as Prime Minister, but only if they concede to him much greater authority than before (1842).

49. B The speaker is addressing a group of his peers, who are the other members of Parliament. The tricky part here is, of course, the repetition of "Sir," a political convention in Great Britain—it is as if the prime minister were addressing each member of Parliament as an individual. We know that he is the minister of England because of the final sentences; and these sentences also reveal definitively that he is speaking to peers: "Sir, I do not wish to be the Minister of England; but while I have the high honour of holding that Office, I am determined to hold it by no servile tenure. I will only hold that office upon the condition of being unshackled by any other obligations than those of consulting the public interests, and of providing for the public safety."

50. **D** Everything before this line is an introduction to the minister's real message; until this point, he has joked, given a general review of his former motivations and actions as the leader of the Conservative party, and explained his reasons for accepting to serve again as prime minister ("feeling of honour") in spite of his failing health and aged mind ("a burden too great for my physical, and far beyond my intellectual structure"). The transition comes with "But, Sir, I will not take the step with mutilated power and shackled authority." He will do the country and his peers a favor, but only if he is granted much more authority to rule.

51. **E** Eliminate (A), (B), and (D), so you're left with (C) and (E), which do not fit neatly into the nautical terminology. Answer (C) is the one to eliminate. All the other terms fit neatly into the nautical terminology. However, one could stretch a point and claim that "fairly" is related to fair weather; whereas "unshackled" is clearly unrelated to this metaphor.

52. **E** Naturally, the first step is to determine the "dominant point" of the final paragraph. Thankfully, the second paragraph is short—it is the rhetorical summation of his ultimatum. The key phrases are "servile tenure" and "unshackled by any other obligations." Of course, "unfettered" and "unshackled" are synonyms, so the best answer is (E), "unfettered."

53. **C** The minister states unequivocally that honor is his motivation, in the following passage in particular: "and to be relieved from it [the position] with perfect honour would be the greatest favour that could be conferred on me. But as a feeling of honour and strong sense of duty require me to undertake those responsible functions, I declare, Sir, that I am ready to incur these risks, to bear these burdens, and to front all these honourable dangers." The word *honor* comes up numerous times in this excerpt.

54. **C** You should be able to narrow your options to (B) and (C). But be careful! Do you think that the speaker, the most powerful man in Great Britain, allowed his mood to shift or to affect his tone? The speech was carefully constructed, and the tone was coolly calculated when William Gladstone wrote it. The prime minister began with a light tone because he was looking to set up his audience, not because he started his speech in a good mood. In fact, his real mood never shifts: He manipulates tone for maximum effect.

ANSWERS TO THE FREE-RESPONSE SECTION

QUESTION 1

Synthesis Essay

Although it is not perfect, this essay below merits an 8. Its use of language is skilled and it is reasonably well constructed. However, several of its assertions stray from the sources, particularly in the end of the second body paragraph and in the final paragraph. As often happens, this goes hand-in-hand with reliance on repetition rather than evidence to make a point; the author repeats several times that full citizenship requires voting rights, without leaning on anything more than the Anthony argument for support.

Embracing responsibility is an essential step on the path toward maturity. No group of people can become full, contributing members of their community if they are systematically denied the chance to be responsible for matters affecting that community. Equal responsibilities and equal citizenship do not necessarily imply identical roles. In theory, that responsibility need not include voting for everyone, and well-intentioned arguments have been made in this direction. But in practice, no other responsibility is equal to or could substitute for this one; someone denied the responsibility of voting cannot be considered an equal citizen. Thus, women's suffrage is a right that springs directly from equal citizenship; it is not a gift of the legislature.

Susan B. Anthony made precisely this argument in her 1872 defense against the charges of unlawful voting. She grounded her defense in the Constitution's acknowledgment of "the natural right of every individual member" of the country "to a voice and a vote." Per Anthony, the Constitution acknowledges rights; it does not claim "the power to create or to confer" them. This is ultimately the meaning of the Constitutional amendment granting women the right to vote, which says that "the right of citizens...to vote shall not be denied or abridged...on account of sex." This amendment follows the form of the rest of the Bill of Rights: it does not lay out a right explicitly, but rather states that the right exists, and that neither Congress nor the states could restrict it.

As Susan B. Anthony and the 66th Congress both saw, it is essential that all people be given the right to vote so that they may be full, responsible citizens. This point had earlier been made in the cartoon printed as Source F, which illustrates the way a lack of civic participation confines women to trivial matters. People do not tend to engage thoughtfully in issues in which they are legally forbidden from having any influence. It is only by acknowledging women's voting rights that the government acknowledges their complete citizenship, for without the responsibility of voting, women would not be involved in the political process, as required of all full citizens.

Arguments to the contrary, such as Source B (a cartoon showing men confined to gossip and child-rearing, and women in positions of authority and political power), miss the point. No one claims that all citizens are the same, or that granting the vote will turn women into men (or vice versa, probably more terrifying for the male population of the time). Roles within a society can be "separate but equal." But in terms of being responsible citizens of a state or of this country, the right to vote is sacrosanct.

QUESTION 2

Rhetorical Analysis Essay

The sample essay that follows is a strong one; the writer could expect to receive a score of 8 with this work. One important thing to note about this essay is the structure. The writer avoids the common error made in comparison and contrast essays; she does NOT write first about one review in one paragraph and another in a second paragraph. That said, inside each paragraph, the discussion of the articles is clearly segregated; this could have been handled more deftly, but this organization gets the job done. The introduction is a bit on the long side, but it provides a clear outline of the material and engages the reader thoroughly.

Mary Shelley's Frankenstein is, in modern times, heralded as a classic, great work of art. However, when it was first published in 1818, few people regarded it as a worthy work of literary art. As seen in the two passages taken from the critics' reviews of the novel, Frankenstein inspired extreme sentiments and reactions—readers either loved and enjoyed it or abhorred it and were disgusted by it. The two reviews presented convey the two contrasting emotions, as if in response to each other. The first, an anonymous piece from The Quarterly Review, criticizes Mary Shelley's work, using vernacular and plain (yet grotesque) language and popular culture allusions and standards to illustrate the author's condemnation of Frankenstein. Conversely, Sir Walter Scott's review from Blackwood's Edinburgh Magazine is itself written in a worthy literary manner, using heightened terms, literary terms, and quotations from other works to demonstrate his positive point of view. In the 1800s, there were many magazines available for the literate to purchase and indulge in, some were professional journals intended for those who worked in a particular industry (like science or literature), while others were broader publications for the general public. The difference between the two kinds was always (and still is) readily apparent in the type of language used by the authors of the magazine's articles. It can be surmised that Blackwood's Edinburgh Magazine was intended for those immersed in literature, or at least those who were highly educated. Scott's writing is romantic, mentioning "daemons," "the lovely and helpless" and "creature" and "persecutor." All these words and phrases are characteristic of a gothic or a romantic novel, in which the reader is presented with a tortured hero who is persecuted in some form and is faced with something lovely (usually a female). Phrases such as "resentment toward the human race," "expedients for exciting terror," and "uncommon powers of poetic imagination" are meant for a reader with a heightened vocabulary; one capable of understanding Scott's references and intentions. However, juxtaposed with Sir Walter Scott's review, the anonymous review from The Quarterly Review (a seemingly plain publication) is straightforward and simple. Instead of embellishing or elaborating, the author uses language like "strong and striking language," "tissue of horrible and disgusting absurdity," and "fatigues the feelings" to criticize the novel. Overall, the article has a condescending tone; in summarizing the conclusion of the novel, the author adds in his own commentary, sarcastically remarking on the implausibility of the entire situation. All his opinions are presented in a clear, plain manner, which serves to make very clear his utter loathing of Mary Shelley's work.

Both Scott and the anonymous author make use of popular conventions, standards, and allusions of their time period. However, their references again establish a distinct difference between the two articles. Scott, in his piece, quotes <u>Macbeth</u>, by William Shakespeare, to illustrate his point that <u>Frankenstein</u>, while shocking, cannot shock an already jaded audience. Furthermore, he speaks of terror being "employed by the romantic writers of the age" mentioning literary conventions. Another convention is brought up when he states that Shelley does not utilize "hyperbolic Germanisms" with which tales of wonder are usually told. The anonymous author, on the other hand, never quotes another literary work to support his ideas. He alludes to Bedlam, "Mad Bess," and "Mad Tom" as popular cultural figures. Continuing with his appeal to the masses, the anonymous author points out that <u>Frankenstein</u> "inculcates no lessons of conduct, manners or morality." Unlikely popular literature of the time, Shelley's novel disregards the conventions of morals and lessons learned.

Though the two reviews were written in highly different forms of language, both convey their point of view clearly. Scott's review was a positive one, meant for an elite readership. The anonymous author, however, wrote a disgusted condemnation for the pious masses.

QUESTION 3

Argumentative Essay

The following sample essay is very strong. The one noticeable flaw is the discussion of Switzerland; this detour pertains to neutrality, but it is not clear how it relates to racism. It is difficult to gauge just how deleterious the flaw may be. Certainly, the essay would earn a score of at least 7 and may get an 8.

Often, it is believed that if one ignores an issue or a problem, it will merely disappear. Mothers tell their children to ignore bullies, and even the Bible instructs us to turn the other cheek. However, when certain issues are not dealt with, they can fester until they become something far more serious than they were originally; racism is one such issue. As the passage suggests, colorblindness and neutrality are not equalizers; they are merely blinders that allow people to continue as though nothing is out of balance. By adopting a "neutral stand" and by failing to recognize the innate differences between racial groups, one not only perpetuates racism, but also promotes the homogenization of cultures and races, in itself a form of racism.

Sooner or later, the issues one faces must be dealt with. Ignorance, in this case, is not bliss; the longer a problem is put aside, the harder it is to conquer when one finally decides to face it. In the United States, the quintessential example of such a problem is racism. The 1950s and 1960s were a demonstration of just what can happen when an entire nation pretends that nothing is wrong or unequal. Race riots all over the country were the culmination of a race's mounting frustrations. The passage states that "identifying problems and actively promoting solutions are necessary to effect useful change." In fact change, in the form of various civil rights legislatures, only took place when racism was recognized and dealt with by the federal government. Only strong action, like the integration of the Central High School in Little Rock, Arkansas, could ever hope to remedy the situation. By bringing the problem into the spotlight and making everyone consider it and its implications, the government steps toward change, progress, and equality.

The only successful neutral stance ever taken in history was by Switzerland, during all the wars that raged around the country's borders. However, a neutral stance requires more effort to maintain than a stance that is evidently one-sided, because neutrality involves denying the "social and historical context for every situation...[and]... ignoring personal contexts." When this occurs, it would seem that one is assenting that we are all the same equal people, yet that very assertion is flawed, since it eliminates the "differences that exist." If one does not take a side or a stance, one is, in effect, resigning oneself to the current state of affairs, the status quo. As the author of the passage points out, ignoring inequalities and differences allows "the inequalities to continue to exist, given that [one] wouldn't do anything to help change them." Until the public began noticing and sympathizing with the victims of racism, it took no collective action to change the status quo. Finally recognizing the inequality which was the status quo, the public could no longer remain neutral—it split into those who wanted to maintain the status quo and those who wanted to change it and improve the situation.

In essence, neutrality is supposed to be an equalizer because it declares that there are no differences between human beings. However, that denial takes away that which makes us inherently human. Without our cultures and races, we would have nothing to separate one person from another. Thus neutrality states that it is better for a group of people to lack differences than to embrace those differences. Racism is looking down on and rejecting the differences between two people. In much the same way, neutrality turns a blind eye to differences, lending validity to ignorance. Without action and discussion, societies become stale. It is only with a firm stance that one can hope to incite progress and reform; there must be recognition and a definite lack of neutrality if racism is to be prevented. "Being neutral is consenting to the status quo," a status quo which is unequal, unfair, and socially unbalanced.

HOW TO SCORE PRACTICE TEST 1

SECTION I: MULTIPLE-CHOICE

$$\underset{\substack{\text{Number of Correct} \\ \text{(out of 54)}}}{\underline{\hspace{3cm}}} \times 1.2500 = \underset{\substack{\text{Weighted} \\ \text{Section I Score} \\ \text{(Do not round)}}}{\underline{\hspace{3cm}}}$$

SECTION II: FREE RESPONSE

(See if you can find a teacher or classmate to score your essays using the guidelines in Chapter 3.)

Question 1 $\underset{\text{(out of 9)}}{\underline{\hspace{2.5cm}}} \times 3.0556 = \underset{\text{(Do not round)}}{\underline{\hspace{2.5cm}}}$

Question 2 $\underset{\text{(out of 9)}}{\underline{\hspace{2.5cm}}} \times 3.0556 = \underset{\text{(Do not round)}}{\underline{\hspace{2.5cm}}}$

Question 3 $\underset{\text{(out of 9)}}{\underline{\hspace{2.5cm}}} \times 3.0556 = \underset{\text{(Do not round)}}{\underline{\hspace{2.5cm}}}$

AP Score Conversion Chart English Language and Composition	
Composite Score Range	AP Score
112–150	5
98–111	4
80–97	3
55–79	2
0–54	1

Sum $= \underset{\substack{\text{Weighted Section II} \\ \text{Score (Do not round)}}}{\underline{\hspace{3cm}}}$

COMPOSITE SCORE

$$\underset{\substack{\text{Weighted} \\ \text{Section I Score}}}{\underline{\hspace{2.5cm}}} + \underset{\substack{\text{Weighted} \\ \text{Section II Score}}}{\underline{\hspace{2.5cm}}} = \underset{\substack{\text{Composite Score} \\ \text{(Round to nearest} \\ \text{whole number)}}}{\underline{\hspace{2.5cm}}}$$

14

Practice Test 2

AP® English Language and Composition Exam

DO NOT OPEN THIS BOOKLET UNTIL YOU ARE TOLD TO DO SO.

At a Glance

Total Time
1 hour
Number of Questions
54
Percent of Total Grade
45%
Writing Instrument
Pencil required

Instructions

Section I of this examination contains 54 multiple-choice questions. Fill in only the ovals for numbers 1 through 54 on your answer sheet.

Indicate all of your answers to the multiple-choice questions on the answer sheet. No credit will be given for anything written in this exam booklet, but you may use the booklet for notes or scratch work. After you have decided which of the suggested answers is best, completely fill in the corresponding oval on the answer sheet. Give only one answer to each question. If you change an answer, be sure that the previous mark is erased completely. Here is a sample question and answer.

Sample Question   Sample Answer

Chicago is a   Ⓐ ● Ⓒ Ⓓ Ⓔ
(A) state
(B) city
(C) country
(D) continent
(E) village

Use your time effectively, working as quickly as you can without losing accuracy. Do not spend too much time on any one question. Go on to other questions and come back to the ones you have not answered if you have time. It is not expected that everyone will know the answers to all the multiple-choice questions.

About Guessing

Many candidates wonder whether or not to guess the answers to questions about which they are not certain. Multiple choice scores are based on the number of questions answered correctly. Points are not deducted for incorrect answers, and no points are awarded for unanswered questions. Because points are not deducted for incorrect answers, you are encouraged to answer all multiple-choice questions. On any questions you do not know the answer to, you should eliminate as many choices as you can, and then select the best answer among the remaining choices.

This page intentionally left blank.

ENGLISH LANGUAGE AND COMPOSITION
SECTION I
Time—1 hour

Directions: This part consists of selections from prose works and questions on their content, form, and style. After reading each passage, choose the best answer to each question and completely fill in the corresponding oval on the answer sheet.

Note: Pay particular attention to the requirement of questions that contain the words NOT, LEAST, or EXCEPT.

Questions 1-11. Read the following passage carefully before you choose your answers.

(The following passage is from Samuel Johnson's Life of Sir Thomas Browne, *1756.)*

His exuberance of knowledge, and plenitude of
ideas, sometimes obstruct the tendency of his reasoning
and the clearness of his decisions: on whatever subject
Line he employed his mind, there started up immediately so
5 many images before him, that he lost one by grasping
another. His memory supplied him with so many
illustrations, parallel or dependent notions, that he
was always starting into collateral considerations;
but the spirit and vigour of his pursuit always gives
10 delight; and the reader follows him, without reluctance,
through his mazes, in themselves flowery and pleasing,
and ending at the point originally in view.
　　"To have great excellencies and great faults, *'magnæ
virtutes nec minora vitia,'* is the poesy," says our author,
15 "of the best natures." This poesy may be properly
applied to the style of Browne; it is vigorous, but
rugged; it is learned, but pedantick; it is deep, but
obscure; it strikes, but does not please; it commands,
but does not allure; his tropes are harsh, and his
20 combinations uncouth.
　　He fell into an age in which our language began
to lose the stability which it had obtained in the time
of Elizabeth; and was considered by every writer as
a subject on which he might try his plastick skill, by
25 moulding it according to his own fancy. Milton, in
consequence of this encroaching license, began to
introduce the Latin idiom: and Browne, though he
gave less disturbance to our structures in phraseology,
yet poured in a multitude of exotick words; many,
30 indeed, useful and significant, which, if rejected, must
be supplied by circumlocution, such as commensality,
for the state of many living at the same table; but many
superfluous, as a paralogical, for an unreasonable
doubt; and some so obscure, that they conceal his
35 meaning rather than explain it, as arthritical analogies,
for parts that serve some animals in the place of joints.
　　His style is, indeed, a tissue of many languages;
a mixture of heterogeneous words, brought
together from distant regions, with terms originally
40 appropriated to one art, and drawn by violence into

the service of another. He must, however, be confessed
to have augmented our philosophical diction; and, in
defence of his uncommon words and expressions, we
must consider, that he had uncommon sentiments, and
45 was not content to express, in many words, that idea
for which any language could supply a single term.
　　But his innovations are sometimes pleasing, and
his temerities happy: he has many "verba ardentia"
forcible expressions, which he would never have found,
50 but by venturing to the utmost verge of propriety; and
flights which would never have been reached, but by
one who had very little fear of the shame of falling.

1. The reader can infer from the first paragraph that
　some critics have

　　(A) chastised Browne for his inability to reason
　　(B) lauded Browne's frequent linear explanations
　　(C) complained about Browne's lack of clarity
　　(D) compared Browne with Shakespeare
　　(E) compared the author of the passage with
　　　　Browne

2. In context, "poesy" (line 14) most nearly means

　　(A) poetry
　　(B) inspiration for writing
　　(C) sentimental thoughts
　　(D) flowery writing
　　(E) poetic dreaming

3. The meaning of the phrase *magnæ virtutes nec minora
　vitia* (lines 13-14)

　　(A) can be ascertained only if one understands
　　　　Latin
　　(B) becomes clear at the end of the paragraph
　　(C) is obvious
　　(D) has been lost over the centuries
　　(E) was known only to Browne

GO ON TO THE NEXT PAGE.

4. In the second paragraph, the author

   (A) is openly critical of Browne's style
   (B) hints that Browne's writing is pedantic
   (C) justifies the strength of Browne's style
   (D) argues in favor of a reexamination of Browne's style
   (E) suggests that Browne's writing is too facile

5. The author modifies the strict parallelism of "it is vigorous, but rugged; it is learned, but pedantick; it is deep, but obscure; it strikes, but does not please; it commands, but does not allure; his tropes are harsh, and his combinations uncouth" (lines 16-20) to

   (A) better define his point of view
   (B) keep the reader off balance
   (C) maintain a sense of imbalance
   (D) show more respect for Browne's accomplishments
   (E) to obfuscate his real opinions

6. According to the author, Browne lived at a time of significant

   (A) linguistic experimentation
   (B) literary conservatism
   (C) linguistic stability
   (D) metaphorical license
   (E) impoverishment of the English language

7. In lines 27-36 ("Browne, though he gave less disturbance...in the place of joints"), the author classifies Browne's diction in a manner that proceeds from

   (A) interesting, to captivating, to intriguing
   (B) appropriate, to inappropriate, to superfluous
   (C) interesting, to intriguing, to disappointing
   (D) useful, to unhelpful, to deleterious
   (E) appropriate, to inappropriate, to intriguing

8. The author posits that Browne's unusual diction can be tied to his desire

   (A) to mystify his readers
   (B) to develop English phraseology
   (C) to enrich the English language
   (D) to set himself apart from other authors of his time
   (E) to express exactly his unusual thoughts

9. According to the author, Browne's style is marked by

   (A) heteroclite diction
   (B) homogeneous words
   (C) mundane vocabulary
   (D) humorous phrases
   (E) heterogeneous tropes

10. Which of the following best summarizes the passage?

    (A) an impartial reconsideration of Browne's style
    (B) a scathing critique by a rival
    (C) a manifesto by one of Browne's colleagues
    (D) a comparative study of Milton and Browne
    (E) a virulent polemic

11. The author's tone in this passage is best described as

    (A) sarcastic and doctrinaire
    (B) analytical and scholarly
    (C) expository and harsh
    (D) indulgent and condescending
    (E) capricious and sentimental

GO ON TO THE NEXT PAGE.

Questions 12-20. Read the following passage carefully before you choose your answers.

(The following passage is excerpted from an article by Virginia Woolf that was first published in 1919.)

But is it upon the heroines that we would cast a final glance. "I have always been finding out my religion since I was a little girl," says Dorothea Casaubon. "I
Line used to pray so much—now I hardly ever pray. I try
5 not to have desires merely for myself..." She is speaking for them all. That is their problem. They cannot live without religion, and they start out on the search for one when they are little girls. Each has the deep feminine passion for goodness, which makes the place
10 where she stands in aspiration and agony the heart of the book—still and cloistered like a place of worship, but that she no longer knows to whom to pray. In learning they seek their goal; in the ordinary tasks of womanhood; in the wider service of their kind. They
15 do not find what they seek, and we cannot wonder. The ancient consciousness of woman, charged with suffering and sensibility, and for so many ages dumb, seems in them to have brimmed and overflowed and uttered a demand for something—they scarcely know
20 what—for something that is perhaps incompatible with the facts of human existence. George Eliot had far too strong an intelligence to tamper with those facts, and too broad a humour to mitigate the truth because it was a stern one. Save for the supreme courage of
25 their endeavour, the struggle ends, for her heroines, in tragedy, or in a compromise that is even more melancholy. But their story is the incomplete version of the story that is George Eliot herself. For her, too, the burden and the complexity of womanhood were
30 not enough; she must reach beyond the sanctuary and pluck for herself the strange bright fruits of art and knowledge. Clasping them as few women have ever clasped them, she would not renounce her own inheritance—the difference of view, the difference
35 of standard—nor accept an inappropriate reward. Thus we behold her, a memorable figure, inordinately praised and shrinking from her fame, despondent, reserved, shuddering back into the arms of love as if there alone were satisfaction and, it might be,
40 justification, at the same time reaching out with "a fastidious yet hungry ambition" for all that life could offer the free and inquiring mind and confronting her feminine aspirations with the real world of men. Triumphant was the issue for her, whatever it may have
45 been for her creations, and as we recollect all that she dared and achieved, how with every obstacle against her—sex and health and convention—she sought more knowledge and more freedom till the body, weighted with its double burden, sank worn out, we must lay
50 upon her grave whatever we have it in our power to bestow of laurel and rose.

12. The speaker in the passage above can be described best as

(A) a family member of George Eliot
(B) a member of the clergy
(C) a student
(D) a chauvinist literary critic
(E) a professional writer

13. According to the speaker, George Eliot's heroines are "cloistered" (line 11) because they are

(A) in a church
(B) essentially alone
(C) in a monastery
(D) imprisoned in cloisters
(E) lost in prayer

14. In context, "the facts of human existence" (line 21)

(A) restrict both men and women
(B) restrict women only
(C) are only applicable to Eliot's heroines
(D) pertain to any literary character
(E) pertain to men only

15. "Save for" (line 24) most nearly means

(A) except for
(B) saving
(C) safe for
(D) guarding against
(E) keeping in mind

16. The "differences" mentioned in line 34 pertain to Eliot's

(A) profession
(B) class
(C) upbringing
(D) education
(E) gender

17. According to the speaker, Eliot

(A) enjoyed excellent health
(B) suffered from her independence and knowledge
(C) was prevented from attaining fame by men
(D) was very unlike the heroines of her books
(E) repudiated her feminine nature

GO ON TO THE NEXT PAGE.

18. In the sentence beginning "Thus we behold her" (lines 36-43), the speaker employs all of the following EXCEPT

    (A) apposition
    (B) hyperbole
    (C) personification
    (D) relative clauses
    (E) parallelism

19. It is reasonable to assume that the phrase "a fastidious yet hungry ambition" (lines 40-41)

    (A) is spoken by one of Eliot's heroines
    (B) comes from one of the speaker's literary works
    (C) is borrowed from one of Eliot's critics
    (D) is not to be taken seriously
    (E) does not represent the speaker's point of view

20. Generally, the style of the entire passage is best defined as

    (A) effusive and disorganized
    (B) pedantic and terse
    (C) sympathetic and concrete
    (D) abstract and metaphysical
    (E) intellectual and cynical

GO ON TO THE NEXT PAGE.

Questions 21-25. Read the following passage carefully before you choose your answers.

(The following passage is excerpted from an address on the significance of education delivered in 1816.)

It will be readily admitted, that a population trained in regular habits of temperance, industry, and sobriety; of genuine charity for the opinions of all
Line mankind, founded on the only knowledge that can
5 implant true charity in the breast of any human being; trained also in a sincere desire to do good to the utmost of their power, and without any exception, to every one of their fellow creatures, cannot, even by their example alone, do otherwise than materially increase
10 the welfare and advantages of the neighbourhood in which such a population may be situated. To feel the due weight of this consideration, only imagine to yourselves 2,000 or 3,000 human beings trained in habits of licentiousness, and allowed to remain in
15 gross ignorance. How much, in such a case, would not the peace, quiet, comfort, and happiness of the neighbourhood be destroyed! But there is not anything I have done, or purpose to do, which is not intended to benefit my fellow-creatures to the greatest extent
20 that my operations can embrace. I wish to benefit all equally; but circumstances limit my present measures for the public good within a narrow circle. I must begin to act at some point; and a combination of singular events has fixed that point at this establishment. The
25 first and greatest advantages will therefore centre here. But, in unison with the principle thus stated, it has ever been my intention that as this Institution, when completed, will accommodate more than the children of parents resident at the village, any persons living
30 at Lanark, or in the neighbourhood anywhere around, who cannot well afford to educate their children, shall be at liberty, on mentioning their wishes, to send them to this place, where they will experience the same care and attention as those who belong to the establishment.
35 Nor will there be any distinction made between the children of those parents who are deemed the worst, and of those who may be esteemed the best, members of society: rather, indeed, would I prefer to receive the offspring of the worst, if they shall be sent at an early
40 age; because they really require more of our care and pity; and by well training these, society will be more essentially benefited, than if the like attention were paid to those whose parents are educating them in comparatively good habits. The system now preparing,
45 and which will ultimately be brought into full practice, is to effect a complete change in all our sentiments and conduct towards those poor miserable creatures whom the errors of past times have denominated the bad, the worthless, and the wicked. A more enlarged and
50 better knowledge of human nature will make it evident

that, in strict justice, those who apply these terms to their fellow-men are not only the most ignorant, but are themselves the immediate causes of more misery in the world than those whom they call the outcasts
55 of society. They are, therefore, correctly speaking, the most wicked and worthless; and were they not grossly deceived, and rendered blind from infancy, they would become conscious of the lamentably extensive evils, which, by their well-intended but most mistaken
60 conduct, they have, during so long a period, inflicted on their fellow-men. But the veil of darkness must be removed from their eyes; their erroneous proceedings must be made so palpable that they shall thenceforth reject them with horror. Yes! They will reject with
65 horror even those notions which hitherto they have from infancy been taught to value beyond price.

21. In general, the passage reveals a point of view that is

(A) philanthropic and utopian
(B) pessimistic and cynical
(C) altruistic and elitist
(D) quixotic and irrational
(E) positivist and unreasonable

22. The Institution (line 27) is

(A) a hospital
(B) a town
(C) an asylum
(D) a school
(E) a church

23. The sentence that begins "They are, therefore, correctly speaking, the most wicked and worthless…" (lines 55-61) serves to

(A) explain a paradox
(B) prepare an antithesis
(C) present an analogy
(D) resolve an inconsistency
(E) summarize a theme

GO ON TO THE NEXT PAGE.

24. "They" (line 64) refers to

    (A) the poor
    (B) the wealthy
    (C) the inhabitants of Lanark
    (D) the inhabitants of neighboring areas
    (E) all of the above

25. The speaker appears most interested in

    (A) establishing mercantile and financial
        establishments
    (B) creating more employment and cultural
        opportunities
    (C) abolishing socioeconomic and cultural
        differences
    (D) discussing social conduct and poverty
    (E) imparting knowledge and moral values

GO ON TO THE NEXT PAGE.

Questions 26-32. Read the following passage carefully before you choose your answers.

The following passage is from The Souls of Black Folk, *by American sociologist W. E. B. Du Bois, published in 1903.)*

And yet, being a problem is a strange experience— peculiar even for one who has never been anything else, save perhaps in babyhood and in Europe. It
Line is in the early days of rollicking boyhood that the
5 revelation first bursts upon one, all in a day, as it were. I remember well when the shadow swept across me. I was a little thing, away up in the hills of New England, where the dark Housatonic winds between Hoosac and Taghkanic to the sea. In a wee wooden schoolhouse,
10 something put it into the boys' and girls' heads to buy gorgeous visiting-cards—ten cents a package—and exchange. The exchange was merry, till one girl, a tall newcomer, refused my card—refused it peremptorily, with a glance. Then it dawned upon me with a certain
15 suddenness that I was different from the others; or like, mayhap, in heart and life and longing, but shut out from their world by a vast veil. I had thereafter no desire to tear down that veil, to creep through; I held all beyond it in common contempt, and lived above it
20 in a region of blue sky and great wandering shadows. That sky was bluest when I could beat my mates at examination-time, or beat them at a foot-race, or even beat their stringy heads. Alas, with the years all this fine contempt began to fade; for the worlds I longed
25 for, and all their dazzling opportunities, were theirs, not mine. But they should not keep these prizes, I said; some, all, I would wrest from them. Just how I would do it I could never decide: by reading law, by healing the sick, by telling the wonderful tales that swam in my
30 head—some way. With other black boys the strife was not so fiercely sunny: their youth shrunk into tasteless sycophancy, or into silent hatred of the pale world about them and mocking distrust of everything white; or wasted itself in a bitter cry, Why did God make me
35 an outcast and a stranger in mine own house? The shades of the prison-house closed round about us all: walls strait and stubborn to the whitest, but relentlessly narrow, tall, and unscalable to sons of night who must plod darkly on in resignation, or beat unavailing palms
40 against the stone, or steadily, half hopelessly, watch the streak of blue above.

26. The speaker was a problem because

  (A) of his ambition
  (B) he was involved in schoolyard fights
  (C) he was contemptuous of his peers
  (D) of his race
  (E) of his upbringing

27. In this passage, the anecdote of the visiting-cards serves as

  (A) an epiphany for the speaker
  (B) a moment of triumph for the speaker
  (C) a revelation for the reader
  (D) a turning point for the school
  (E) a chance for redemption for the speaker

28. After presenting the incident of the visiting-cards, the speaker controls the rest of the passage by employing

  (A) repeated appeals to authority
  (B) a series of euphemisms
  (C) a series of analogies
  (D) two extended metaphors
  (E) self-deprecating humor

29. The "sons of night" (line 38) are

  (A) evil young men
  (B) African American boys
  (C) sons of evil parents
  (D) lost souls
  (E) prisoners

30. One can infer from the passage all of the following EXCEPT that

  (A) the speaker considered himself inferior to his white peers
  (B) the speaker considered himself superior to his African American peers
  (C) the other African American boys treated their white peers with deference
  (D) the speaker was superior to his white peers in many ways
  (E) the speaker felt isolated from both white and African American peers

31. The speaker's contempt wanes and is replaced by

  (A) a commitment to become a famous professional
  (B) a pledge to beat his peers in athletic contests
  (C) a helpless rage against society
  (D) a spirit of revenge
  (E) actions that eventually lead him to prison

32. The tone of this passage can NOT be described as

  (A) self-aware
  (B) decisive
  (C) fervent
  (D) reflective
  (E) laudatory

GO ON TO THE NEXT PAGE.

Questions 33-39. Read the following passage carefully before you choose your answers.

(The following passage is from the Lincoln-Douglas Debates of 1858.)

Now, I hold that Illinois had a right to abolish and prohibit slavery as she did, and I hold that Kentucky has the same right to continue and protect slavery
Line that Illinois had to abolish it. I hold that New York
5 had as much right to abolish slavery as Virginia has to continue it, and that each and every State of this Union is a sovereign power, with the right to do as it pleases upon this question of slavery, and upon all its domestic institutions. Slavery is not the only
10 question which comes up in this controversy. There is a far more important one to you, and that is, what shall be done with the free negro? We have settled the slavery question as far as we are concerned; we have prohibited it in Illinois forever, and in doing so, I think
15 we have done wisely, and there is no man in the State who would be more strenuous in his opposition to the introduction of slavery than I would; but when we settled it for our selves, we exhausted all our power over that subject. We have done our whole duty, and
20 can do no more. We must leave each and every other State to decide for itself the same question. In relation to the policy to be pursued toward the free negroes, we have said that they shall not vote; whilst Maine, on the other hand, has said that they shall vote. Maine is
25 a sovereign State, and has the power to regulate the qualifications of voters within her limits. I would never consent to confer the right of voting and of citizenship upon a negro, but still I am not going to quarrel with Maine for differing from me in opinion. Let Maine take
30 care of her own negroes, and fix the qualifications of her own voters to suit herself, without interfering with Illinois, and Illinois will not interfere with Maine. So with the State of New York. She allows the negro to vote provided he owns two hundred and fifty dollars'
35 worth of property, but not otherwise. While I would not make any distinction whatever between a negro who held property and one who did not, yet if the sovereign State of New York chooses to make that distinction it is her business and not mine, and I will
40 not quarrel with her for it. She can do as she pleases on this question if she minds her own business, and we will do the same thing. Now, my friends, if we will only act conscientiously and rigidly upon this great principle of popular sovereignty, which guarantees to
45 each State and Territory the right to do as it pleases on all things, local and domestic, instead of Congress interfering, we will continue at peace one with another. Why should Illinois be at war with Missouri, or Kentucky with Ohio, or Virginia, with New York,
50 merely because their institutions differ? Our fathers intended that our institutions should differ. They knew that the North and the South, having different climates, productions, and interests, required different institutions. This doctrine of Mr. Lincoln, of uniformity
55 among the institutions of the different States, is a new doctrine, never dreamed of by Washington, Madison, or the framers of this government. Mr. Lincoln and the Republican party set themselves up as wiser than these men who made this government, which has
60 flourished for seventy years under the principle of popular sovereignty, recognizing the right of each State to do as it pleased. Under that principle, we have grown from a nation of three or four millions to a nation of about thirty millions of people; we have
65 crossed the Allegheny mountains and filled up the whole Northwest, turning the prairie into a garden, and building up churches and schools, thus spreading civilization and Christianity where before there was nothing but savage barbarism. Under that principle we
70 have become, from a feeble nation, the most powerful on the face of the earth, and if we only adhere to that principle, we can go forward increasing in territory, in power, in strength, and in glory until the Republic of America shall be the north star that shall guide the
75 friend of freedom throughout the civilized world. And why can we not adhere to the great principle of self-government upon which our institutions were originally based? I believe that this new doctrine preached by Mr. Lincoln and his party will dissolve
80 the Union if it succeeds. They are trying to array all the Northern States in one body against the South, to excite a sectional war between the free States and the slave States, in order that the one or the other may be driven to the wall.

33. In this passage the speaker's purpose is to

(A) analyze the causes of slavery
(B) argue in favor of states' rights
(C) criticize individual states
(D) describe the advantages of a federal government
(E) argue in favor of slavery

34. Which of the following best describes the tone of the passage?

(A) mock enthusiasm
(B) righteous indignation
(C) well-reasoned polemic
(D) objective rationalization
(E) ironic detachment

GO ON TO THE NEXT PAGE.

35. In the first two sentences (lines 1-9), the speaker grounds his central idea on which of the following rhetorical strategies?

    (A) inductive reasoning
    (B) deductive reasoning
    (C) description
    (D) classification
    (E) appeal to ignorance

36. The most significant rhetorical shift in the passage begins with

    (A) "So with the State of New York." (lines 32-33)
    (B) "Now, my friends…" (line 42)
    (C) "Why should Illinois be at war with Missouri…" (line 48)
    (D) "Under that principle…" (line 69)
    (E) "I believe that this new doctrine…" (line 78)

37. The speaker substantiates his central idea with

    (A) clever anecdotes
    (B) innovative symbols
    (C) unusual paradoxes
    (D) extended metaphors
    (E) appeal to authority

38. From the passage, it appears that the speaker's personal view is that African Americans

    (A) should be slaves and should not be allowed to hold property
    (B) should not be slaves and should be allowed to vote
    (C) should not be free but should be allowed to hold some property
    (D) should be free but not allowed to vote
    (E) should be allowed to hold property and to vote

39. In the final lines of the passage, the speaker attempts to win over his audience by

    (A) inspiring confidence
    (B) shifting blame
    (C) instilling fear
    (D) reconciling differences
    (E) overstating a problem

GO ON TO THE NEXT PAGE.

Questions 40-46. Read the following passage carefully before you choose your answers.

(The following passage is excerpted from an essay published in a literary journal in 1860.)

Observe, the merchant's function (or manufacturer's, for in the broad sense in which it is here used the word must be understood to include
Line both) is to provide for the nation. It is no more his
5 function to get profit for himself out of that provision than it is a clergyman's function to get his stipend. This stipend is a due and necessary adjunct, but not the object of his life, if he be a true clergyman, any more than his fee (or honorarium) is the object of life
10 to a true physician. Neither is his fee the object of life to a true merchant. All three, if true men, have a work to be done irrespective of fee—to be done even at any cost, or for quite the contrary of fee; the pastor's function being to teach, the physician's to heal, and the
15 merchant's, as I have said, to provide. That is to say, he has to understand to their very root the qualities of the thing he deals in, and the means of obtaining or producing it; and he has to apply all his sagacity and energy to the producing or obtaining it in perfect state,
20 and distributing it at the cheapest possible price where it is most needed.
And because the production or obtaining of any commodity involves necessarily the agency of many lives and hands, the merchant becomes in the course
25 of his business the master and governor of large masses of men in a more direct, though less confessed way, than a military officer or pastor; so that on him falls, in great part, the responsibility for the kind of life they lead: and it becomes his duty, not only to be
30 always considering how to produce what he sells, in the purest and cheapest forms, but how to make the various employments involved in the production, or transference of it, most beneficial to the men employed.
And as into these two functions, requiring for
35 their right exercise the highest intelligence, as well as patience, kindness, and tact, the merchant is bound to put all his energy, so for their just discharge he is bound, as soldier or physician is bound, to give up, if need be, his life, in such way as it may be demanded of
40 him. Two main points he has in his providing function to maintain: first, his engagements (faithfulness to engagements being the real root of all possibilities, in commerce); and, secondly, the perfectness and purity of the thing provided; so that, rather than fail
45 in any engagement, or consent to any deterioration, adulteration, or unjust and exorbitant price of that which he provides, he is bound to meet fearlessly any form of distress, poverty, or labour, which may, through maintenance of these points, come upon him.

40. The author relies principally on which rhetorical strategy?

(A) appeal to authority
(B) classification
(C) description
(D) induction
(E) analogy

41. According to the author, a merchant is

(A) not motivated primarily by the prospect of making a profit
(B) more devoted to material gain than a clergyman
(C) less focused on making money than is a physician
(D) essentially different from a manufacturer
(E) wholly dedicated to material gain

42. In line 7, "adjunct" most nearly means

(A) accompaniment
(B) evil
(C) adjustment
(D) bonus
(E) addition

43. "Agency" (line 23) is directly related semantically to

(A) "business" (line 25)
(B) "merchant" (line 24)
(C) "master" (line 25)
(D) "commodity" (line 23)
(E) "duty" (line 29)

44. The author uses "hands" (line 24)

(A) as a synecdoche
(B) to reinforce the manual aspect of most labor of his time
(C) to attenuate the repetition of the word "men"
(D) as a concrete image
(E) all of the above

GO ON TO THE NEXT PAGE.

45. The "two functions" in line 34 are

    (A) earning high profits and pacifying the workers
    (B) manufacturing a good, cheap product and providing for workers
    (C) exploiting the workers and maximizing profits
    (D) manufacturing good products and making good profits
    (E) dealing with unions and keeping profits high

46. Most likely, the author would

    (A) support Marxism
    (B) neither like nor dislike socialism
    (C) support capitalism
    (D) support anticlerical groups
    (E) dislike the medical profession

GO ON TO THE NEXT PAGE.

Questions 47-50. Read the following passage carefully before you choose your answers.

(The following passage is excerpted from an influential work published in 1839.)

This archipelago consists of ten principal islands, of which five exceed the others in size. They are situated under the Equator, and between five and six hundred
Line miles westward of the coast of America. They are all
5 formed of volcanic rocks; a few fragments of granite curiously glazed and altered by the heat, can hardly be considered as an exception. Some of the craters, surmounting the larger islands, are of immense size, and they rise to a height of between three and four
10 thousand feet. Their flanks are studded by innumerable smaller orifices. I scarcely hesitate to affirm, that there must be in the whole archipelago at least two thousand craters. These consist either of lava or scoriae, or of finely-stratified, sandstone-like tuff. Most of the latter
15 are beautifully symmetrical; they owe their origin to eruptions of volcanic mud without any lava: it is a remarkable circumstance that every one of the twenty-eight tuff-craters which were examined had their southern sides either much lower than the other
20 sides, or quite broken down and removed. As all these craters apparently have been formed when standing in the sea, and as the waves from the trade wind and the swell from the open Pacific here unite their forces on the southern coasts of all the islands, this singular
25 uniformity in the broken state of the craters, composed of the soft and yielding tuff, is easily explained.

47. This passage is most notable for its

(A) meticulous classification
(B) unusual point of view
(C) precise description
(D) resourceful analogies
(E) lyrical prose

48. Most likely, the passage is extracted from

(A) an entry in a scientific journal
(B) a nineteenth-century novel
(C) a book on tourism
(D) a letter from a poet
(E) a book on volcanoes

49. In context, one can infer that tuff is

(A) an alternate spelling for tough
(B) a kind of sand
(C) made up principally of grass
(D) volcanic rock
(E) dense and resistant

50. In this passage, the speaker is most notably impressed by

(A) the flora on the islands
(B) the force of the Pacific Ocean
(C) the fragments of granite
(D) the symmetrical craters on the islands
(E) the topography of the smaller islands

GO ON TO THE NEXT PAGE.

Questions 51-54. Read the following passage carefully before you choose your answers.

(The following passage is excerpted from an essay by a nineteenth-century British writer.)

Art begins with abstract decoration, with purely imaginative and pleasurable work dealing with what is unreal and non-existent. This is the first stage. Then
Line Life becomes fascinated with this new wonder, and
5 asks to be admitted into the charmed circle. Art takes life as part of her rough material, re-creates it, and refashions it in fresh forms, is absolutely indifferent to fact, invents, imagines, dreams, and keeps between herself and reality the impenetrable barrier of beautiful
10 style, of decorative or ideal treatment. The third stage is when Life gets the upper hand, and drives Art out into the wilderness. That is the true decadence, and it is from this that we are now suffering.
Take the case of the English drama. At first in
15 the hands of the monks Dramatic Art was abstract, decorative and mythological. Then she enlisted Life in her service, and using some of life's external forms, she created an entirely new race of beings, whose sorrows were more terrible than any sorrow man has
20 ever felt, whose joys were keener than lover's joys, who had the rage of the Titans and the calm of the gods, who had monstrous and marvelous sins, monstrous and marvelous virtues. To them she gave a language different from that of actual use, a language full of
25 resonant music and sweet rhythm, made stately by solemn cadence, or made delicate by fanciful rhyme, jeweled with wonderful words, and enriched with lofty diction. She clothed her children in strange raiment and gave them masks, and at her bidding the antique
30 world rose from its marble tomb. A new Caesar stalked through the streets of risen Rome, and with purple sail and flute-led oars another Cleopatra passed up the river to Antioch. Old myth and legend and dream took shape and substance. History was entirely rewritten,
35 and there was hardly one of the dramatists who did not recognize that the object of Art is not simple truth but complex beauty. In this they were perfectly right. Art itself is really a form of exaggeration; and selection, which is the very spirit of art, is nothing more than an
40 intensified mode of over-emphasis.
But Life soon shattered the perfection of the form. Even in Shakespeare we can see the beginning of the end. It shows itself by the gradual breaking-up of the blank-verse in the later plays, by the predominance
45 given to prose, and by the overimportance assigned to characterization. The passages in Shakespeare—and they are many—where the language is uncouth, vulgar, exaggerated, fantastic, obscene even, are entirely due to Life calling for an echo of her own voice, and rejecting
50 the intervention of beautiful style, through which alone

should life be suffered to find expression. Shakespeare is not by any means a flawless artist. He is too fond of going directly to life, and borrowing life's natural utterance. He forgets that when Art surrenders her
55 imaginative medium she surrenders everything.

51. The author of this passage is most likely

(A) a poet
(B) a novelist
(C) an art critic
(D) a journalist
(E) an actor

52. The author relies principally on which of the following to substantiate his thesis?

(A) a faulty analogy
(B) process analysis
(C) deductive reasoning
(D) an accumulation of facts
(E) illustration by example

53. "...when Art surrenders her imaginative medium she surrenders everything" (lines 54-55) is in the form of

(A) a maxim
(B) a chiasmus
(C) an antithesis
(D) an understatement
(E) an analogy

54. Above all else, the author reveres

(A) beauty
(B) life
(C) Shakespeare
(D) Caesar
(E) English drama

END OF SECTION I

AP® English Language and Composition Exam

SECTION II: Free-Response Questions

DO NOT OPEN THIS BOOKLET UNTIL YOU ARE TOLD TO DO SO.

At a Glance

Total Time
2 hours, plus a 15-minute reading period
Number of Questions
3
Percent of Total Grade
55%
Writing Instrument
Pen required

Instructions

Section II of this examination requires answers in essay form. To help you use your time well, the coordinator will announce the time at which each question should be completed. If you finish any question before time is announced, you may go on to the following question. If you finish the examination in less than the time allotted, you may go back and work on any essay question you want.

Each essay will be judged on its clarity and effectiveness in dealing with the requirements of the topic assigned and on the quality of the writing. After completing each question, you should check your essay for accuracy of punctuation, spelling, and diction; you are advised, however, not to attempt many longer corrections. Remember that quality is far more important than quantity.

Write your essays with a pen, preferably in black or dark blue ink. Be sure to write CLEARLY and LEGIBLY. Cross out any errors you make.

The questions for Section II are printed in the green insert. You are encouraged to use the green insert to make notes and to plan your essays, but be sure to write your answers in the pink booklet. Number each answer as the question is numbered in the examination. Do not skip lines. Begin each answer on a new page in the pink booklet.

ENGLISH LANGUAGE AND COMPOSITION
SECTION II
Total Time—2 hours

Question 1

(Suggested writing time—40 minutes. This question counts for one-third of the total essay section score.)

Countries define effective leadership in different ways. Some focus on fear and power, while others point to respect and propriety.

Carefully read the following six sources, including the introductory information for each source. Then synthesize information from at least three of the sources and incorporate it into a coherent, well-developed essay that defends, challenges, or qualifies the claim that authoritative leadership is more effective than collaborative leadership.

Make sure that your argument is central; use the sources to illustrate and support your reasoning. Avoid merely summarizing the sources. Indicate clearly which sources you are drawing from, whether through direct quotation, paraphrase, or summary. You may cite the sources as Source A, Source B, etc., or by using the descriptions in parentheses.

Source A   (Patton)
Source B   (Machiavelli)
Source C   (Plato)
Source D   (Confucius)
Source E   (David)
Source F   (Hobbes)

GO ON TO THE NEXT PAGE.

Source A

George S. Patton

The following is a quote from one of the most highly regarded generals in World War II.

"Don't tell people how to do things, tell them what to do and let them surprise you with their results."

GO ON TO THE NEXT PAGE.

Source B

Machiavelli, Niccolo. The Prince. 1513.

The following passage is excerpted from a famous treatise on leadership.

Upon this a question arises: whether it be better to be loved than feared or feared than loved? It may be answered that one should wish to be both, but, because it is difficult to unite them in one person, it is much safer to be feared than loved, when, of the two, either must be dispensed with…that prince who, relying entirely on [the] promises [of his subjects], has neglected other precautions, is ruined;…men have less scruple in offending one who is beloved than one who is feared, for love is preserved by the link of obligation which, owing to the baseness of men, is broken at every opportunity for their advantage; but fear preserves you by a dread of punishment which never fails.

Nevertheless a prince ought to inspire fear in such a way that, if he does not win love, he avoids hatred; because he can endure very well being feared whilst he is not hated, which will always be as long as he abstains from the property of his citizens and subjects and from their women…But when a prince is with his army, and has under control a multitude of soldiers, then it is quite necessary for him to disregard the reputation of cruelty, for without it he would never hold his army united or disposed to its duties.

GO ON TO THE NEXT PAGE.

> ### Source C
>
> Plato. <u>The Republic</u>. Translated by
> Benjamin Jowett.

The following passage is an excerpt from Plato's best-known work.

I said: Until philosophers are kings, or the kings and princes of this world have the spirit and power of philosophy, and political greatness and wisdom meet in one (and those commoner natures who pursue either to the exclusion of the other are compelled to stand aside) cities will never have rest from their evils—nor will the human race, as I believe—and then only will this our State have a possibility of life and behold the light of day. Such was the thought, my dear Glaucon, which I would fain have uttered if it had not seemed too extravagant; for to be convinced that in no other State can there be happiness private or public is indeed a hard thing.

GO ON TO THE NEXT PAGE.

Source D

Confucius. <u>The Analects</u>. Translated by James
Legge, with alterations for clarity.

The following passage is excerpted from a collection of philosophical sayings and ideas.

13. The Master said, "If a prince can govern his kingdom with tolerance and propriety, what difficulty will he have? If he cannot govern it with that tolerance, how can there be propriety?"

18. The Master said, "In serving his parents, a son may remonstrate with them, but gently; when he sees that they do not incline to follow his advice, he shows an increased degree of reverence, but does not abandon his purpose; and should they punish him, he does not allow himself to murmur."

26. Ziyu said, "In serving a prince, frequent remonstrances lead to disgrace. Between friends, frequent reproofs make the friendship distant."

GO ON TO THE NEXT PAGE.

Source E

David, Jacques-Louis. <u>Napoleon Crossing the Alps</u>, oil on canvas, c. 1800.

The following painting shows Napoleon Bonaparte, the French Emperor, crossing the Alps to invade Italy. The name at the lower left refers to Hannibal, the Carthaginian general who led elephants over the Alps, posing the most serious threat the Roman Empire ever faced.

GO ON TO THE NEXT PAGE.

Source F

Hobbes, Thomas. <u>Leviathan</u>. 1651. Updated to
modern English.

*The following passage is excerpted from a book concerning the structure of society and legitimate
government.*

The only way to erect such a Common Power [as can] make [the people] secure...is to confer
all their power and strength upon one man...that may reduce all their wills, by plurality of
voices, unto one will: which is as much as to say, to appoint one man...to represent them all.
And every person to own, and acknowledge himself to be author of, whatever this Man shall
do, or cause to be done, in those things which concern the common peace and safety; and
therein to submit their wills, every one, to that Man's will, and their judgments, to that Man's
judgment. This is more than consent...it is a covenant of every man with every man...as if
every man should say to every man, "I authorize and give up my right of governing myself to
this Man...on the condition that you give up your right to him, and authorize all his actions
in like manner."...For by this authority, given him by every particular man in the commonwealth, he hath the use of so much power and strength conferred on him, that by terror
thereof, he is enabled to form the wills of them all, to peace at home, and mutual aid against
their enemies abroad.

GO ON TO THE NEXT PAGE.

Question 2

(Suggested time—40 minutes. This question counts for one-third of the total essay section score.)

The passage below is excerpted from one of Mark Twain's most famous essays, "Fenimore Cooper's Literary Offenses." At the time Twain wrote his essay, Cooper's novels were generally well liked and respected. Read the entire passage carefully. Then write an essay analyzing the rhetorical strategies that Twain uses to convey his attitude.

If Cooper had been an observer his inventive faculty would have worked better; not more interestingly, but more rationally, more plausibly. Cooper's proudest
Line creations in the way of "situations" suffer noticeably
5 from the absence of the observer's protecting gift. Cooper's eye was splendidly inaccurate. Cooper seldom saw anything correctly. He saw nearly all things as through a glass eye, darkly. Of course a man who cannot see the commonest little every-day
10 matters accurately is working at a disadvantage when he is constructing a "situation." In the *Deerslayer* tale Cooper has a stream which is fifty feet wide where it flows out of a lake; it presently narrows to twenty as it meanders along for no given reason, and yet when a
15 stream acts like that it ought to be required to explain itself. Fourteen pages later the width of the brook's outlet from the lake has suddenly shrunk thirty feet, and become "the narrowest part of the stream." This shrinkage is not accounted for. The stream has bends in
20 it, a sure indication that it has alluvial banks and cuts them; yet these bends are only thirty and fifty feet long. If Cooper had been a nice and punctilious observer he would have noticed that the bends were often nine hundred feet long than short of it.
25 Cooper made the exit of that stream fifty feet wide, in the first place, for no particular reason; in the second place, he narrowed it to less than twenty to accommodate some Indians. He bends a "sapling" to form an arch over this narrow passage, and conceals six
30 Indians in its foliage. They are "laying" for a settler's scow or ark which is coming up the stream on its way to the lake; it is being hauled against the stiff current by rope whose stationary end is anchored in the lake; its rate of progress cannot be more than a mile an hour.
35 Cooper describes the ark, but pretty obscurely. In the matter of dimensions "it was little more than a modern canal boat." Let us guess, then, that it was about one hundred and forty feet long. It was of "greater breadth than common." Let us guess then that it was about
40 sixteen feet wide. This leviathan had been prowling

down bends which were but a third as long as itself, and scraping between banks where it only had two feet of space to spare on each side. We cannot too much admire this miracle. A low-roofed dwelling occupies
45 "two-thirds of the ark's length"—a dwelling ninety feet long and sixteen feet wide, let us say—a kind of vestibule train. The dwelling has two rooms—each forty-five feet long and sixteen feet wide, let us guess. One of them is the bedroom of the Hutter girls, Judith
50 and Hetty; the other is the parlor in the daytime, at night it is papa's bedchamber. The ark is arriving at the stream's exit now, whose width has been reduced to less than twenty feet to accommodate the Indians—say to eighteen. There is a foot to spare on each side of the
55 boat. Did the Indians notice that there was going to be a tight squeeze there? Did they notice that they could make money by climbing down out of that arched sapling and just stepping aboard when the ark scraped by? No, other Indians would have noticed these things,
60 but Cooper's Indian's never notice anything. Cooper thinks they are marvelous creatures for noticing, but he was almost always in error about his Indians. There was seldom a sane one among them.
The ark is one hundred and forty-feet long; the
65 dwelling is ninety feet long. The idea of the Indians is to drop softly and secretly from the arched sapling to the dwelling as the ark creeps along under it at the rate of a mile an hour, and butcher the family. It will take the ark a minute and a half to pass under. It will
70 take the ninety-foot dwelling a minute to pass under. Now, then, what did the six Indians do? It would take you thirty years to guess, and even then you would have to give it up, I believe. Therefore, I will tell you what the Indians did. Their chief, a person of quite
75 extraordinary intellect for a Cooper Indian, warily watched the canal-boat as it squeezed along under him and when he had got his calculations fined down to exactly the right shade, as he judged, he let go and dropped. And missed the boat! That is actually what
80 he did. He missed the house, and landed in the stern of

GO ON TO THE NEXT PAGE.

the scow. It was not much of a fall, yet it knocked him silly. He lay there unconscious. If the house had been ninety-seven feet long he would have made the trip. The error lay in the construction of the house. Cooper
85 was no architect.

There still remained in the roost five Indians. The boat has passed under and is now out of their reach. Let me explain what the five did—you would not be able to reason it out for yourself. No. 1 jumped for
90 the boat, but fell in the water astern of it. Then No. 2 jumped for the boat, but fell in the water still further astern of it. Then No. 3 jumped for the boat, and fell a good way astern of it. Then No. 4 jumped for the boat, and fell in the water away astern. Then even No. 5
95 made a jump for the boat—for he was a Cooper Indian. In that matter of intellect, the difference between a Cooper Indian and the Indian that stands in front of the cigar-shop is not spacious. The scow episode is really a sublime burst of invention; but it does not thrill,
100 because the inaccuracy of details throw a sort of air of fictitiousness and general improbability over it. This comes of Cooper's inadequacy as observer.

GO ON TO THE NEXT PAGE.

Question 3

(Suggested time—40 minutes. This question counts for one-third of the total essay section score.)

Read and think carefully about the following quotation. Then write an essay in which you refute, support, or qualify Voltaire's claim. Make sure to use appropriate evidence from literary, historical, or personal sources to develop your argument.

It is dangerous to be right in matters about which the established authorities are wrong.

—*Voltaire*

STOP

END OF EXAM

15

Practice Test 2: Answers and Explanations

EXPLANATIONS TO THE MULTIPLE-CHOICE SECTION

1. **C** Remember that oftentimes AP questions will ask you to infer—to draw a conclusion based on what is said in the text.

   The best course of action to take when approaching this question is POE. Answer (B) is the only one that posits a positive answer (to "laud" means to praise), and it can be eliminated easily because of the word "linear." The final sentence of the first paragraph does laud Browne's writing, but the author suggests that the reading process is like going through a series of mazes. This is anything but straightforward—or linear. Later in the text, there is an oblique allusion to William Shakespeare ("the time of Elizabeth"), but there is nothing resembling a comparison between Browne and Shakespeare; eliminate (D). There is even less reason to suspect that there is any suggestion of a comparison between the author of the passage (Samuel Johnson, by the way) and Browne; so you can eliminate answer (E). Now you're down to two choices. The author criticizes the exuberance and lack of clarity that makes it difficult to understand his reasoning; he does not suggest that Browne reasons poorly (or not at all); thus, answer (A) is not correct. You're left with (C), which fits: The author complains about Browne's lack of clarity.

2. **B** This question also requires you to use POE. The first answer should be suspect—it would be far too easy if they just expected you to equate "poesy" and "poetry." Remember that the author applies the poesy to Browne's style, which the author qualifies with a combination of positive and negative attributes. In essence, you must match the positive qualities ("excellencies") and negative ones ("faults") with one of the answers. None of the last three answers, which all are tied to "poetry" to keep you leaning toward a simplistic answer, is appropriate. Browne says that greatness is connected to certain extremes (both good and bad) in an individual's character; the author of the passage suggests that the extremes of Browne's character help explain the eccentricities of his style.

   More often than not the correct answer will be similar, but not identical, to the answer that you come up with from reading the passage. Your goal is to identify the best answer, and (B) is the only plausible one.

3. **C** The meaning is obvious because the author translates the expression for us, putting the translation just before the Latin phrase: "To have great excellencies and great faults." By the way, more often than not, authors who insert foreign words or phrases will tip their hands and either suggest the meaning or simply state it.

4. **A** Here's another example where POE comes in handy. At first glance, answer (B) seems plausible, but the problem lies in the word "hints." The author does not hint; rather, he says outright that the style is pedantic. The author describes, but does not justify or argue, so (C) and (D) are out. Choice (E) can't be correct; Browne's style is many things (including complex), but it is definitely not facile (easy). True, there are some positive elements in the author's evaluation, but these are outweighed by the negative epithets: rugged, pedantic (overly bookish), obscure, harsh, and uncouth. This appears to be open criticism, so (A) is the best answer.

5. **A** The key to answering this question correctly is to recognize that the author establishes a clear parallel pattern: a sequence of positive qualifiers contrasted with related negative ones (this, but that). At the end of the sentence, however, the author combines two pejorative statements (this and that). This parallelism tips the balance toward the negative, revealing

the author's point of view. Remember that the passage begins with Browne's own comment that suggests that greatness originates in a sort of balance between the great qualities and great faults. By adding on only faults at the end of the sentence describing Browne's style, the author of the passage shows that he sees more faults than "excellencies." Some of the answers are deliberately misleading. Both (B) and (C) pertain to "balance," although each has nothing to do with our answer. Choice (D) appears to function only as "filler." If you chose this answer, you should review the meaning of parallelism before going any further. Choice (E) is the exact opposite of the correct answer; "obfuscate" means to intentionally mislead.

6. **A** The first sentence of the third paragraph allows you to use POE to begin eliminating incorrect answer choices: "He fell into an age in which our language began to lose the stability…." Right away, you can eliminate answers (B), (C), and (E). You should be suspicious of (D) because of the word "metaphorical." Where does "metaphorical" come in? It doesn't, which is why (D) is not the best answer. Browne lived in a time of linguistic experimentation, and the author of the passage takes the time to discuss this to put some of Browne's excesses in context.

7. **D** The author at first classifies Browne's use of vocabulary as "useful" then goes on to describe some of it as "superfluous" and then "obscure." You can use POE to eliminate all but the correct answer. The last word in the correct answer, "deleterious," may have given you problems; this word means "harmful." The idea that some of his vocabulary is, in fact, harmful to his writing is given in the lines that say that some words "conceal his meaning rather than explain it."

8. **E** For this question, all of the answers probably seemed plausible. Your first step should have been to find the appropriate part of the text. In the last paragraph, the author writes: "in defence of his uncommon words and expressions, we must consider that he had uncommon sentiments, and was not content to express, in many words, that idea for which any language could supply a single term." Thus, the author attributes Browne's unusual diction (word choice) to his desire to find the exact word that expresses his uncommon thoughts or feelings, instead of circuitously expressing them through the use of many words.

9. **A** This question does not ask anything new; in essence, it addresses the same content as the preceding question, but in a slightly different way and while also indirectly testing your knowledge of a couple of words. If you understand that "heteroclite diction" signifies the use of words that are unusual or unusually varied, you can probably pick out the correct answer immediately. If not, use POE. You can eliminate (D) right away. Hopefully, you are familiar with the word "homogeneous" and can eliminate choice (B), too. Even if you aren't sure about the meaning of "mundane" (ordinary, usual, worldly) or "trope" (similar in meaning to rhetorical figure, for example, metaphor), you will have narrowed your choices to three, and should guess and move on.

10. **A** This question is relatively straightforward; using POE would enable you to eliminate answers (B) and (D). You may have been tempted by (C), but you should have noticed that the author of the passage discusses Browne as though he were writing in the past; for example, the third paragraph begins, "He fell into an age in which our language began to lose the stability which it had obtained in the time of Elizabeth." Finally, if you know that polemic means "debate" and that "virulent polemic" means something like a "heated debate," then you can dismiss answer (E). If not, then you should have guessed and moved on.

11. **B** Remember that with this type of question, if you can determine that half of the answer is untrue, then you can eliminate the entire answer. Thus, the fact that "sarcastic" seems way off-base allows you to eliminate (A), the inappropriateness of "harsh" allows you to discard (C), and the use of "sentimental" (or "capricious") disqualifies (E). It may not seem unreasonable to claim that the author of the passage is somewhat condescending, but it would be inaccurate to say that he is indulgent; the author appears to genuinely appreciate and admire certain aspects of Browne's style. In fact, he analyzes the style in a scholarly manner, which is why (B) is the best answer.

12. **E** One of the most important questions that you can ask while reading is: Who is speaking? With more modern literary texts, the question is often difficult to answer. Clearly, in this case, the speaker is a talented writer who knows the works of George Eliot (a nineteenth-century female writer). We have no reason to suspect that the speaker is a family member, so choice (A) is incorrect. Answer (B) is a trap for those casual readers who note that in the initial part of the text there is a discussion of religion, but fail to see how this fits into a discussion of the heroines in a feminist construct. Answer (D) would be a legitimate answer were it not for the qualifier, "chauvinist." If you had to attach a label to the speaker, it would probably be feminist, not chauvinist. After using POE, the only answer choice left is (E), and it seems appropriate enough.

13. **B** This question digs deeper into the relevance of the discussion of religion as it applies to the speaker's view of Eliot as a feminist writer (or as a writer about the feminine condition). Don't let the simile ("like a place of worship") mislead you. The speaker claims that at the heart of Eliot's novels the reader finds a young woman's struggle "in aspiration and agony" for "something that is perhaps incompatible with the facts of human existence." There is no statement about where the heroine might be physically, so answers (A), (C), and (D) should be eliminated right away. Answer (E) may have seemed plausible, but in fact, the heroine, as a woman in a world dominated by men, is shut off from "the real world" and forced into herself, not necessarily "lost in prayer." She is more precisely "essentially alone."

14. **B** The great fact of human existence in the context of this passage is that it's a man's world (remember that Eliot wrote in nineteenth-century England). The entire passage is about women and their place in "the human condition." Answer (C) may have tempted you, but "the facts of human existence" cannot be limited to these women protagonists. You may have felt that answer (A) was correct because human existence restricts both men and women in some way; however, the aspirations of the heroines are incompatible only with "the facts of human existence." In this context, the incompatibility pertains only to women.

15. **A** Every once in a while, the exam will surprise you with a question as easy as this one. "Save for," which you may have seen written before, is sometimes substituted for the phrase "except for."

16. **E** "The difference of [point of] view" and "the difference of standard" are Eliot's "inheritance." Like men, Eliot sought and achieved a significant grasp of art and culture, but, according to the speaker, she did not renounce the feminine qualities—the results of her gender—that made her different.

17. **B** At the end of the passage, the speaker calls Eliot's knowledge and freedom a "double burden" and suggests that the burden led directly to Eliot's death, in the phrase "sank worn out." Clearly, Eliot was not in good health, since she has died, and answer (A) can be

eliminated. The other answer choices are very obviously incorrect; choice (C) is incorrect since Eliot was in fact famous. Choice (D) is also untrue according to the passage, and (E) is the opposite of what is stated in the passage. Choice (B) is the best answer.

18. **D** The best way to approach this type of question is to use POE. The apposition ("her, a memorable figure") appears almost at the beginning of the sentence, so (A) is not the correct answer. The claim that Eliot reached out "for all that life could offer" may be intended literally, but the statement is hyperbolic (it is an overstatement). As for choice (C), there is a clear example of personification when Eliot shrinks "back into the arms of love." One could also argue that there are multiple examples of not very noteworthy parallelism, but perhaps the most obvious one is the construction "reaching out with ... confronting her feminine aspirations with." You may expect to find a relative clause in such a long periodic sentence, however, there is none, and the correct answer is (D).

19. **A** The question boils down to this: Who is speaking? Let's use POE. The speaker put the phrase in quotation marks to show that it is not hers; therefore, (B) is incorrect. If the speaker borrowed it from one of Eliot's critics, she would need to identify the citation somehow; (C), therefore, does not seem plausible. From context, it is clear that the reader should, indeed, take the phrase seriously, and the phrase *does* represent the speaker's point of view, which is why the phrase is there in the first place. So answers (D) and (E) can be eliminated. The entire text centers on Eliot's relationship to her feminine protagonists, and so it seems very probable (in this case, certain) that the speaker would integrate a phrase from one of Eliot's heroines. Choice (A) is the best answer.

20. **C** It would be difficult to accept either qualifier in (A), but "disorganized" is far too pejorative and couldn't possibly be appropriate for this passage. Answer (B) is far off the mark too, especially if you can discern between "scholarship" and "pedantry." Pedantic means "characterized by a narrow, often ostentatious concern for book learning and formal rules." You could probably dismiss both terms in answer (D), also; this passage cannot accurately be described as "metaphysical." Answer (E) is half right; the style could be called "intellectual," but there is no cynicism here. POE leaves us with "sympathetic and concrete." This answer may not be ideal, but it's the best choice available.

21. **A** Choice (A) is the only answer that lists two appropriate adjectives, but go through the other choices to make sure none of them is equally good: Both parts of (B) are untrue. Answer (C) starts out well; the point of view could be considered "altruistic." The second term ("elitist"), however, does not seem appropriate at all. Remember that you need to eliminate only one element of the answer to discount the entire answer. "Quixotic" (overly idealistic) might fit, but the plan is presented in a rational manner, so you can eliminate (D). The point of view is "positivist" (having to do with faith in progress), but "unreasonable" is too strong. Although (E) is a possibility, (A) is a better answer.

22. **D** The key in this question is to recognize that the "Institution" the author of this passage describes is meant to serve only children. The other answer choices are institutions that serve both children and adults. The author, who did, in fact, establish a utopian community (Lanark, in Southern Scotland) never uses the word *school*, but it is clear what kind of institution he is proposing because of this sentence: "It has ever been my intention that as this Institution, when completed, will accommodate more than the children of parents resident at the village, any persons living at Lanark, or in the neighbourhood anywhere around, who

cannot well afford to educate their children, shall be at liberty, on mentioning their wishes, to send them to this place, where they will experience the same care and attention as those who belong to the establishment."

23. **A** The pronoun at the beginning of the sentence refers to "those who apply these terms to their fellow-men," and we can infer that the "those" referred to are the wealthy and privileged middle class. Essentially, the sentence states that the "men of worth" (the wealthy) are the worthless. That is a paradox or apparent contradiction. The wealthy who believe that the poor are worthless creatures help perpetuate their poverty; this, states the author, is far worse than the condition of being poor. The entire sentence both states, and partly explains, the paradox.

24. **B** This question is merely a continuation of the previous one. The pronoun that they're asking about in this question is the same one they asked about in question 23—"they." Again, "they" refers to "those who apply these terms to their fellow-men." We can infer that the author most nearly means "the wealthy."

25. **E** At first glance, all of the answers seem to be correct. But what is the speaker most interested in? The passage is centered on the establishment of the (educational) "Institution" and its goals. Note that the author blames poor upbringing (education) for the "wicked" attitude of the privileged classes. Thus, the real focus of the passage is on education—"imparting knowledge and moral values."

26. **D** The incorrect answers are all related to the text, but only (D) explains the opening sentence of the passage ("And yet, being a problem is a strange experience"). The passage is written by an African American author (W. E. B. Du Bois) and deals with racism.

27. **A** An epiphany is a sudden realization; in this passage, there is a rhetorical statement that announces the moment of epiphany: "Then it dawned upon me with a certain suddenness...." Even if you didn't know the meaning of epiphany, you could use POE to arrive at the correct answer. The author is definitely not describing the incident as a moment of triumph (B). Answer (C) is partly true because the moment is a revelation, but the epiphany is for the boy, not for the reader. The remaining answers have no grounding in the passage.

28. **D** The more obvious of the metaphors is the sky, which is extended by "dazzling," "sunny," and "streak of blue." The blue, dazzling, and sunny sky represents the world of opportunity that shines above the white children and, for a while, the author. As the child matures, he realizes the narrowness of his opportunities (the blue is reduced to a streak). The other metaphor is the house/prison with its straight, narrow, tall, and unscalable walls of stone; of course, this edifice is not a real prison, but the limiting restrictions of racism. You may have noticed that the walls of the prison are white.

You can eliminate the other answers with ease, unless you are not familiar with "euphemism," which means "a word or words that replace a crass, crude, or simply inappropriate word or phrase."

29. **B** This is a common AP exam phenomenon: Two questions so closely linked that you are more likely to get both right or both wrong. In light of the previous explanation, the "night" is used metonymically to suggest the color of the boys' skin. (In metonymy, one term is substituted for another term with which it is closely associated.)

30. **A** You can eliminate (C), (D), and (E) with certainty. The author states that his comrades shrank into "sycophancy" (obsequiousness, or, in the vernacular, "brown-nosing"); he implies that he had moments of intellectual and physical triumph over his white peers; he also sets himself somewhat apart from his African American comrades ("other black boys"). Choosing between (A) and (B) is the tricky part. On the one hand, even though the author does finally include himself ("the shades of the prison-house closed around us all"), the author places himself above them by accusing the other black boys of being sycophants, and saying that only he wrested his share of opportunity. On the other hand, he suggests that he is superior to his white peers by saying that he could win his share of prizes and contests at school, he suggests that he could at least hold his own in professional life (law, medicine, literature), if given the opportunity.

31. **A** The previous explanation hints at the answer to this question. The author's first reaction was to remain aloof and "above" the racism at school; however, he realizes that this attitude would do nothing to change one stark reality: that he would not be able to remain apart if he were to somehow "wrest from them" the opportunities open to white boys. He vows to succeed in a field restricted almost exclusively to white men: law, medicine, or literature.

32. **E** Laudatory means "praiseworthy or congratulatory," and if you know this, the question is not too difficult. If you didn't know this, then POE will enable you to eliminate all of the answers except (E). Watch out for questions that say "EXCEPT" or "NOT"—in these questions, you're looking for the opposite of what you'd usually look for.

33. **B** This passage is from one of the famous Lincoln-Douglas debates; here, Douglas argues in favor of states' rights.

You should note that it is possible to eliminate several of the choices based on the verb used. The speaker presents an argument; he does not analyze (A), criticize (C), or describe (D). Douglas says directly that he is vehemently opposed to the idea of slavery in his home state of Illinois; he argues in favor of letting each state decide the issue for itself and goes on to claim that the greatness of the country rests on the sovereignty of the states to do so.

34. **C** You might not agree with what Douglas is saying in this passage, but he controls his tone carefully; remember, he is engaged in a debate at a time when people turned out in droves, expecting not colossal home runs, spectacular slam-dunks, hockey fights, or touchdown passes, but brilliantly conceived, expertly delivered rhetoric.

If you use POE, you can narrow it down to three choices by eliminating (A) and (E). Answer (D) may be alluring, but be careful not to apply a twenty-first-century point of view to nineteenth-century reality. It may be tempting to see Douglas's defense of states' rights as a mask for his true feelings on slavery or, at least, as a poor veil for a racist bias. However, none of that is appropriate to the task at hand. The tone is best described as the tone of a debate; in other words, the speaker attempts to step back and let the force of his words (the voice of reason, if you will) carry the day. Also, remember that polemic means "controversial argument."

35. **A** The speaker uses inductive reasoning (which is defined as reasoning derived from detailed facts, to form general principles) that goes something like this: You all agree that it was right for Illinois to vote as it chose and abolish slavery; thus, every state should be able to make its own choice on this issue. Moreover, every state should be able to make its own choices on just about everything.

36. **B** The shift that begins with "Now, my friends…" is important because at this point in the passage, Douglas shifts from the issue of states' rights and slavery to what the consequences will be if voters do not support his platform—the consequences are civil war. This is a scare tactic. Douglas is saying that voters should support states' rights because that is the only way to maintain peace between North and South.

37. **E** The correct answer may not have been readily apparent, but using POE allows you to eliminate (A) through (D). Douglas uses no anecdotes, much less clever ones; likewise, there are no symbols, paradoxes, or metaphors. The authorities in this case are not only the other states (meaning the voters in the other states), but also the founding fathers: "Washington, Madison, or the framers of this government."

38. **D** Douglas states his own opinion on slavery (his official opinion, at least) at the beginning of the passage ("there is no man in the State who would be more strenuous in his opposition to the introduction of slavery than I would"). Douglas also presents a clear position on voting: "I would never consent to confer the right of voting and of citizenship upon a negro…." Finally, there is a clear position on property: "I would not make any distinction whatever between a negro who held property and one who did not…." Of course, this implies that he would allow African Americans to have property, but he states that, propertied or not, they should not be able to vote. With this information, it is possible to answer the question with certainty; the correct answer is (D).

39. **C** In a way, this is simply a reprise of Question 36, but here Douglas pushes his scare tactic even further by saying that Lincoln and his party are deliberately infringing on states' rights to incite a civil war. We hope you were not fooled by (B). While it is true that Douglas is blaming the war (that hadn't yet begun) on Lincoln and his political party, he is not shifting any blame; nowhere does he imply that anyone was blaming or accusing Douglas and his party of trying to provoke a war, and to shift blame, Douglas would have to have *had* blame at some point.

40. **E** In this passage, the author builds his case by claiming that the role of the merchant is analogous to that of a physician or clergyman; this is a clear analogy. Note that the author is not referring to physicians and clergymen as authorities; so answer choice (A), "appeal to authorities," is not correct.

41. **A** If you understood the previous question, you could probably have eliminated (B) and (C) immediately. At the beginning of the passage, the author tells us that he includes manufacturer in the category of merchant, so (D) is not correct, and you have already narrowed down the answer choices significantly. You may have expected (E) to be true, but in the context of this particular passage, the merchant is said to be motivated by the same altruistic motives that guide a doctor or clergyman.

42. **A** The author claims that "the stipend" (salary or profit) is a necessary adjunct to the work of a merchant, physician, or clergyman, but not the true motivational force. Only answer choice (A) comes close to sounding right in context: "This stipend is a due and necessary <u>accompaniment</u>, but not the object of his life, if he be a true clergyman, any more than his fee (or honorarium) is the object of life to a true physician." The best answer is (A).

43. **C** In this context, agency means "direction" or "governance," and the term is, therefore, tied to "master and governor of large masses of men." The question asks you to tie together words by semantics; that is, to tie them together by *meaning*. The merchant must oversee or govern all his workers, and this leads logically to the role of governor. It is the semantic connection that allows the reader to understand the writer's logic in this sentence. By using POE, you can narrow the answers to (C) and (E). If you're not sure, guess and move on.

44. **E** This is a tricky question. If you understand the term "synecdoche," you increase your odds of getting the question right. This rhetorical figure is a limited form of metonymy (which is defined as any time a characteristic represents something, or something stands for its characteristic). Synecdoche is when a part stands for the whole. In this case, the merchant doesn't govern hands, he governs workers, but the workers are mostly manual laborers, so the hands represent the workers (by synecdoche) and reinforce the idea of manual labor. The author employs the word *men* twice in the paragraph, and the synecdoche also helps with diction. Answer (D) is less important, but surely "hands" is a concrete, rather than an abstract, image. Thus, all four answers are appropriate.

45. **B** The answer to this question is embedded in the final part of the paragraph discussed above. If you read and understood the passage, you should have been fine; the question should cause problems only for those who guess by using the context of the twenty-first century. He says that the merchant's two obligations are to produce quality, affordable goods and take care of his workers. From the initial paragraph, we saw that according to this author, profits are only secondary to the merchants' real functions, so you can eliminate every answer but (B) right off the bat.

46. **C** This passage is a kind of an ode to the merchant, and this is tantamount to an ode to capitalism.

   If you decide to use POE, then you can eliminate (D) and (E) right away: The author posits merchants, clerics, and physicians in a decidedly positive light. By extolling the virtues of the merchant (and manufacturer), he cannot possibly be a supporter of socialism, so even (B) is an unreasonable choice.

47. **C** This is a scientifically precise description of the Galapagos Islands. Choice (A) is incorrect since nothing is being classified in this passage. Choice (B) is also wrong—no point of view is presented here—just facts. The passage is not dominated by analogies, so (D) can't be right. Finally, you know that (E) is incorrect, since "lyrical" pertains to personal sentiment, and there are practically no personal feelings expressed at all; the closest we get to personal sentiment is the statement that some of the craters are "beautifully symmetrical."

48. **A** You can use POE to answer this question. Answer (D) is the easiest to eliminate; the passage is neither lyrical nor poetic—it was not written by a poet. The passage is about the islands themselves, not about volcanoes as (E) suggests. Answers (B) and (C) are somewhat plausible; however if this passage were emblematic of an entire novel, what boring reading that would be. Finally, a book for tourists about the Galapagos Islands would make the islands far more alluring than this passage does.

49. **D** In this case, the answer is made clear from the passage; the craters have a border of soft stone (tuff) that has worn away on the southern side. The specific line from the passage that allows you to answer this question is: "These consist either of lava or scoriae, or of finely-

stratified, sandstone-like tuff." Sandstone is a type of rock. The definition of "tuff" is actually "a rock composed of compacted volcanic ash varying in size from fine sand to coarse gravel."

50. **D** The author doesn't address (A) or (E), so you can eliminate those and look more closely at the middle three choices. While it is true that the speaker mentions the Pacific Ocean and the fragments of granite, he incorporates these elements in his overarching discussion of the symmetrical craters.

51. **A** In reality, the author is both a poet and a novelist, but you are asked to make a judgment based on the passage. To answer this question correctly, you would need to use POE and your best judgment to eliminate all of the least likely answer choices. The passage is an attack against the intrusion of prosaic life into the realm of art. The panegyric (high praise) of classical language is a key to understanding the author's point of view: "a language different from that of actual use, a language full of resonant music and sweet rhythm, made stately by solemn cadence, or made delicate by fanciful rhyme, jeweled with wonderful words, and enriched with lofty diction." In a word, this is poetry.

The writing is far too lyrical for the author of the passage to be a journalist (D) or an actor (E); the latter choice is thrown in for those superficial readers who assume that a passage that purports to deal with English drama should be somehow related to a theatrical term. The same may be said for (C). The author capitalizes "art" because he is not discussing painting specifically, but the general realm of artistic creation that encompasses all the arts.

52. **E** The example is stated rhetorically: "Take the case of the English drama," and lasts for most of the passage. "Illustration by example" is definitely the defining rhetorical device of this passage.

53. **A** A maxim is a truism or pithy saying, a gnomic statement similar to a proverb, so (A) is the best answer.

POE can help you narrow down your choices. Clearly, the statement does not compare Art to something else, so you can eliminate (E). If anything, the statement is overstatement (hyperbole), and for that reason (D) can be discarded. For the statement to be an antithesis, the author would have needed to put two things or concepts in opposition, but we have only one element (Art); thus, you can eliminate answer (C). At this point, your chances are fifty-fifty, so you could guess and move on.

But let's look at (B). A "chiasmus" is a syntactic figure wherein the elements in one clause are reversed in another. The most famous example is President Kennedy's statement: "Ask not what your country can do for you, but what you can do for your country."

54. **A** The author does not revere life above everything else—for example, he clearly states that he doesn't like life as an intrusion on Art, at the very least or as it appears in certain parts of William Shakespeare's work. He includes these examples of Caesar and English drama for rhetorical reasons, and while he admires English drama, he does not appear to revere it. (By the way, to "revere" something is "to regard it with awe, deference, and devotion.") Beauty is held up as an ideal, and this is clear when the author says, "the object of Art is not simple truth but complex beauty."

EXPLANATIONS TO THE FREE-RESPONSE SECTION

QUESTION 1

Synthesis Essay

This sample essay is above average, but winds up being unnecessarily repetitive. The author does a good job of bringing in outside knowledge to round out information in the sources. However, he does not fully engage with the sources—he treats the David painting, in particular, as though its meaning was obvious and required no further explanation. The author lays out a very clear framework for his views on leadership, which also guides the structure of the essay. However, he does not attempt to engage two of the more difficult sources, the quotations from Plato and Confucius, which might not fit well into that framework. At the level of writing, this essay is solid; however, some of its sentences get away from the author and become unwieldy. Further, the essay becomes repetitive in the final paragraph, where the author relies more on repeating his thesis, rather than demonstrating it by use of the sources. Finally, the conclusion, while clear, is a little too pat. The author fails to acknowledge that leaders of all kinds have been successful in history, and that his examples do not necessarily fall into his desired categories as clearly as he might like. Overall, this essay likely merits a 7.

There are perhaps as many approaches to leadership and governing as there are leaders and rulers. However, in general, these styles can be separated into two categories: collaborative leadership and authoritative leadership. Collaborative leaders view their subjects as allies with useful skills and viewpoints, who may have worthwhile insights and who can be trusted, even if they need direction. Authoritative leadership, however, considers followers to be untrustworthy unless closely supervised, and claims that one cannot befriend the common people; one can only overawe them. Of these two ways of ruling, the collaborative style produces better results, even though strong believers in authority are not able to trust that a collaborative process can work.

In The Prince, Niccolo Machiavelli laid out a handbook for an authoritative leadership style. He claimed that a ruler cannot put his faith in the common people, because they will always betray the leader when times are difficult. A prince who relies "entirely on...promises" will fail, because only "the dread of punishment" can ensure compliance. Thomas Hobbes, in Leviathan, makes a similar point: security for the people is so important that they themselves must embrace a tyrannical ruler. People cannot trust each other unless they set up some absolute authority, which, once it exists, is unquestionable, and can ensure safety by intimidation.

History gives the lie to the assertions of these political thinkers. Machiavelli wanted a prince to unify the Italian city-states through force of arms; no such person would come about until the 19th Century, and then it was a king whose main appeal was that he was a limited, constitutional monarch, rather than a dictator. Hobbes claimed that security could only be assured by government that overwhelmed the will of the people; but the most secure states today are the ones which are run by democracies that respond to people's complaints.

Instead, the most successful leaders in history have been collaborative ones: those who inspire greatness, rather than fear, in their followers, and who help their followers to achieve greatness without micromanaging them. For example, General George Patton's view on leadership was that the leader should trust his subordinates. By making sure not to restrain his subordinates' creativity, Patton became one of the most successful generals in World War II. Napoleon Bonaparte was another kind of collaborative leader. He definitely gave his subordinates clear orders and goals, but he "led from the trenches." He was directly involved in their struggles. His personal boldness and character inspired greatness in his followers. Without needing to intimidate his people, Napoleon succeeded where even the great general Hannibal failed, becoming one of the greatest rulers in history. This collaborative leadership style—trusting people to do the right thing—is characteristic of highly successful leaders in history, as well as the most important form of government in the modern world: democracy.

QUESTION 2

Rhetorical Analysis Essay

The following sample is a slightly better than adequate response; the strong writing would probably carry it to a 7 or 8, despite the tenuous grasp of rhetorical strategies. It would be possible to question the student's assertion that Mark Twain's comment that "the scow episode is really a sublime burst of invention" proves that "he is a reasonable critic and not bent on purely insulting the popular author." Most likely, this represents more of Twain's sarcasm.

Mark Twain's well-known essay "Fenimore Cooper's Literary Offenses" seeks to mock both the work itself and its devoted readers. Though Twain's piece has a decidedly ironic tone and is not meant to be serious literary criticism, he employs a variety of rhetorical tactics to argue his point and persuade the audience that not only is Cooper's work flawed and ridiculous, but also that they are mislead in having enjoyed Cooper's writing. Twain uses rhetorical devices rooted in both language and content to convince the reader of the validity of his scathing conclusion about Cooper.

By subtle choices of persuasive writing, Twain conveys his meaning through his language. He uses the first person plural as his point of view to connect with the reader and to give an impression of a sympathetic guide alerting the reader to literary inadequacy. Instead of always presenting his evidence outright, Twain uses rhetorical questions to intensify his essay and to catch the reader's attention. By demanding "Did the Indians notice [...]?" he highlights the unrealistic nature of Cooper's work. In the final paragraph, he employs an anaphora, beginning several successive sentences with "Then No...." This repetitive wording emphasizes his message of Cooper's inadequacy. His phrasing plays a key role in convincing the reader of his point.

In addition, Twain's choice of evidence is clearly intended to strengthen his argument. He uses a simile, "He saw nearly all things as through a glass eye, darkly" to help the audience visualize and better comprehend his meaning. To dramatize his critique, Twain writes "It would take you thirty years to guess," an obvious hyperbole that vividly depicts the ridiculousness of Cooper's work. Throughout the essay, Twain relies on mathematical computations and logic to undermine Cooper's credibility, hoping that objective reasoning will sway his readers. Finally, in a concession to Cooper's competency, Twain admits that "the scow episode is really a sublime burst of invention" to illustrate that he is a reasonable critic and not bent on purely insulting the popular author.

Twain's wide range of rhetorical techniques serve to convince his audience in as many different ways as possible that he is a logical, credible critic and that his argument is valid.

QUESTION 3

Argumentative Essay

The sample essay below serves as a great model, for it exudes an ease that can come only with great practice with the art of writing. There is a clear thesis and organizational structure. Quality replaces quantity, and the clarity is pristine. Remember that above all else, the AP reader craves clarity. The work might not earn a 9, but it would definitely receive an 8.

For as long as authority has existed, there have been those who have challenged it, rebelled against it, and even refused to acknowledge it. Institutions that hold great power—the government, the church, public opinion—have dictated what is right and wrong to those under their control. However, when an individual's personal convictions come into conflict with authority's established morality, persecution, isolation, and other such punishments often follow. Voltaire was correct in his assertion that "it is dangerous to be right" in opposition to the status quo, as demonstrated in history and literature.

As science developed during the Renaissance and humans began to have a more objective understanding of the world, the church held vehemently to its tenets and persecuted those who contradicted its teachings. Italian astronomer Galileo Galilei, whose observations played a pivotal role in our model for the solar system, was one such man who suffered greatly for his non-Christian hypotheses. Though Galileo's theories were indeed correct, the Church nonetheless suppressed his work and placed him under house arrest. Similarly, during the 1950s, McCarthyism swept America, as the government tried to root out "Communists." For the few who condemned the inherent immorality of McCarthy's campaign and tactics, the result was that they too would be blacklisted and effectively ruined. In contradicting the Church and the government, independent thinkers have suffered greatly for "being right" throughout history.

The dangers of questioning authority have not been neglected in world literature. In Milan Kundera's The Joke, the protagonist Ludvik is expelled from the university and the Communist Party for making comments derogatory to the Party. Though his criticisms would certainly be deemed valid by later generations, his correct thinking is rewarded with isolation and prison-like punishment in the military. Fighting against both the establishment and the majority, Arthur Miller's character John Proctor is indeed "right" that the Salem witch trials depicted in The Crucible are madness, and ruining the lives of innocent people. However, his unpopular beliefs only cause him danger as he, too, is soon labeled as a witch. These two protagonists, whose lone voices of reason decry the authorities' "wrong" stance, suffer great dangers as a result of their challenges to the establishment. Voltaire's claim has been continually confirmed by history and literature.

HOW TO SCORE PRACTICE TEST 2

SECTION I: MULTIPLE-CHOICE

$$\underline{\hspace{3cm}} \times 1.2500 = \underline{\hspace{3cm}}$$

Number of Correct (out of 54)   Weighted Section I Score (Do not round)

SECTION II: FREE RESPONSE

(See if you can find a teacher or classmate to score your essays using the guidelines in Chapter 3.)

Question 1 $\underline{\hspace{3cm}}$ $\times$ 3.0556 = $\underline{\hspace{3cm}}$
             (out of 9)   (Do not round)

Question 2 $\underline{\hspace{3cm}}$ $\times$ 3.0556 = $\underline{\hspace{3cm}}$
             (out of 9)   (Do not round)

Question 3 $\underline{\hspace{3cm}}$ $\times$ 3.0556 = $\underline{\hspace{3cm}}$
             (out of 9)   (Do not round)

AP Score Conversion Chart English Language and Composition

Composite Score Range	AP Score
112–150	5
98–111	4
80–97	3
55–79	2
0–54	1

Sum = $\underline{\hspace{3cm}}$

Weighted Section II Score (Do not round)

COMPOSITE SCORE

$$\underline{\hspace{3cm}} + \underline{\hspace{3cm}} = \underline{\hspace{3cm}}$$

Weighted Section I Score   Weighted Section II Score   Composite Score (Round to nearest whole number)

Completely darken bubbles with a No. 2 pencil. If you make a mistake, be sure to erase mark completely. Erase all stray marks.

1. YOUR NAME:
(Print) _____
　　　Last　　　　　　First　　　　　　M.I.
SIGNATURE: _____　DATE: _____ / _____ / _____

HOME ADDRESS: _____
(Print)　　　　　　　Number and Street
_____
　　City　　　　　State　　　　　Zip Code
PHONE NO. : _____
(Print)

IMPORTANT: Please fill in these boxes exactly as shown on the back cover of your test book.

2. TEST FORM

6. DATE OF BIRTH

Month	Day	Year
◯ JAN		
◯ FEB		
◯ MAR	⓪	⓪ ⓪ ⓪
◯ APR	①	① ① ①
◯ MAY	②	② ② ②
◯ JUN	③	③ ③ ③
◯ JUL		④ ④ ④
◯ AUG		⑤ ⑤ ⑤
◯ SEP		⑦ ⑦ ⑦
◯ OCT		⑧ ⑧ ⑧
◯ NOV		⑨ ⑨ ⑨
◯ DEC		

3. TEST CODE　　**4. REGISTRATION NUMBER**

Test Code bubbles: ⓪ Ⓐ, ① Ⓑ, ② Ⓒ, ③ Ⓓ, ④ Ⓔ, ⑤ Ⓕ, ⑦ Ⓖ, ⑧, ⑨
Registration number columns: 0–9

7. SEX
◯ MALE
◯ FEMALE

The Princeton Review®
© The Princeton Review, Inc.
FORM NO. 00001-PR

5. YOUR NAME

First 4 letters of last name				FIRST INIT	MID INIT
Ⓐ	Ⓐ	Ⓐ	Ⓐ	Ⓐ	Ⓐ
Ⓑ	Ⓑ	Ⓑ	Ⓑ	Ⓑ	Ⓑ
Ⓒ	Ⓒ	Ⓒ	Ⓒ	Ⓒ	Ⓒ
Ⓓ	Ⓓ	Ⓓ	Ⓓ	Ⓓ	Ⓓ
Ⓔ	Ⓔ	Ⓔ	Ⓔ	Ⓔ	Ⓔ
Ⓕ	Ⓕ	Ⓕ	Ⓕ	Ⓕ	Ⓕ
Ⓖ	Ⓖ	Ⓖ	Ⓖ	Ⓖ	Ⓖ
Ⓗ	Ⓗ	Ⓗ	Ⓗ	Ⓗ	Ⓗ
Ⓘ	Ⓘ	Ⓘ	Ⓘ	Ⓘ	Ⓘ
Ⓙ	Ⓙ	Ⓙ	Ⓙ	Ⓙ	Ⓙ
Ⓚ	Ⓚ	Ⓚ	Ⓚ	Ⓚ	Ⓚ
Ⓛ	Ⓛ	Ⓛ	Ⓛ	Ⓛ	Ⓛ
Ⓜ	Ⓜ	Ⓜ	Ⓜ	Ⓜ	Ⓜ
Ⓝ	Ⓝ	Ⓝ	Ⓝ	Ⓝ	Ⓝ
Ⓞ	Ⓞ	Ⓞ	Ⓞ	Ⓞ	Ⓞ
Ⓟ	Ⓟ	Ⓟ	Ⓟ	Ⓟ	Ⓟ
Ⓠ	Ⓠ	Ⓠ	Ⓠ	Ⓠ	Ⓠ
Ⓡ	Ⓡ	Ⓡ	Ⓡ	Ⓡ	Ⓡ
Ⓢ	Ⓢ	Ⓢ	Ⓢ	Ⓢ	Ⓢ
Ⓣ	Ⓣ	Ⓣ	Ⓣ	Ⓣ	Ⓣ
Ⓤ	Ⓤ	Ⓤ	Ⓤ	Ⓤ	Ⓤ
Ⓥ	Ⓥ	Ⓥ	Ⓥ	Ⓥ	Ⓥ
Ⓦ	Ⓦ	Ⓦ	Ⓦ	Ⓦ	Ⓦ
Ⓧ	Ⓧ	Ⓧ	Ⓧ	Ⓧ	Ⓧ
Ⓨ	Ⓨ	Ⓨ	Ⓨ	Ⓨ	Ⓨ
Ⓩ	Ⓩ	Ⓩ	Ⓩ	Ⓩ	Ⓩ

Section 1

Start with number 1 for each new section.
If a section has fewer questions than answer spaces, leave the extra answer spaces blank.

1. Ⓐ Ⓑ Ⓒ Ⓓ
2. Ⓐ Ⓑ Ⓒ Ⓓ
3. Ⓐ Ⓑ Ⓒ Ⓓ
4. Ⓐ Ⓑ Ⓒ Ⓓ
5. Ⓐ Ⓑ Ⓒ Ⓓ
6. Ⓐ Ⓑ Ⓒ Ⓓ
7. Ⓐ Ⓑ Ⓒ Ⓓ
8. Ⓐ Ⓑ Ⓒ Ⓓ
9. Ⓐ Ⓑ Ⓒ Ⓓ
10. Ⓐ Ⓑ Ⓒ Ⓓ
11. Ⓐ Ⓑ Ⓒ Ⓓ
12. Ⓐ Ⓑ Ⓒ Ⓓ
13. Ⓐ Ⓑ Ⓒ Ⓓ
14. Ⓐ Ⓑ Ⓒ Ⓓ
15. Ⓐ Ⓑ Ⓒ Ⓓ
16. Ⓐ Ⓑ Ⓒ Ⓓ
17. Ⓐ Ⓑ Ⓒ Ⓓ
18. Ⓐ Ⓑ Ⓒ Ⓓ
19. Ⓐ Ⓑ Ⓒ Ⓓ
20. Ⓐ Ⓑ Ⓒ Ⓓ
21. Ⓐ Ⓑ Ⓒ Ⓓ
22. Ⓐ Ⓑ Ⓒ Ⓓ
23. Ⓐ Ⓑ Ⓒ Ⓓ
24. Ⓐ Ⓑ Ⓒ Ⓓ
25. Ⓐ Ⓑ Ⓒ Ⓓ
26. Ⓐ Ⓑ Ⓒ Ⓓ
27. Ⓐ Ⓑ Ⓒ Ⓓ
28. Ⓐ Ⓑ Ⓒ Ⓓ
29. Ⓐ Ⓑ Ⓒ Ⓓ
30. Ⓐ Ⓑ Ⓒ Ⓓ

31. Ⓐ Ⓑ Ⓒ Ⓓ
32. Ⓐ Ⓑ Ⓒ Ⓓ
33. Ⓐ Ⓑ Ⓒ Ⓓ
34. Ⓐ Ⓑ Ⓒ Ⓓ
35. Ⓐ Ⓑ Ⓒ Ⓓ
36. Ⓐ Ⓑ Ⓒ Ⓓ
37. Ⓐ Ⓑ Ⓒ Ⓓ
38. Ⓐ Ⓑ Ⓒ Ⓓ
39. Ⓐ Ⓑ Ⓒ Ⓓ
40. Ⓐ Ⓑ Ⓒ Ⓓ
41. Ⓐ Ⓑ Ⓒ Ⓓ
42. Ⓐ Ⓑ Ⓒ Ⓓ
43. Ⓐ Ⓑ Ⓒ Ⓓ
44. Ⓐ Ⓑ Ⓒ Ⓓ
45. Ⓐ Ⓑ Ⓒ Ⓓ
46. Ⓐ Ⓑ Ⓒ Ⓓ
47. Ⓐ Ⓑ Ⓒ Ⓓ
48. Ⓐ Ⓑ Ⓒ Ⓓ
49. Ⓐ Ⓑ Ⓒ Ⓓ
50. Ⓐ Ⓑ Ⓒ Ⓓ
51. Ⓐ Ⓑ Ⓒ Ⓓ
52. Ⓐ Ⓑ Ⓒ Ⓓ
53. Ⓐ Ⓑ Ⓒ Ⓓ
54. Ⓐ Ⓑ Ⓒ Ⓓ
55. Ⓐ Ⓑ Ⓒ Ⓓ
56. Ⓐ Ⓑ Ⓒ Ⓓ
57. Ⓐ Ⓑ Ⓒ Ⓓ
58. Ⓐ Ⓑ Ⓒ Ⓓ
59. Ⓐ Ⓑ Ⓒ Ⓓ
60. Ⓐ Ⓑ Ⓒ Ⓓ

61. Ⓐ Ⓑ Ⓒ Ⓓ
62. Ⓐ Ⓑ Ⓒ Ⓓ
63. Ⓐ Ⓑ Ⓒ Ⓓ
64. Ⓐ Ⓑ Ⓒ Ⓓ
65. Ⓐ Ⓑ Ⓒ Ⓓ
66. Ⓐ Ⓑ Ⓒ Ⓓ
67. Ⓐ Ⓑ Ⓒ Ⓓ
68. Ⓐ Ⓑ Ⓒ Ⓓ
69. Ⓐ Ⓑ Ⓒ Ⓓ
70. Ⓐ Ⓑ Ⓒ Ⓓ
71. Ⓐ Ⓑ Ⓒ Ⓓ
72. Ⓐ Ⓑ Ⓒ Ⓓ
73. Ⓐ Ⓑ Ⓒ Ⓓ
74. Ⓐ Ⓑ Ⓒ Ⓓ
75. Ⓐ Ⓑ Ⓒ Ⓓ
76. Ⓐ Ⓑ Ⓒ Ⓓ
77. Ⓐ Ⓑ Ⓒ Ⓓ
78. Ⓐ Ⓑ Ⓒ Ⓓ
79. Ⓐ Ⓑ Ⓒ Ⓓ
80. Ⓐ Ⓑ Ⓒ Ⓓ
81. Ⓐ Ⓑ Ⓒ Ⓓ
82. Ⓐ Ⓑ Ⓒ Ⓓ
83. Ⓐ Ⓑ Ⓒ Ⓓ
84. Ⓐ Ⓑ Ⓒ Ⓓ
85. Ⓐ Ⓑ Ⓒ Ⓓ
86. Ⓐ Ⓑ Ⓒ Ⓓ
87. Ⓐ Ⓑ Ⓒ Ⓓ
88. Ⓐ Ⓑ Ⓒ Ⓓ
89. Ⓐ Ⓑ Ⓒ Ⓓ
90. Ⓐ Ⓑ Ⓒ Ⓓ

91. Ⓐ Ⓑ Ⓒ Ⓓ
92. Ⓐ Ⓑ Ⓒ Ⓓ
93. Ⓐ Ⓑ Ⓒ Ⓓ
94. Ⓐ Ⓑ Ⓒ Ⓓ
95. Ⓐ Ⓑ Ⓒ Ⓓ
96. Ⓐ Ⓑ Ⓒ Ⓓ
97. Ⓐ Ⓑ Ⓒ Ⓓ
98. Ⓐ Ⓑ Ⓒ Ⓓ
99. Ⓐ Ⓑ Ⓒ Ⓓ
100. Ⓐ Ⓑ Ⓒ Ⓓ
101. Ⓐ Ⓑ Ⓒ Ⓓ
102. Ⓐ Ⓑ Ⓒ Ⓓ
103. Ⓐ Ⓑ Ⓒ Ⓓ
104. Ⓐ Ⓑ Ⓒ Ⓓ
105. Ⓐ Ⓑ Ⓒ Ⓓ
106. Ⓐ Ⓑ Ⓒ Ⓓ
107. Ⓐ Ⓑ Ⓒ Ⓓ
108. Ⓐ Ⓑ Ⓒ Ⓓ
109. Ⓐ Ⓑ Ⓒ Ⓓ
110. Ⓐ Ⓑ Ⓒ Ⓓ
111. Ⓐ Ⓑ Ⓒ Ⓓ
112. Ⓐ Ⓑ Ⓒ Ⓓ
113. Ⓐ Ⓑ Ⓒ Ⓓ
114. Ⓐ Ⓑ Ⓒ Ⓓ
115. Ⓐ Ⓑ Ⓒ Ⓓ
116. Ⓐ Ⓑ Ⓒ Ⓓ
117. Ⓐ Ⓑ Ⓒ Ⓓ
118. Ⓐ Ⓑ Ⓒ Ⓓ
119. Ⓐ Ⓑ Ⓒ Ⓓ
120. Ⓐ Ⓑ Ⓒ Ⓓ

Completely darken bubbles with a No. 2 pencil. If you make a mistake, be sure to erase mark completely. Erase all stray marks.

1. YOUR NAME:
(Print) _____ Last _____ First _____ M.I.

SIGNATURE: _____ DATE: ___ / ___ / ___

HOME ADDRESS: _____
(Print) Number and Street

_____
City State Zip Code

PHONE NO. : _____
(Print)

IMPORTANT: Please fill in these boxes exactly as shown on the back cover of your test book.

2. TEST FORM
_____

3. TEST CODE   **4. REGISTRATION NUMBER**

6. DATE OF BIRTH

Month	Day	Year
○ JAN		
○ FEB		
○ MAR	⓪ ⓪	⓪ ⓪
○ APR	① ①	① ①
○ MAY	② ②	② ②
○ JUN	③ ③	③ ③
○ JUL		④ ④ ④
○ AUG		⑤ ⑤ ⑤
○ SEP		⑦ ⑦ ⑦
○ OCT		⑧ ⑧ ⑧
○ NOV		⑨ ⑨ ⑨
○ DEC		

7. SEX
○ MALE
○ FEMALE

The Princeton Review.
© The Princeton Review, Inc.
FORM NO. 00001-PR

5. YOUR NAME

First 4 letters of last name | FIRST INIT | MID INIT

(A)(B)(C)(D)(E)(F)(G)(H)(I)(J)(K)(L)(M)(N)(O)(P)(Q)(R)(S)(T)(U)(V)(W)(X)(Y)(Z)

Section 1

Start with number 1 for each new section.
If a section has fewer questions than answer spaces, leave the extra answer spaces blank.

1. (A)(B)(C)(D)
2. (A)(B)(C)(D)
3. (A)(B)(C)(D)
4. (A)(B)(C)(D)
5. (A)(B)(C)(D)
6. (A)(B)(C)(D)
7. (A)(B)(C)(D)
8. (A)(B)(C)(D)
9. (A)(B)(C)(D)
10. (A)(B)(C)(D)
11. (A)(B)(C)(D)
12. (A)(B)(C)(D)
13. (A)(B)(C)(D)
14. (A)(B)(C)(D)
15. (A)(B)(C)(D)
16. (A)(B)(C)(D)
17. (A)(B)(C)(D)
18. (A)(B)(C)(D)
19. (A)(B)(C)(D)
20. (A)(B)(C)(D)
21. (A)(B)(C)(D)
22. (A)(B)(C)(D)
23. (A)(B)(C)(D)
24. (A)(B)(C)(D)
25. (A)(B)(C)(D)
26. (A)(B)(C)(D)
27. (A)(B)(C)(D)
28. (A)(B)(C)(D)
29. (A)(B)(C)(D)
30. (A)(B)(C)(D)

31. (A)(B)(C)(D)
32. (A)(B)(C)(D)
33. (A)(B)(C)(D)
34. (A)(B)(C)(D)
35. (A)(B)(C)(D)
36. (A)(B)(C)(D)
37. (A)(B)(C)(D)
38. (A)(B)(C)(D)
39. (A)(B)(C)(D)
40. (A)(B)(C)(D)
41. (A)(B)(C)(D)
42. (A)(B)(C)(D)
43. (A)(B)(C)(D)
44. (A)(B)(C)(D)
45. (A)(B)(C)(D)
46. (A)(B)(C)(D)
47. (A)(B)(C)(D)
48. (A)(B)(C)(D)
49. (A)(B)(C)(D)
50. (A)(B)(C)(D)
51. (A)(B)(C)(D)
52. (A)(B)(C)(D)
53. (A)(B)(C)(D)
54. (A)(B)(C)(D)
55. (A)(B)(C)(D)
56. (A)(B)(C)(D)
57. (A)(B)(C)(D)
58. (A)(B)(C)(D)
59. (A)(B)(C)(D)
60. (A)(B)(C)(D)

61. (A)(B)(C)(D)
62. (A)(B)(C)(D)
63. (A)(B)(C)(D)
64. (A)(B)(C)(D)
65. (A)(B)(C)(D)
66. (A)(B)(C)(D)
67. (A)(B)(C)(D)
68. (A)(B)(C)(D)
69. (A)(B)(C)(D)
70. (A)(B)(C)(D)
71. (A)(B)(C)(D)
72. (A)(B)(C)(D)
73. (A)(B)(C)(D)
74. (A)(B)(C)(D)
75. (A)(B)(C)(D)
76. (A)(B)(C)(D)
77. (A)(B)(C)(D)
78. (A)(B)(C)(D)
79. (A)(B)(C)(D)
80. (A)(B)(C)(D)
81. (A)(B)(C)(D)
82. (A)(B)(C)(D)
83. (A)(B)(C)(D)
84. (A)(B)(C)(D)
85. (A)(B)(C)(D)
86. (A)(B)(C)(D)
87. (A)(B)(C)(D)
88. (A)(B)(C)(D)
89. (A)(B)(C)(D)
90. (A)(B)(C)(D)

91. (A)(B)(C)(D)
92. (A)(B)(C)(D)
93. (A)(B)(C)(D)
94. (A)(B)(C)(D)
95. (A)(B)(C)(D)
96. (A)(B)(C)(D)
97. (A)(B)(C)(D)
98. (A)(B)(C)(D)
99. (A)(B)(C)(D)
100. (A)(B)(C)(D)
101. (A)(B)(C)(D)
102. (A)(B)(C)(D)
103. (A)(B)(C)(D)
104. (A)(B)(C)(D)
105. (A)(B)(C)(D)
106. (A)(B)(C)(D)
107. (A)(B)(C)(D)
108. (A)(B)(C)(D)
109. (A)(B)(C)(D)
110. (A)(B)(C)(D)
111. (A)(B)(C)(D)
112. (A)(B)(C)(D)
113. (A)(B)(C)(D)
114. (A)(B)(C)(D)
115. (A)(B)(C)(D)
116. (A)(B)(C)(D)
117. (A)(B)(C)(D)
118. (A)(B)(C)(D)
119. (A)(B)(C)(D)
120. (A)(B)(C)(D)

Navigate the admissions process with more guidance from the experts.

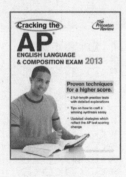

Ace the APs:

Cracking the AP Biology Exam, 2013 Edition
978-0-307-94508-2 • $18.99/$21.99 Can.
Ebook: 978-0-307-94580-8

Cracking the AP Calculus AB & BC Exams, 2013 Edition
978-0-307-94486-3 • $19.99/$23.99 Can.
Ebook: 978-0-307-94451-1

Cracking the AP Chemistry Exam, 2013 Edition
978-0-307-94488-7 • $18.99/$21.99 Can.
Ebook: 978-0-307-94452-8

Cracking the AP Economics Macro & Micro Exams, 2013 Edition
978-0-307-94509-9 • $18.00/$21.00 Can.
Ebook: 978-0-307-94581-5

Cracking the AP English Language & Composition Exam, 2013 Edition
978-0-307-94511-2 • $18.00/$21.00 Can.
Ebook: 978-0-307-94582-2

Cracking the AP English Literature & Composition Exam, 2013 Edition
978-0-307-94512-9 • $18.00/$21.00 Can.
Ebook: 978-0-307-94583-9

Cracking the AP Environmental Science Exam, 2013 Edition
978-0-307-94513-6 • $18.99/$21.99 Can.
Ebook: 978-0-307-94584-6

Cracking the AP European History Exam, 2013 Edition
978-0-307-94489-4 • $18.99/$21.99 Can.
Ebook: 978-0-307-94453-5

Cracking the AP Human Geography Exam, 2013 Edition
978-0-307-94514-3 • $18.00/$21.00 Can.

Cracking the AP Physics B Exam, 2013 Edition
978-0-307-94515-0 • $18.99/$21.99 Can.
Ebook: 978-0-307-94585-3

Cracking the AP Physics C Exam, 2013 Edition
978-0-307-94516-7 • $18.99/$21.99 Can.

Cracking the AP Psychology Exam, 2013 Edition
978-0-307-94517-4 • $18.00/$21.00 Can.
Ebook: 978-0-307-94586-0

Cracking the AP Spanish Exam with Audio CD, 2013 Edition
978-0-307-94518-1 • $24.99/$28.99 Can.

Cracking the AP Statistics Exam, 2013 Edition
978-0-307-94519-8 • $19.99/$23.99 Can.

Cracking the AP U.S. Government & Politics Exam, 2013 Edition
978-0-307-94520-4 • $18.99/$21.99 Can.
Ebook: 978-0-307-94587-7

Cracking the AP U.S. History Exam, 2013 Edition
978-0-307-94490-7 • $18.99/$21.99 Can.
Ebook: 978-0-307-94447-4

Cracking the AP World History Exam, 2013 Edition
978-0-307-94491-7 • $18.99/$21.99 Can.
Ebook: 978-0-307-94445-0

Essential AP Biology (flashcards)
978-0-375-42803-6 • $18.99/$20.99 Can.

Essential AP Psychology (flashcards)
978-0-375-42801-2 • $18.99/$20.99 Can.

Essential AP U.S. Government & Politics (flashcards)
978-0-375-42804-3 • $18.99/$20.99 Can.

Essential AP U.S. History (flashcards)
978-0-375-42800-5 • $18.99/$20.99 Can.

Essential AP World History (flashcards)
978-0-375-42802-9 • $18.99/$20.99 Can.

Get the scores you need:

11 Practice Tests for the SAT and PSAT, 2013 Edition
978-0-307-94481-8 • $24.99/$28.99 Can.

ACT or SAT?
978-0-375-42924-8 • $15.99/$19.99 Can.

College Essays that Made a Difference, 5th Edition
978-0-307-94521-1 • $13.99/$16.99
Ebook: 978-0-375-42715-2

Cracking the ACT, 2012 Edition
978-0-375-42744-2 • $19.99/$22.99 Can.
Ebook: 978-0-307-94454-2

Cracking the ACT with DVD, 2012 Edition
978-0-375-42745-9 • $31.99/$36.99 Can.

Cracking the SAT, 2013 Edition
978-0-307-94478-8 • $21.99/$25.99 Can.
Ebook: 978-0-307-94479-5

Cracking the SAT with DVD, 2013 Edition
978-0-307-94480-1 • $34.99/$41.99 Can.

Crash Course for the SAT, 4th Edition
978-0-375-42831-9 • $9.99/$10.99 Can.

Math Workout for the SAT, 3rd Edition
978-0-375-42833-3 • $16.99/$18.99 Can.

Reading and Writing Workout for the SAT, 2nd Edition
978-0-375-42832-6 • $16.99/$18.99 Can.

Essential ACT (Flashcards)
978-0-375-42806-7 • $17.99/$19.99 Can.

Essential SAT Vocabulary (Flashcards)
978-0-375-42964-4 • $16.99/$21.99 Can.

Find and fund the best school for you:

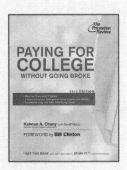

The Best 377 Colleges, 2013 Edition
978-0-307-94487-0 • $23.99/$27.99 Can.

The Complete Book of Colleges, 2013 Edition
978-0-307-94492-4 • $26.99/$32.00 Can.

Paying for College Without Going Broke, 2013 Edition
978-0-307-94532-7 • $20.00/$24.00
Ebook: 978-0-307-94533-4

Boost your scores on the SAT Subject Tests:

Cracking the SAT Biology E/M Subject Test, 2011–2012 Edition
978-0-375-42810-4 • $19.99/$22.99 Can.

Cracking the SAT Chemistry Subject Test, 2011–2012 Edition
978-0-375-42814-2 • $19.99/$22.99 Can.

Cracking the SAT French Subject Test, 2011–2012 Edition
978-0-375-42815-9 • $19.99/$22.99 Can.

Cracking the SAT Literature Subject Test, 2011–2012 Edition
978-0-375-42811-1 • $19.99/$22.99 Can.

Cracking the SAT Math 1 & 2 Subject Tests, 2011–2012 Edition
978-0-375-42812-8 • $19.99/$22.99 Can.

Cracking the SAT Physics Subject Test, 2011–2012 Edition
978-0-375-42813-5 • $19.99/$22.99 Can.

Cracking the SAT Spanish Subject Test, 2011–2012 Edition
978-0-375-42817-3 • $19.99/$22.99 Can.

Cracking the SAT U.S. & World History Tests, 2011–2012 Edition
978-0-375-42816-6 • $19.99/$22.99 Can.

Available everywhere books are sold and at PrincetonReviewBooks.com